Real-Time UML

Developing Efficient Objects for Embedded Systems

Bruce Powel Douglass

ADDISON-WESLEY

An Imprint of Addison Wesley Longman, Inc.

Reading, Massachusetts • Harlow, England • Menlo Park, California
Berkeley, California • Don Mills, Ontario • Sydney
Bonn • Amsterdam • Tokyo • Mexico City

Many of the designations used by manufacturers and sellers to distinguish their products are claimed as trademarks. Where those designations appear in this book, and Addison Wesley Longman was aware of a trademark claim, the designations have been printed in initial capital letters or all capital letters.

The UML logo is a registered trademark of the Rational Software Corporation (http://www.rational.com). Used by permission.

The author and publisher have taken care in preparation of this book, but make no expressed or implied warranty of any kind and assume no responsibility for errors or omissions. No liability is assumed for incidental or consequential damages in connection with or arising out of the use of the information or programs contained herein.

The publisher offers discounts of this book when ordered in quantity for special sales. For more information, please contact:

Corporate & Professional Publishing Group
Addison Wesley Longman, Inc.
One Jacob Way
Reading, Massachusetts 01867

Library of Congress Cataloging-in-Publication Data

Douglass, Bruce Powel.
    Real-time UML : developing efficient objects for embedded systems
/ Bruce Powel Douglass.
        p.   cm.
    Includes bibliographical references and index.
    ISBN 0-201-32579-9
    1. Embedded computer systems—Programming.   2. Real-time data
processing.   3. Object-oriented methods (Computer science)
I. Title.
QA76.6.D66   1998
005.1'17—dc21   97–39889
                                                                  CIP

Text printed on recycled paper.

4 5 6 7 8 9   MA   01 00 99 98

4th Printing August, 1998

This book is dedicated to my two boys—Scott Powel Douglass and Blake William Douglass—who, despite their few years, have more to teach me than I have to teach them.

Contents

Figure List

Additional figures appear in the Appendix.

About the Author

Bruce was raised by wolves in the Oregon wilderness. He taught himself to read at age 3 and calculus before age 12. He dropped out of school when he was 14 and traveled around the U.S. for a few years before entering the University of Oregon as a mathematics major. He eventually received his M.S. in exercise physiology from the University of Oregon and his Ph.D. in neurophysiology from the USD Medical School, where he developed a branch of mathematics called autocorrelative factor analysis for studying information processing in multicellular biological neural systems.

Bruce is a well-known speaker and author in the area of real-time embedded systems. He has worked as a software developer in real-time systems for almost 20 years. He is on the Advisory Board of the Embedded Systems Conference and has taught courses in software estimation and scheduling, project management, object-oriented analysis and design, communications protocols, finite state machines, and safety-critical systems design. He has taught his own week-long course in real-time object-oriented analysis and design for many years and continues to teach it in open public courses and at a variety of companies. He is currently working on a comprehensive overview of object-oriented analysis and design for real-time systems called *Doing Hard Time: Objects and Patterns in Real-Time Software Development* to be published by Addison Wesley Longman at the end of 1998.

He is currently employed as the Manager of Technical Marketing for i-Logix, a leading producer of tools for real-time systems development. Bruce has been working with Rational and the other UML partners on the specification of the UML. He also does consulting and mentoring for a number of companies building large-scale real-time safety-critical systems. He is the author of three other books on software as well as a short textbook on table tennis.

Bruce enjoys classical music and has played classical guitar professionally. He has competed in several sports, including table tennis, bicycle racing, running, and full-contact Tae Kwon Do, although he currently only fights inanimate objects that don't hit back. He and his two sons now ponder interesting questions in Wisconsin. He can be reached at: bpd@ilogix.com

Foreword

Embedded computerized systems are here to stay. Reactive and real-time systems likewise. As this book aptly points out, one can see embedded systems everywhere; there are more computers hidden in the guts of things than there are conventional desktops or laptops.

Wherever there are computers and computerized systems, there has to be software to drive them—and software doesn't just happen. People have to write it, people have to understand and analyze it, people have to use it, and people have to maintain and update it for future versions. It is this human aspect of programming that calls for modeling complex systems on levels of abstraction that are higher than that of "normal" programming languages. From this also comes the need for methodologies to guide software engineers and programmers in coping with the modeling process itself.

There is broad agreement that one of the things to strive for in devising a high-level modeling approach is good diagrammatics. All other things being equal, pictures are usually better understood than text or symbols. But we are not interested just in pictures or diagrams, since constructing complex software is not an exclusively human activity. We are interested in *languages* of diagrams, and these languages require computerized support for validation and analysis. Just as high-level programming languages require not only editors and version control utilities but also—and predominantly!—compilers and debugging tools, so do modeling languages require not only pretty graphics, document generation utilities, and project management aids, but also means for executing models and for synthesizing code. This means that we need *visual formalisms* that come complete with a syntax to determine what is allowed and semantics to determine what the allowed things mean. Such formalisms should be as visual as possible (obviously, some things do not lend themselves to natural visualization) with the main emphasis placed on topological relationships between diagrammatic entities, and then, as next-best options, geometry, metrics, and perhaps iconics, too.

Over the years, the main approaches to high-level modeling have been *structured analysis* (SA), and *object orientation* (OO). The two are about a decade apart in initial conception and evolution. SA started in the late 1970s by DeMarco, Yourdon, and others, and is based on "lifting" classical, procedural programming concepts up to the modeling level. The result calls for modeling system structure by functional decomposition and flow of information, depicted by (hierarchical) data-flow diagrams. As to system behavior, the early- and mid-1980s saw several methodology teams (such as Ward/Mellor, Hatley/Pirbhai, and the STATEMATE team from i-Logix) making detailed recommendations that enriched the basic SA model with means for capturing behavior based on state diagrams or the richer language of statecharts. Carefully defined behavioral modeling is especially crucial for embedded, reactive, and real-time systems.

OO modeling started in the late 1980s, and, in a way, its history is very similar. The basic idea for system structure was to "lift" concepts from object-oriented programming up to the modeling level. Thus, the basic structural model for objects in Booch's method, in the OMT and ROOM methods, and in many others, deals with classes and instances, relationships and roles, operations and events, and aggregation and inheritance. Visuality is achieved by basing this model on an embellished and enriched form of entity-relationship diagrams. As to system behavior, most OO modeling approaches adopted the statecharts language for this (I cannot claim to be too upset about that decision). A statechart is associated with each class, and its role is to describe the behavior of the instance objects. The subtle and complicated connections between structure and behavior, i.e., between object models and statecharts, were treated by OO methodologists in a broad spectrum of degrees of detail—from vastly insufficient to adequate. The test, of course, is whether the languages for structure and behavior and their interlinks are defined sufficiently well to allow the "interpretation" and "compilation" of high-level models, i.e., full model execution and code synthesis. This has been achieved only in a couple of cases, namely in the ObjecTime tool (based on the ROOM method of Selic, Gullekson, and Ward), and the Rhapsody tool (from i-Logix, based on the Executable Object Modeling method of Gery and the undersigned).

In a remarkable departure from the similarity in evolution between the SA and OO paradigms for system modeling, the last two or three years have seen OO methodologists working together. They have compared notes, debated the issues, and finally cooperated in formulating a general Unified Modeling Language (UML) in the hope of bringing together the best of the various OO modeling approaches. This sweeping effort, which in its teamwork is reminiscent of the Algol60 and Ada efforts, is taking place under the auspices of Rational Corporation, spearheaded by G. Booch (of the Booch method), J. Rumbaugh (codeveloper of the OMT method), and I. Jacobson (czar of use cases). Version 0.8 of the UML was released in 1996 and was rather open-ended, vague, and not nearly as well-defined as some expected. For about a year, the UML team went into overdrive, with a lot of help from methodologists and language designers from outside Rational Corporation (the undersigned contributing his 10 cents worth, too), and version 1.1, whose defining documents were released in early 1997, is much tighter and more solid. The UML has very recently been adopted as a standard by the object management group (OMG), and with more work there is a good chance that it will become not just an officially approved, if somewhat dryly documented, standard, but the main modeling mechanism for the software that is constructed according to the object-oriented doctrine. And this is no small matter, as more software engineers are now claiming that more kinds of software are best developed in an OO fashion.

For capturing system structure, the UML indeed adopts an entity-relationship-like diagrammatic language for classes and objects. For early-stage behavioral thinking it recommends use cases and utilizes sequence diagrams (often called message sequence charts or MSCs). For the full constructive specification of behavior it adopts statecharts.

In this book, Bruce Douglass does an excellent job of dishing out engineering wisdom to people who have to construct complex software—especially real-time, embedded, reactive software. Moreover, it does this with UML as the main underlying vehicle, a fact which, given the recent standardization of the UML and its fast-spreading usage, makes the book valuable to anyone whose daily worry is the expeditious and smooth development of such systems. Moreover, Bruce's book is clear and very well written, and it gives the reader the confidence boost that stems from the fact that the author is not writing from the ivy-clouded heights of an academic institution or the religiously-tainted vantage point of a professional methodologist, but that he has extensive experience in engineering the very kinds of systems the book discusses.

The recent wave of popularity that the UML is enjoying will bring with it not only the official UML books written by Rational Corporation authors, but a true flood of books, papers, reports, seminars, and tools, describing, utilizing, and elaborating upon the UML, or purporting to do so.

Readers will have to be extra careful in finding the really worthy trees in this messy forest. I have no doubt that Bruce's book will remain one of those.

Despite all of this, one must remember that right now UML is a little *too* massive. We understand well only parts of it; the definition of other parts has yet to be carried out in sufficient depth to make crystal clear their relationships with the constructive core of UML (the class diagrams and the statecharts). For example, use cases and their associated sequence and collaboration diagrams are invaluable to users and requirements engineers trying to work out the system's desired behavior in terms of scenarios. In the use case world we describe a single scenario (or a single cluster of closely related scenarios) for all relevant objects—we might call it *interobject behavior*. In contrast, a statechart describes all the behavior for a single object—*intraobject behavior*. I would like to term this stark difference as *the grand duality of system behavior.* We are far from having a good algorithmic understanding of this duality. We don't know yet how to derive one view from the other, or even how to efficiently test whether descriptions presented in the two are mutually consistent.

Other serious challenges remain, for which only the surface has been scratched. Examples include true formal verification of object-oriented software modeled using the high-level means afforded by the UML, automatic eye-pleasing and structure-enhancing layout of UML diagrams, satisfactory ways of dealing with hybrid systems that involve discrete as well as continuous parts, and much more.

As a general means for dealing with complex software, OO is also here to stay, and hence, so is the UML. OO is a powerful and wise way to think about systems and to program them, and will for a long time to come be part and parcel of the body of knowledge required by any self-respecting software engineer. This book will greatly help in that. On the other hand, OO doesn't solve *all* problems, and hence, neither does the UML. There is still much work to be done. In fact, it is probably no great exaggeration to say that there is a lot more that we *don't* know and *can't* achieve yet in this business than what we do and can. Still, what we have is tremendously more than we would have hoped for five years ago, and for this we should be thankful and humble.

David Harel
The Weizmann Institute of Science
Rehovot, Israel
October 1997

Preface

Goals

Real-Time UML: Developing Efficient Objects for Embedded Systems is an introduction to object-oriented analysis and design for hard real-time systems using the Unified Modified Language (UML). UML is a third-generation modeling language that rigorously defines the semantics of the object metamodel and provides a notation for capturing and communicating object structure and behavior. Many methodologists—including Grady Booch (Booch Method), Jim Rumbaugh (Object Modeling Technique [OMT], Ivar Jacobson (Object-Oriented Software Engineering [OOSE], and David Harel (Statecharts)—collaborated to achieve UML. Many more participated, myself included, in the specification of the UML, and we believe that it is the leading edge in modeling for complex systems.

There are very few books on the use of objects in real-time systems and even fewer on UML. Virtually all object-oriented books focus primarily on business or database application domains and do not mention real-time aspects at all. On the other hand, texts on real-time systems have largely ignored object-oriented methods. For the most part, they fall into two primary camps: those that bypass methodological considerations altogether and focus solely on "bare metal" programming, and those that are highly theoretical with little advice for actually implementing workable systems. *Real-Time UML: Developing Efficient Objects for Embedded Systems* is meant to be a concise and timely bridge for these technologies, presenting the development of deployable real-time systems using the object semantics and notation of the UML. This has many advantages, including focusing the development process of real-time systems into logical, concrete steps that progress in an orderly fashion with a standardized notation.

Audience

The book is oriented towards the practicing professional software developer and the computer science major, in the junior or senior year. This book could also serve as an undergraduate or graduate level text, but the focus is on practical development rather than a theoretical introduction. Very few equations will be found in this book, but more theoretical and mathematical approaches are referenced where appropriate. The book assumes a reasonable proficiency in at least one programming language and at least a cursory exposure to the fundamental concepts of both object orientation and real-time systems.

Organization

The book follows the normal analysis → design → implementation approach followed by most development projects. The first chapter identifies the fundamental concepts of objects and real-time systems. The next two discuss analysis—the identification and specification of the problem to be solved. Analysis is divided into two portions: black box requirements analysis using context diagrams, use cases and scenarios (Chapter 2), and capturing the key concepts and their relationships from the problem domain (Chapter 3).

Design follows analysis and adds details as to how the analysis model should be implemented. Design is broken up into three parts, each taken up in a separate chapter—Architectural, Mechanistic, and Detailed design. The parts differ in the scope of their concerns. Architectural design deals with very broad scope strategic decisions, such as tasking models and inter-processor design. Mechanistic design focuses on how groups of objects collaborate to achieve common purposes. Both architectural and mechanistic design chapters include a number of patterns that have been found generally applicable in real-time systems. Finally, detailed design specifies the internal structure and function of individual objects.

Throughout the book, the UML notation is introduced as needed. However, a notational summary is provided in the appendix so that this book can continue to serve as a reference guide as your projects evolve.

Examples

Two different approaches to examples are used in different texts. Some authors (and readers) prefer a single example taken throughout the entire book to illustrate the various concepts. The other approach is to use many different examples with the idea that it is more useful to see the concepts used in a wide variety of applications. This book uses a compromise approach. A variety of real-time examples illustrate the concepts and notation of UML in several real-time application domains, but the examples reappear in different chapters of the book. This approach reinforces the concepts by showing how they apply in various situations. Special care has been taken to select real-time examples with rich behavioral semantics; however, examples that are not strictly real-time are used where appropriate.

Bruce Powel Douglass, Ph.D.
Summer 1997

Acknowledgments

I wish to express thanks to my reviewers who tried hard to keep me honest and on topic, and who, I think, more or less succeeded:

> Douglas Thomae, Compuware, Inc.
> Kevin Dahlhausen, Morse Controls
> Jeffrey Fischer, Rational Software Corporation
> Glenn Jones, Raytheon E-systems
> Johan Galle, E2S nv
> Bruce Lerner, Otis Elevator Company

I would also like to thank Jerri Pries and Gene Robinson of i-Logix for their support in allowing me to spend so much effort on this book; Sylvia Pacheco, also of i-Logix, for her input; and the editorial and production teams at Addison Wesley Longman, including Carter Shanklin, Angela Buenning, Rachel Beavers, Maureen Hurley, and others.

I would like to add a special thanks to Catherine Joy who assisted me by providing emotional, as well as editorial, support during the development and editing process.

Chapter 1

Introduction to Real-Time Systems and Objects

Real-time applications vary in size and scope from wristwatches and microwave ovens to factory automation and nuclear power plant control systems. Applying a general methodology to the development of real-time systems means that it must meet the tight performance and size constraints of small 4-bit and 8-bit controllers, yet scale up to networked arrays of powerful processors coordinating their activities to achieve a common purpose. Object-oriented methodologies are no silver bullet, but they offer significant improvements over traditional structured methodologies for the development of real-time systems.

Real-time systems are ones in which timeliness is essential to correctness. Object-oriented modeling is a natural fit for capturing the various characteristics and requirements of systems that have hard deadlines on performance.

Notation and Concepts Discussed

What is special about real-time systems?

Dealing with time

Real-time operating systems

Advantages of objects

Objects and the UML

UML notation

1.1 What Is Special about Real-Time Systems?

If you read the popular computer press, you would come away with the impression that most computers sit on a desktop (or lap) and run Windows. In terms of the numbers of deployed systems, embedded real-time systems are orders of magnitude more common than their more visible desktop cousins. A tour of the average affluent American home might find one or even two standard desktop computers, but literally dozens of smart consumer devices, each containing one or more processors. From the washing machine and microwave oven to the telephone, stereo, television, and automobile, embedded computers are everywhere. They help us evenly toast our muffins and identify mothers-in-law calling on the phone. Embedded computers are even more prevalent in industry. Trains, switching systems, aircraft, chemical process control, and nuclear power plants all use computers to improve our productivity and quality of life safely and conveniently (not to mention that they also keep a significant number of us gainfully employed).

The software for these embedded computers is more difficult to construct than it is for the desktop. Real-time systems have all the problems of desktop applications plus many more. Non-real-time systems do not concern themselves with timelines, robustness, or safety—at least not nearly to the same extent as real-time systems. Real-time systems often do not have a conventional computer display or keyboard, but lie at the heart of some apparently noncomputerized device. The user of these devices may never be aware of the CPU embedded within making decisions about how and when the system should act. The user is not intimately involved with such a device as a computer *per se*, but rather as an electrical or mechanical appliance that provides services. Such systems must often operate for days or even years without stopping, in the most hostile environments. The services and controls provided must be autonomous and timely. Frequently, these devices have the potential to do great harm if they fail unsafely.

Real-time systems encompass all devices with performance constraints. *Hard deadlines* are performance requirements that absolutely must be met. A missed deadline constitutes an erroneous computation and a system failure. In these systems, *late* data is *bad* data. *Soft* real-time systems are constrained only by average time constraints—examples include on-line databases and flight reservation systems. In these systems, *late* data is still *good* data. The methods presented in this text may be applied to the development of all performance-constrained systems, hard and soft alike. When we use the term *real-time* alone, we are specifically referring to hard real-time systems.

An *embedded system* contains a computer as part of a larger system, and does not exist primarily to provide standard computing services to a user. A desktop PC is not an embedded system, unless it is within a tomographical imaging scanner or some other device. A computerized microwave oven or VCR is an embedded system because it does no "standard computing." In both cases, the embedded computer is part of a larger system that provides some noncomputing feature to the user, such as popping corn or showing Schwarzenegger ripping telephone booths from the floor (*Commando*, a heart-warming tale if there ever was one).

Most real-time systems interact directly with electrical devices and indirectly with mechanical ones. Frequently, custom software, written specifically for the application, must control the device. This is why real-time programmers have the reputation of being "bare metal code pounders." You cannot buy a standard device driver or Windows VxD to talk to custom hardware components. Programming these device drivers requires very low-level manipulation. This kind of programming requires intimate knowledge of the electrical properties and timing characteristics of the actual devices.

Virtually all real-time systems either monitor or control hardware, or both. Sensors provide information to the system about the state of its external environment. Medical monitoring devices, such as electrocardiography (ECG) machines use sensors to monitor patient and machine status. Air speed, engine thrust, attitude, and altitude sensors provide aircraft information for proper execution of flight control plans. Linear and angular position sensors sense a robot's arm position and adjust it via DC or stepper motors.

Many real-time systems use actuators to control their external environment or guide some external processes. Flight control computers command engine thrust and wing and tail flap orientation to meet flight parameters. Chemical process control systems control when, what kind, and the amounts of different reagents added to mixing vats. Pacemakers make the heart beat at appropriate intervals with electrical leads attached to the inside walls of the heart.

Naturally, most systems containing actuators also contain sensors. Although there are some open loop control systems, the majority of control systems use environmental feedback to ensure that the control loop is acting properly.

Standard computing systems react almost entirely to the user and nothing else.[1] Real-time systems, on the other hand, may interact with the user, but have more concern for interactions with their sensors and actuators.

One of the problems that arises with environmental interaction is that the universe has an annoying habit of disregarding our opinions of how and when it ought to behave. External events are frequently not predictable. Systems must react to events when they occur rather than when it might be convenient. An ECG monitor must alarm quickly following the cessation of cardiac activity if it is to be of value. The system cannot delay alarm processing until later that evening when the processor load is less. Many hard real-time systems are *reactive* in nature, and their responses to external events must be tightly bounded in time. Control loops, as we shall see later, are very sensitive to time delays. Delayed actuations destabilize control loops.

Most real-time systems do one or a small set of high-level tasks. The actual execution of those high-level tasks requires many simultaneous lower level activities. This is called *concurrency*. Since single processor systems can do only a single thing at a time, they implement a *scheduling policy* that controls when tasks execute. In multiple processor systems, true concurrency is achievable since the processors execute asynchronously. Individual processors within such systems schedule many threads pseudoconcurrently as well.

---

[1] It is true that behind the scenes even desktop computers must interface with printers, mice, keyboards, and networks. The point is that they do this only to facilitate the user's whim.

Embedded systems are usually constructed with the least powerful computers that can meet the functional and performance requirements. Real-time systems ship the hardware along with the software as part of a complete system package. As many products are extremely cost sensitive, marketing and sales concerns push for using smaller processors and less memory. Providing smaller CPUs with less memory lowers the manufacturing cost. This per-shipped-item cost is called *recurring cost,* because it recurs as each device is manufactured. Software has no significant recurring cost—all the costs are bound up in development, maintenance, and support activities, making it appear to be free.[2] This means that most often, choices are made that decrease hardware costs while increasing software development costs.

Under UNIX, if a developer needs a big array, he might just allocate space for 1,000,000 floats with little thought of the consequences. If the program doesn't use all that space—who cares? The workstation has dozens of megabytes of RAM and gigabytes of virtual memory in the form of hard disk storage. The embedded systems developer cannot make these simplifying assumptions. He must do more with less, resulting in convoluted algorithms and extensive performance optimization. Naturally, this makes the real-time software more complex and expensive to develop and maintain.

Real-time developers often use tools hosted on PCs and workstations, but targeted to smaller, less capable computer platforms. This means that they must use cross-compiler tools, which are often more temperamental than the more widely used desktop tools. Additionally, the hardware facilities available on the target platform—such as timers, A/D converters, and sensors—cannot easily be simulated on a workstation. The discrepancy between the development and the target environments adds time and effort for the developer wanting to execute and test his code. The lack of sophisticated debugging tools on most small targets complicates testing as well. Small embedded targets often do not even have a display on which to view error and diagnostic messages.

Frequently, real-time developers must design and write software

---

[2] Unfortunately, many companies opt for decreasing hardware recurring costs without considering all of the development cost ramifications, but that's fodder for another book.

for hardware that does not yet exist. This creates very real challenges since they cannot validate their understanding of how the hardware functions. Integration and validation testing become more difficult and lengthy.

Embedded real-time systems must often run continuously for long periods of time. It would be awkward to have to reset your flight control computer because of a GPF[3] while in the air above Newark. The same applies to cardiac pacemakers, which last up to *10 years* after implantation. Unmanned space probes must function properly for years on nuclear or solar power supplies. This is different from desktop computers that are reset at least daily. It may be acceptable to reboot your desktop PC when you discover one of those hidden Excel "features," but it is much less acceptable for a life support ventilator or the control avionics of a 767 passenger jet.

Embedded system environments are often adverse and computer-hostile. In surgical operating rooms, electrosurgical units create electrical arcs to cauterize incisions. These produce extremely high EMI (electromagnetic interference) and can physically damage unprotected computer electronics. Even if the damage is not permanent, it is possible to corrupt memory storage, degrading performance or inducing a systems failure.

Apart from increased reliability concerns, software is finding its way ever more frequently into safety systems. Medical devices are perhaps the most obvious safety-related computing devices, but computers control many kinds of vehicles such as aircraft, spacecraft, trains, and even automobiles. Software controls weapons systems and ensures the safety of nuclear power and chemical plants. There is compelling evidence that the scope of industrial and transportation accidents is increasing [1,2].[4] Clearly, greater care must be taken in the development of systems that have potentially catastrophic effects.

For all the reasons mentioned previously, developing real-time software is generally much more difficult than developing non-real-time software. The development environments have fewer tools, and the

---

[3] *General Protection Fault,* a term that was introduced to tens of millions of people with Microsoft's release of Windows 3.1.

[4] It is not a question as to whether or not safety-critical software developers are paranoid. The real question is "Are they paranoid enough?"

ones that exist are often less capable than those for desktop environments or for "Big Iron" mainframes. Embedded targets are slower and have less memory, yet must still perform within tight deadlines. These additional concerns translate into more complexity for the developer, which means more time, more effort, and (unless we're careful indeed) more defects than standard desktop software of the same size.

1.2 Dealing with *Time*

A critical aspect of real-time systems is how time itself is handled. The design of a real-time system must identify the timing requirements of the system and ensure that the system performance is both correct *and* timely.

The three types of time constraints on computation are:

Hard   The correctness of response includes a description of timeliness. A late answer is incorrect and constitutes a system failure. A cardiac pacemaker must avoid pacing during specific periods of time following a contraction, or fibrillation (uncoordinated contraction of random myocardial cells—this is a *bad* thing) can occur. The time of pacing is an example of a hard real-time requirement.

Soft   Soft timeliness requirements are specified using an average response time. If a single computation is late, it is not usually significant, although consistently late computation can result in system failures. If an airline reservation system takes a few extra seconds, the data remains valid.

Firm   Firm deadlines are a combination of both hard and soft timeliness requirements. The computation has a shorter soft requirement, and a longer hard requirement. A patient ventilator must mechanically ventilate the patient a certain amount in the long run. A breath could come a few seconds late without affecting patient safety. However, a several minute delay in the initiation of a breath is unacceptable. Many requirements specified as soft are truly firm in nature.

The basic concepts of timeliness in real-time systems are straight-forward. Most time requirements come from bounds on the performance of reactive systems. The system must react in a timely way to external events. The reaction may be a simple digital actuation, such as turning on a light, or a complicated control loop controlling dozens of actuators simultaneously. Typically, many subroutines or tasks must execute between the causative event and the resulting system action. External requirements bound the overall performance of the control path. Each of the processing activities in the control path is assigned a portion of the overall time budget. The sum of the time budgets for any path must be less than or equal to the overall performance constraint.

1.2.1 Real-Time Operating Systems

Most moderate to complex real-time systems use a Real-Time Operating System (RTOS). The functions of an RTOS are much the same as those for a normal operating system:

- Managing the interface to the underlying computer hardware
- Scheduling and preempting tasks
- Managing memory
- Providing common services including I/O to standard devices such as keyboards, video, LCD displays, pointing devices, and printers

RTOSs differ from normal operating systems in a variety of ways. The most important of these are:

- Scalability
- Scheduling policies
- Support for embedded, diskless target environments

First of all, the RTOS is usually *scaleable*. That means the RTOS is structured like the growth rings on a redwood tree. The inner-most ring, called the kernel, provides the most essential features of the RTOS. Other features are added as necessary. Scalability makes an RTOS widely applicable to both small single-processor applications, and large distributed ones. RTOS vendors call this a *microkernel architecture*, emphasizing the small size of the minimalist kernel.

Fairness doctrines determine task scheduling in many operating systems. This ensures that all tasks have equal access to the CPU. Non-preemptive scheduling relies heavily on the proper execution of the application threads. Such schedulers cannot schedule other tasks until the currently executing thread explicitly releases control. One misbehaved task can starve all other threads by not releasing control to the OS in a timely fashion. RTOSs most commonly provide priority-based pre-emption[5] for control of scheduling. In this kind of scheduling, the higher priority task always preempts lower priority tasks when the former becomes ready to run. In real-time systems, average performance is a secondary concern. The primary concern is that the system meets all computational deadlines even in the absolute worst case.

RTOSs are tailored for embedded systems. They typically provide the ability to boot from ROM—a real advantage in systems without disk storage. Many can even operate out of ROM. This decreases the time necessary for system boot. Furthermore, EMI is less likely to corrupt ROM, so executing out of ROM increases the reliability of most systems.

1.3 Advantages of Objects

The previous section was all about the hard luck story that is our profession, developing real-time embedded systems. The good news is that although these issues will never go away, advances in the technology of representing and developing complex systems make them more tractable. Just as Fred Brooks said, there is no "silver bullet" that magically will make software development easy, but we can make incremental improvements in the way we think about systems and the way we develop them. This new technology is called object-oriented development, and it has been around for almost two decades now.

The primary advantages of object-oriented development are:

---

[5] The *priority* of a task is a measure of its timeliness requirement, not its criticality. The tighter the deadline, the higher the priority. This concern is orthogonal with the criticality or importance of the task.

- Consistency of model views
- Improved problem domain abstraction
- Improved stability in the presence of changes
- Improved model facilities for reuse
- Improved scalability
- Better support for reliability and safety concerns
- Inherent support for concurrency

The net result is that the object way is *better.* It's not dramatically better in the sense that software development will suddenly become easy, but better in that it enables us to build more complex systems in less time with fewer defects. Let's discuss each of these benefits in turn.

1.3.1 Consistency of Model Views

One of the problems with structured methods is the difficulty in mapping analysis views to design views and vice versa. Even though both representations are views of the very same system, it is nontrivial to show the exact correspondence between the analysis views (data flow and entity relationship diagrams) and the design views (structure charts). The fact that an infinite set of designs can fulfill the same analysis model doesn't help either. Once you're down in the code, it is difficult to show which data flow or process the code implements. The concepts used in data flow modeling and code writing are fundamentally disjoint. This makes it hard to show that the code in fact implements the analysis model.

In object-oriented systems, the same set of modeling views is used in all phases of development. Objects and classes identified in the analysis model have direct representations in the code so it is almost trivial to show the relationship between the definition of the problem (analysis) and its solution (the code).

Object-oriented systems are developed using one of two approaches. Either the analysis model is elaborated by adding design concepts (the *elaborative* development model) or a translator is built that embodies the design decisions directly (the *translative* development model). In either case, the analysis model maps directly to the implementation.

1.3.2 Improved Problem Domain Abstraction

Structured methods have some limited facilities for abstraction and encapsulation. However, they enforce an artificial separation of structure and behavior that greatly weakens their effectiveness. A *sensor* must be modeled on one hand as some data values and on the other as a set of operations, but the inherent link between them that exists in the real world is not maintained.

Object-oriented modeling maintains the strong cohesion among data items and the operations that manipulate them. Because this is how the real world exists, object-oriented abstractions are more intuitive and powerful. Even the vocabulary for naming the objects comes from the problem domain. Users and marketers can understand the implications of their requirements much more clearly because it is constructed using their own concepts. The object perspective is at a higher level, closer to the problem domain and further away from the computer science implementation domain. This results in a system that has loose coupling between independent aspects of your system while maintaining good cohesion of aspects that are inherently tightly coupled.

1.3.3 Improved Stability in the Presence of Changes

Every developer has had the experience that a small change in requirements has a catastrophic effect on the software structure. This is because the foundation of structured systems is *fundamentally unstable* and subject to radical changes. The structured development world is rather like a Dali painting in which *a priori* truths are subject to *a posteriori* modification. It works fine for art, but that's no way to live.

Because object-oriented system abstractions are based on the real world, they tend to be much more stable. The fundamental structure of the real universe doesn't undergo daily fluctuations.[6] Changing requirements is usually a matter of adding or removing aspects of the model rather than a total restructuring of the system.

---

[6] I understand that this means that politics must be excluded from the "real universe," but I'm OK with that. Ever since the Tennessee State Senate tried to legislate the value of pi to be 3.0 I think they've been banished to an alternative universe anyway.

1.3.4 Improved Model Facilities for Reuse

Structured systems have had limited success with reuse. If the component does exactly what you need, great—you can reuse it (provided that it links properly to your compiler on your operating system, even though it was developed with an older revision of a now-unavailable compiler). Reuse in structured systems is generally a matter of modifying the source code of the component to meet your new requirements or integrate with your new environment. The net result has been a truly abysmal record of reuse.

Object-oriented modeling includes two tactical means for improving reuse—generalization and refinement. Generalization (a.k.a. *inheritance*) supports reuse by adding and extending existing components with no changes to their source code. This is the powerful notion of "programming by difference" and allows the developer to code only the things that are different.

Refinement is similar to generalization but allows the incomplete specification of objects, which are then refined by adding the missing pieces. The same basic structure is reused by using different missing parts. It is possible to write a sort routine once and refine it for different data types, like integers, floats, accounts, EEG measurements, and target coordinates. The code that actually sorts the collection had to be written only one time but it can be applied to many different circumstances.[7]

1.3.5 Improved Scalability

The whole point of any kind of method for developing software is to manage complexity. Small systems are less complex than larger ones (Duh!), and if the system is small enough no method is required at all. At the other end of the spectrum, where we *really* need development methods is when the systems are large and complicated. Structured methods work well for small to medium scale systems, but they fail when confronted with large scale problems.

The lack of scalability of structured systems is due to a number of weaknesses within the structured way of thinking and modeling.

---

[7] The reuse facilities in object-oriented methods are an enabling technology permitting reuse to occur. They do not automatically guarantee that reuse *will* occur—that is a sociological issue beyond the scope of this book.

Structured systems have weaker abstraction and encapsulation facilities, meaning that structured systems tend to have some level of pathological coupling that becomes more severe as the scale of the problem grows. The use of different modeling notations and concepts in different phases means that "getting to there from here" is harder and more error-prone. Lastly, too many system aspects aren't directly modeled, meaning that *ad hoc* approaches must be applied. As the system grows, these *ad hoc* approaches become less tenable.

Objects do it better. Improved abstraction and encapsulation maintains looser coupling among components, decreasing pathological coupling. The use of the same notation throughout the development process means that there is no "can't get there from here" syndrome when moving from analysis to design to code. The notation itself is obvious and simple and not full of *ad hoc* artifacts necessary to circumvent the deficiencies in the method.

1.3.6 Better Support for Reliability and Safety Concerns

Because of better abstraction and encapsulation, the interaction of different object-oriented components can be limited to a few well-defined interfaces. This improves reliability because it is possible to control how the components interact. Additionally, it is possible to more clearly and cleanly enforce pre- and post-conditions required to make your system run properly. For example, C standard arrays require the user of the component to make sure that array bounds are not exceeded; object language allows you to build the reliability checking into the array itself. Also, object systems offer exception handling for ensuring that exceptional and fault conditions are handled correctly. Finally, because of the improved support for reuse, better-tested components can be reused so that less of each new system must be developed from scratch.

1.3.7 Inherent Support for Concurrency

Concurrency is a fact of life—and a very important fact for real-time embedded systems developers. Structured methods have no notion of concurrency, task management, or task synchronization. These important aspects of your system can't even be represented using standard structured methods.

Object-oriented systems are inherently concurrent, and the details of tasking and task synchronization can be represented explicitly using orthogonal components in statecharts, active objects, and object messaging. These are powerful tools in the struggle to build correct systems that meet tight performance requirements.

1.4 Object Orientation with UML

The Unified Modeling Language (UML) is a language for expressing the constructs and relationships of complex systems. It began as a response to the Object Modeling Group's (OMG) request for a proposal for a standard object-oriented methodology. Spearheaded by Rational's Grady Booch, Jim Rumbaugh, and Ivar Jacobson, the UML is being submitted to the OMG by some of the major software companies in the world, including i-Logix, Digital, HP, ICON Computing, Microsoft, MCI Systemhouse, Oracle, Texas Instruments, and Unysis. Contributions have been made by many of the top object modelers, such as David Harel, Peter Coad, Jim Odell, and others.

UML is more complete than other methods in its support for modeling complex systems and is particularly suited for including real-time embedded systems. Its major features include:

- Object model
- Use cases and scenarios
- Behavioral modeling with statecharts
- Packaging of various kinds of entities
- Representation of tasking and task synchronization
- Models of physical topology
- Models of source code organization
- Support for object-oriented patterns

Throughout the course of this book, these features will be described in more detail, and their use shown by examples. For now, let's explore the fundamental aspects of the UML object model.

1.4.1 Objects

Structured methods look at a system as a collection of functions decomposed into more primitive functions. Data is secondary in structured view and concurrency isn't dealt with at all. The object perspective is different in that the fundamental decompositional unit is the *object*. So, what is an object?

The short form: An object is a cohesive entity that has attributes, behavior, and (optionally) state.

The long form: Objects represent things that have both data and behavior. Objects may represent real world things, like dogs, airfoil control surfaces, sensors, or engines. They may represent purely conceptual entities like bank accounts, trademarks, marriages, or lists. They can be visual things, like fonts, letters, ideographs, histograms, polygons, lines, or circles. All these things have various aspects, such as:

- Attributes (data)
- Behavior (operations or methods)
- State (memory)
- Identity
- Responsibilities

Let's take an example from each of these object categories. A real-world thing might be a sensor that can detect and report both a linear value and its rate of change (Table 1-1).

Table 1-1: *Sensor Object*

Attributes	Behavior	State	Identity	Responsibility
Linear value Rate of Change (RoC)	Acquire Report Reset Zero Enable Disable	Last value Last RoC	Instance for robot arm joint	Provides information for the precise location of the end of the robot arm in absolute space coordinates.

The sensor object contains two attributes; the monitored sensor value and its computed Rate of Change (RoC). The behaviors support data acquisition and reporting, and permit configuration of the sensor. The object state consists of the last acquired/computed values. The identity specifies exactly which object instance is under discussion. The responsibility of the sensor is defined to be how it contributes to the overall system functionality. Its attributes and behaviors must collaborate together to help the object achieve its responsibilities.

A bank account is a conceptual entity, but is nonetheless an important object (Table 1-2).

The account object also has enabling attributes and behaviors. The attributes include the balance, interest rate, and the amount of money accrued due to interest. The behaviors allow you to deposit and withdraw money, create and destroy the account, and get information about it.

A font is a visual object—see Table 1-3. Certain characteristics of an object may be more important for some objects than for others. One could envision a sensor class that had no state—whenever you asked it for information, it sampled the data and returned it, rather than storing it internally. An array of numbers is an object that doesn't have any really interesting behaviors.

The key idea of objects is that they combine these properties into a single cohesive entity. The structured approach to software design deals with data and functions as totally separate entities. Data flow

Table 1.2: *Bank Account Object*

Attributes	Behavior	State	Identity	Responsibilities
Balance Interest Rate Accrued Interest	Debit Credit Report Open Close	Current balance	Sam's checking account	Stores money for Sam providing access via checks. Provides interest on balance as long as it remains above a specific value.

Table 1-3: *Font Object*

Attributes	Behavior	State	Identity	Responsibility
Point size Serif Color	Draw Char Erase Char Load Unload Set color	Current character set	Times New Roman 16 pt. normal san serif (first load)	Provides a visually attractive typeface in a particular size for the display of readable English text messages.

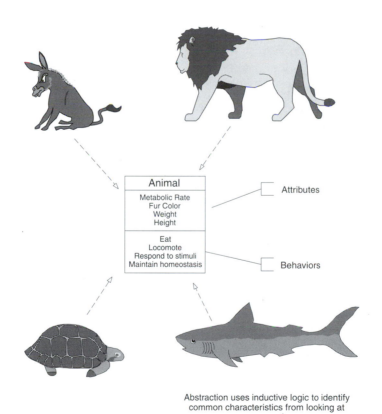

Abstraction uses inductive logic to identify
common characteristics from looking at
many examples

Figure 1-1: *Object Abstraction*

diagrams show both data flow and data processes. Data can be decomposed if necessary. Independently, structure charts show the static call tree to decompose functions (somewhat loosely related to the data processes). Objects fuse related data and functions together. The *object* is the fundamental unit of decomposition in object-oriented programming (see Figure 1-1).

Abstraction is the process of identifying the key aspects of the entity and ignoring the rest. A chair is an abstraction defined as "a piece of furniture with at least one leg, a back, and a flat surface for sitting." That some chairs are made of wood while others may be plastic or metal is inessential to the abstraction of "chair." When we abstract objects we select only those aspects that are important, relative to our point of view. For example, as a runner, my abstraction of dogs is as "high-speed teeth delivery systems." The fact that they may have a pancreas or a tail is immaterial to my modeling domain.

The object metaphor is powerful for a couple of reasons. First and foremost, it aligns well with common daily experience. In the real world, we deal with objects all the time, and each one has all the properties we've assigned to the preceding objects. Rocks may not have interesting behavior—but they do have attributes, like color, weight, and size. They certainly have responsibilities, such as intimidating hungry pit bulls. Most objects have behavior as well. Engines turn on or off, deliver torque, guzzle gas, and require maintenance. Object-oriented decomposition allows us to use our hard-won intuition that we've gained by simply living in the world and interacting with it. This is not true of functional decomposition.

ALGOL-based languages introduced the concept of an Abstract Data Type (ADT). Rather than defining only the underlying data bit patterns, ADTs include the operations that make sense in terms of their use and purpose. An enumerated type is an example of an ADT. Pascal provides three operators for enumerated types: ord(), pred(), and succ(), or ordinal value, predecessor, and successor, respectively. Ada provides the same operators as attributes A'POS, A'PRED, and A'SUCC, in addition to a few more. C has much weaker abstraction facilities. It short-circuits the abstraction by making visible the internal unsigned integer structure of enumerations. It is important to consider the ADTs and the operations defined on them together.

In their simplest expression, objects are nothing more than ADTs

Table 1-4: *Common ADTs*

Data Structure	Operations
Stack	Push Pop Full Empty
Queue	Insert Remove Full Empty
Linked List	Insert Remove Next Previous
Tree	Insert Remove Next Previous

bound together with related operators. This is a low-level perspective and doesn't capture all of the richness available in the object paradigm. Software developers use such ADTs and operators as low level mechanisms all the time—stacks, queues, trees, and all the other basic data structures are nothing more than objects with specific operations defined. Consider the common ADTs in Table 1-4.

At a low-level of abstraction, these are merely objects that provide these operations intrinsically rather than ADTs with separate functions to provide the services. In Pascal, to insert an item in a stack, you might have code that looks like this:

```
type
   OKType = {NoCanDo, CanDo}
   stackFrame = array [1..100] of float;
   record stack
      st: stackFrame; { holds stack values }
      top: integer; { holds top of stack }
   end;
```

```
function insert(var s: stack; f: float) : OKType;
begin
   if s.top > 100 then
      insert := NoCanDo
   else
      begin
      s.st[s.top] := f;
      s.top:= s.top + 1;
      insert := CanDo;
   end;
end; { insert }

var
   s: stack;
   result: OKType;
begin
   s.top := 1; { start at the beginning }
   result:= insert(s, 3.14159265);
end.
```

There are some open issues. Who ensures that s.top is initially set to 1? Here it is decoupled from the declaration of the stack variables and appears after the main BEGIN. Does the insert() function apply to other stack-type objects that might store integers or strings instead of floats? These questions arise because in Pascal there is no way to bind the ADT to the operations defined for it. Compare the preceding code with a C++ implementation:

```
class stack {
   int size;
   int top;
   float *st;
public:
   // constructor sets up top ok
   stack(int s=100) : size(s), top(0) {
      // st = new float[size]; };
   void insert(float f) {
      if (top > size)
         throw StackOverflow;
      else
         st[top++] = f;
      };
   ~stack() { delete[]st};
};
```

```
void main() {
    stack s, t(400);
    s.insert(3.14159265);
    t.insert(2.7182818284);
};
```

Although in this case it may not look like much of an improvement, the stack object binds the data and its associated operations together. Because the concept of a stack is meaningless without both the operations and the data, it makes the most sense to bind these things tightly together—they are different aspects of a single concept. This is called *strong cohesion*—the appropriate binding together of inherently tightly coupled properties. The result of the cohesion is that we can easily create a different sized stack (the default gives us our 100-element stack). The stack object itself handles the details of creation and deletion of variables of type stack. The insert operation is also a part of the stack object.

In a more general sense, objects may be thought of as autonomous machines. Our bodies are constructed of diverse sets of cells that have different attributes, roles, behavior, state, and responsibilities. They come together in higher level collaborations called *organs* to achieve some higher level systemic function, like digestion, locomotion, or thermoregulation. The cells themselves are autonomous and take care of their internal details, just like software objects.

Since objects are autonomous machines, it is easier to ensure that they are loosely coupled with the objects around them. In fact, the execution of behaviors is far more general under this notion than in the standard functional model. In the functional model, it is assumed that the caller calls a function and waits until it is complete and returns, whereupon the caller resumes. This is only one of several available models of interobject communication. Objects may implement this synchronous (direct function) call, but may also implement asynchronous calls as well, as when the called object runs within a different thread of execution or even a different processor. Different mechanisms for handling guards and blocking are also available. The model of object-as-machine is a very general one.

Rather than depict one object calling a service of another, the general model is that one object sends a message to the other requesting a service or operation (see Figure 1-2). Messages may be implemented in

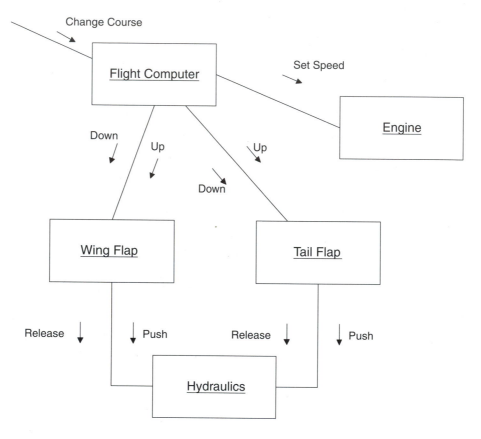

Figure 1-2: *Objects Collaborate to Achieve System Functionality*

many different ways to achieve different effects. At the modeling stage, message implementation is not an essential detail, and as such, it should not be visible.

1.4.2 Attributes

Attributes, in OO-speak, refer to the data encapsulated within an object. It might be the balance of a bank account, the current picture number in an electronic camera, the color of a font, or the owner of a trademark. Some objects may have just one or a small number of simple attributes. Others may be quite rich. In some object-oriented languages, all instances of data types are objects, from the smallest integer type to the most complex aggregate. In C++, in deference to minimizing the difference between C and C++, variables of the elementary data types, such as *int* and *float,* are not really objects. Programmers may treat them as if they are objects (well, almost anyway—but that's a programming, rather than a modeling, issue) but C++ does not require it.

1.4.3 Behavior

Interesting objects do interesting things. Passive objects supply behaviors for other objects; that is, they provide services that other objects may request. ADTs are typically passive objects. In the previous C++ example, the stack objects provide storage for simple data values, the means for inserting and removing them from storage, and some simple error checking to ensure their integrity. Active objects form the roots of threads and invoke the services (behaviors) of the passive objects.

Logically, behavior can be modeled as three distinct types: simple, automaton, and continuous. All three are important, although the second has a particular importance in real-time systems.

The first kind of behavior is called *simple.* The object performs services on request and keeps no memory of previous services. Each action is atomic and complete, at least from an external perspective. A simple object may maintain a collection of primitive data types and operations defined on them. A binary tree object, for instance, shows simple behavior. Another example is a cos(x) function. $\cos(\pi/2)$ always returns the same value, regardless of what value it was invoked with before. It retains no memory of previous invocations. This kind of object is also called *primitive.*

The second type of object behavior treats the object as a particular type of machine, called an *automaton* or Finite State Machine (FSM). This kind of object possesses a bounded (*finite*) set of conditions of existence (*states*). It must be in one and only one state at a time. An automaton exhibits modal behavior—each mode constituting a state. A state is an independent condition of existence defined by the set of events it processes and the actions it performs. Because objects with state machines react to events in well-defined ways, they are also called *reactive objects.*

Incoming events can induce transitions between object states in some predefined manner. Some object-oriented methods claim that all objects exhibit state behavior. A sample-and-hold A/D converter is such an object, as shown in Figure 1-3. It shows the states of

- Enabled
- Sampling
- Holding
- Disabled

The third kind of object behavior is called *continuous.* An object with continuous behavior is one with an infinite, or at least unbounded, set of existence conditions. One example is an *algorithmic object.* This is an object that executes some algorithm on a possibly infinite data stream. A moving average algorithm performs a smoothing function over an incoming data stream. Objects with continuous behavior are objects whose current behavior is dependent on past behavior and inputs, but the dependency is of a continuous, rather than discrete nature. Fuzzy systems and PID control loops are examples of continuous systems, as are pseudo-random number generators and digital filters. Their current behavior depends on past history, but in a quantitative not qualitative way.

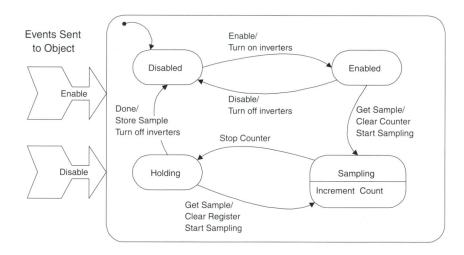

Figure 1-3: *State Machine for a Sample-and-Hold A/D Converter*

1.4.4 Messaging

The logical interface between objects is done with the passing of *messages*. A message is an abstraction of data and/or control information passed from one object to another. Many different implementations are possible. For example:

- A function call
- Mail via a Real-Time Operating System (RTOS)
- An event via an RTOS
- An interrupt
- A semaphore-protected shared resource
- An Ada rendezvous
- A Remote Procedure Call (RPC) in a distributed system

Early analysis identifies the key messages. Later design elaborates an implementation strategy that defines the synchronization and timing requirements for each message. Internally, the object translates the messages into acceptor operations, state transitions, commands, or data to munch on, as appropriate. Messages occur only between objects that have an association (see Figure 1-4).

Use of message passing enforces loose coupling. In analysis, one does not specify interface details such as synchronicity, function call format, rendezvous, time outs, etc. These are design and implementation details that can be decided later, once the overall problem is better understood.

An object's interface is the facade that it presents to the world, and is defined by the set of protocols within which the object participates. An interface protocol consists of three things:

- Preconditions
- Signature
- Postconditions

The preconditions are the conditions guaranteed to be true before the message is sent or received. Preconditions are normally the responsibility of the object sending the message. Postconditions are the things guaranteed to be true by the time the message is processed and are the

Figure 1-4: *Sending a Message to an Object*

responsibility of the receiver of the message. The message signature is the exact mechanism used for message transfer. This can be a function call with the parameters and return type or RTOS message post/pend pair, or bus message protocol.

The interface should reflect the essential characteristics of the object that require visibility to other objects. Objects should hide inessential details. Objects enforce strong encapsulation. In C++, for example, common practice is to hide data members but publish the operations that manipulate the data.

1.4.5 Responsibility

The responsibilities of an object are the roles that it serves within the system. The interface and the behaviors provide the means by which responsibilities are met, but do not define them. Consider a front-end loader tractor as an object, as described in Table 1-5.

The responsibilities are the roles the tractor will play for the road construction firm that uses it. The behaviors must be sufficiently rich to enable the responsibilities to be fulfilled, but do not of themselves define those responsibilities.

1.4.6 Concurrency

Unlike subroutines in structure charts, objects are inherently concurrent unless otherwise specified. It is theoretically possible for each object to run on its own processor. It is the physical structure of modern computers that drives sequential threads.

Table 1-5: *Tractor Characteristics*

Attributes	Carrying capacity Wheel size Maximum engine output Clearance height Weight
Behaviors	Lift Drop Move Set direction Change gear
Responsibilities	Move dirt from road bed to truck Dig holes for bridge supports Fill holes mistakenly dug

A thread is a set of operations executed in sequence. Concurrent threads can run on separate processors, meaning that the relative speeds with which they progress are uncoupled. On the same processor, we must rely on pseudo-concurrency provided by the underlying operating system, or write our own executive. These concurrency mechanisms allow the threads to progress more or less independently.

1.4.7 Objects as Autonomous Machines

Taken together, the characteristics of objects, such as attributes, behaviors, interfaces, encapsulation, and concurrency, allow each object to act as a separate entity—an autonomous machine. This machine does not have to be very smart, but must own its responsibilities and collaborate with other machines to achieve some higher order goals. At a minimum, objects must ensure:

• Data integrity
• Interface protocols are followed
• Their own behavior

This is true of small simple objects as well as more complex elaborate ones. Simple objects are akin to biological cells. Cells manage their own metabolism, absorb nutrients, maintain intracellular homeostasis, and fulfill whatever small function they provide to the system as a whole. Large groups of cells collaborate to form organs that excrete hormones, locomote, maintain systemic homeostasis, and play video games. Even larger collaborations form individual people, and collaborations of these (in pathological cases) form ANSI standards committees! Within the context of their responsibilities, these objects protect their own interests (especially in the standards committees).

This leads to a fundamental rule of object systems—*distributed intelligence.* Each object, however lowly and simple, has enough brains to manage its own resources and perform its own behaviors. This is different from functional decomposition in which it is common to have elaborately complex master subroutines that know everything about everybody. The truth of the matter is that it is far easier to construct dozens of semismart objects than a single really smart object that knows everything.

1.4.8 Classes

In the object-oriented world the term *class* is used in precisely the same way as in philosophy. A class is an abstraction of the common properties from a set containing many similar objects.

A class can be thought of as the type of an object.[8] The values 0, –3, and 7879 are all instances (objects) of the class integer. Further, all instances of a class have all the properties defined by the class. A mammal may have fur, bears its young live, and is homeothermic. This is true of all members of the class mammals—cats, mice, bears, and even rock stars. This does not mean that instances of the class are all the same—cats are certainly different from rock stars—but they share at least some set of common properties (most notably: fur, indifference to the needs of others, and a universal inability to sing). The values of these properties may be different among instances, but all properties must be present. For example, an account class may define a balance attribute—that is, all accounts have balances. Some accounts may have positive values, while others hover around zero or even dip into negative numbers.

Object-oriented designers uncover classes much the same way as philosophers—by observing a number of objects and abstracting the common properties. Table 1-6 contains some example classes.

In each of these cases, it is possible to imagine specific object instances of these classes. Just as a *struct* in C defines data structure, a class defines the type of objects created in its likeness (see Figure 1-5).

A class defines the attributes and behaviors of the objects it instantiates,[9] but not their responsibilities. All properties of objects of a class are all the same in *type*, but not in *value*. That is, if a class has an attribute, such as color or charm, then instances of the class have the characteristic although their particular value of the attribute may differ. Responsibilities, however, are context-specific, and are determined by the use of the object within that context. A simple container object may

---

[8] Strictly speaking, the *type* refers to the interface of the object—objects with the same interface are of the same type, regardless of their class. The class of an object defines its internal implementation. This is not normally a useful distinction unless you are using languages that make the difference visible, such as Java.

[9] The term *instantiation* comes from the term *instance,* as in *making an instance* (i.e., object) of a class.

Table 1-6: *Class Examples*

Class	Attributes	Behaviors	Example Objects	Responsibilities
Bank account	Account type Account number Balance	Open Close Credit Debit	Sam's checking account Julie's savings account	Maintain updated balance to account for credits, debits, and interest. Also maintain an account history.
Elevator	Capacity Current floor Current direction	Go to floor Stop Open door Close door	Elevator 1 Blg 6 Elevator 3 Blg 1	Carry passengers to their desired floor.
Marriage	Wedding Date Number of Children Children	Wed Divorce Create Children	Cindy's first marriage	Maintain stable social group.
Airline flight	Flight number Date Point of origin Destination Departure time	Takeoff Land Lose Luggage	My flight to Jamaica	Carry passengers and luggage to destination safely.
ECG signal	Heart rate PVC count ST segment height Display rate Scalefactor	Get heart rate Set alarm limits Display waveform	George's ECG signal	Monitor and report status of patient's cardiac function to the attending physician; alarm for possibly dangerous conditions.

hold checking accounts and be responsible for coordinating access to these accounts. A container object of the same class may hold inventory records and coordinate access for an inventory control system. The responsibilities are similar in type but differ in the specifics. An object's class defines the responsibilities of an object only when all such objects are all used in the same context and in the same way.

UML classes are shown using rectangles with the name of the class

Human (class)

Bruce (object)

Susan (object)

Sam (object)

Figure 1-5: *Classes and Objects*

inside the rectangle. A variation uses a three-segment box; the top segment has the name of the class, the middle segment contains a list of attributes, and the bottom segment contains a list of operations. Not all of the attributes or operations need to be listed. Figure 1-6 shows a simple autopilot system consisting of an autopilot class and various sensor and actuator classes it uses.

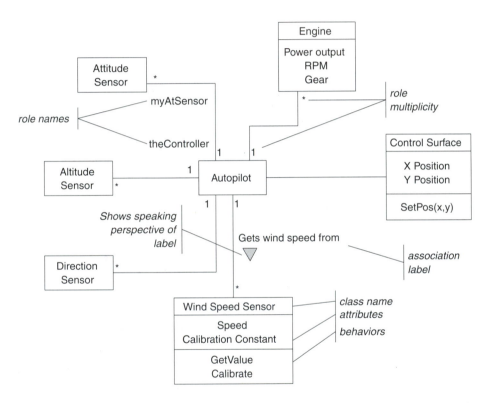

Figure 1-6: *A Simple Class Diagram*

1.4.9 Associations among Classes and Objects

For one object to send messages to another, they must associate with each other in some way. You can imagine that some association exists between the following pairs of objects:

Object	Association	Object
Engine	?	Piston
Flight computer	?	Engine
Linear position sensor	?	Sensor
Ship	?	Planks
Elevator	?	Call button
Bank customer	?	Bank account

As we will see later, the process of analysis identifies the key objects in the system as well as how they relate to each other. All associations can be (optionally) named when they clarify the association. The preceding relationships can be refined:

Object	Association	Object
Engine	*has a*	Piston
Flight computer	*controls an*	Engine
Linear position sensor	*is a type of*	Sensor
Ship	*contains some*	Planks
Elevator	*is called by*	Call button
Bank customer	*stores money in a*	Bank account

In UML, relationships exist between classes. Five elementary types of object relationships exist: *association, aggregation, composition, generalization,* and *refinement.*

Associations are relationships that manifest themselves at run-time to permit the exchange of messages among objects. Associations are shown using simple lines connecting two objects. Unless otherwise specified, UML associations are bidirectional and support messaging in either direction. When it is clear that messages go in only one direction, an open arrowhead points to the receiving object.

Aggregation associations are shown with diamonds at the owner end of the relationship. Aggregation is used when one object logically or physically contains another. *Composition* is a strong form of aggregation in which the owner is explicitly responsible for the creation and destruction of the part objects. The directed lines with closed arrowheads indicate a *generalization* or *is-a-kind-of* relationship. *Refinement* is shown with a closed arrowhead, like generalization, but uses dashed lines. Refinement relationships support generic or template elaborations of incomplete class specifications.

The numbers at each end of the relationship line denote the number of objects that participate in the relationship at each end—this is called the *multiplicity* of the role. We see in Figure 1-7 that one Window object can have 0, 1, or 2 scroll bars. Because the Window can have no scroll bars, this is an *optional* relationship. The scroll bar, for its side, works with only a single window, so the number at the Window side of the relationship is one. If multiple windows shared a scroll bar, then the cardinality would be "*" (an indicator for "unspecified but greater than or equal to 0") or the fixed number, if known. Figure 1-8 shows a more real-time example, a sensor.

Association

When one object uses the services of another, but does not own it, the objects have an association. *Associations* are appropriate when any of the following is true:

- One object uses the services of another but is not an aggregate of it
- The lifecycle of the used class is not the responsibility of the user class; that is, it is not responsible for both the used object's creation and destruction
- The association between objects is looser than one of aggregation
- The association can be characterized as client-server
- The used object is shared and used equally by many others

The class diagrams show that a Window class *uses* (specifically, gets user input from) various input devices. The two types shown are a mouse and keyboard, but other devices are conceivable, including tablets, microphones, and even a modem for a remote session.

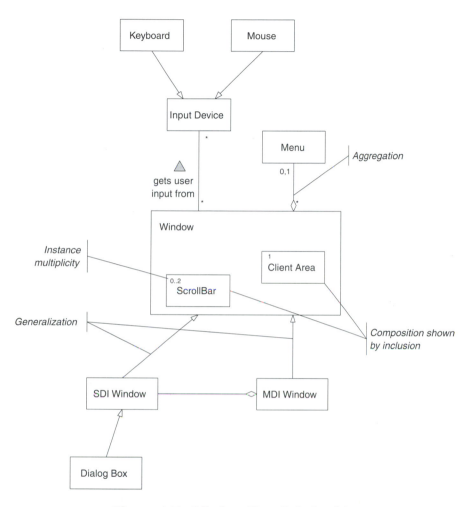

Figure 1-7: *Window Class Relationships*

Aggregation

An *aggregation* relationship applies when one object physically or conceptually contains another. The larger class is referred to as the *owner* or *whole*, and contains the diamond end of the aggregation. The smaller class is the *owned*, *part*, or *component* class. The owner is typically responsible for the creation and destruction of the owned class. UML al-

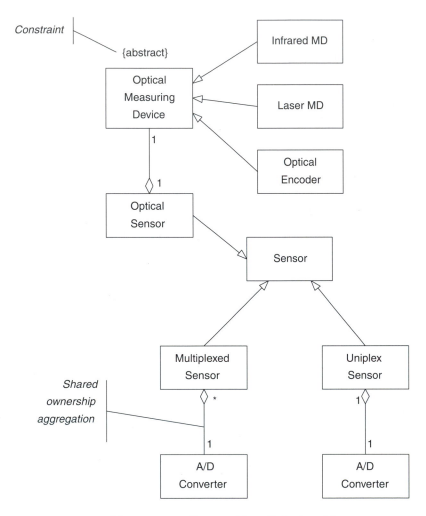

Figure 1-8: *Sensor Class Relationships*

lows components of aggregates to be shared among owners. When an object has shared ownership, some ad hoc rule must specify who has the responsibility for its creation and destruction.

In Windows programming, a *window* is a kind of object that contains a *client area*. The client area cannot stand on its own without being contained by a window. The client area comes into existence during the creation of the window and is destroyed when the window is destroyed. In the Sensor class shown, a Sensor class has an A/D converter.

Composition

Composition is a strong form of aggregation. Components normally are shown by actual inclusion of the component class within the composite. Alternatively, an aggregation association can be used, but shown with a filled diamond. Components of composites cannot be shared (that is, they can have only one owner) and the composite is required to create and destroy its components. A common use of composites is as active objects—that is, objects that are the roots of threads. These active objects create the threads in which to operate, and their components execute within this thread. The composite receives messages and events from the RTOS and other threads, and dispatches them to the appropriate components within its own thread.

Generalization

When one class is a specialization of another, the relationship is called *generalization* or *inheritance.* It means that the child or descendent class has all the characteristics defined by the parent, although it might specialize them. The child may also extend its parent class by adding additional attributes and behaviors. Fundamental to generalization is that it is an "is-a-kind-of" relationship between classes. A mammal is-a-kind-of animal and an infrared sensor is-a-kind-of sensor.

Type hierarchies are created from classes and their inheritance relationships. Such hierarchies form the basis of some kinds of frameworks, such as MFC (Microsoft Foundation Classes) and Borland's OWL (Object Windows Library).

In the Window class diagram in Figure 1-7, the Window parent class has two direct descendants, SDI (Single Document Interface) and MDI (Multiple Document Interface) classes. The SDI class is further subtyped into a Dialog Box class. A Dialog Box is an SDI window that does not have a menu[10] and has visual controls placed in its client area. Mul-

---

[10] Note that all subtypes of the class Windows *can* have a menu (the multiplicity of "0,1" makes it optional), but dialog boxes commonly do not.

tiplicity makes no sense for inheritance relationships, and so is not depicted. Since the parent Window class has a client area, all of its descendants do as well.

Inheritance is an extraordinarily powerful facility, despite its seeming simplicity. It allows objects to be *specified by difference* rather than from scratch each time. In standard structured methods, extending or specializing a function requires modification of the source code to produce a new routine that meets your needs. In object-oriented systems, you may subclass the parent to create a child class and merely add the additional attributes and behaviors needed. If a behavior needs to be implemented differently for a subclass, that's no problem either. You redefine the behavior in the subclass. The object-oriented paradigm ensures the correct version of the behavior will be called based on the object type you have.

What we have discussed so far is called *single inheritance*—a class has one parent. Some languages, such as Ada and Smalltalk, support only single inheritance. Other languages, such as C++, allow you to inherit from more than one parent class—this is called *multiple inheritance.*

The primary reason for multiple inheritance is that you may want to use or create objects that share characteristics from multiple class libraries. One of the goals of object-orientation is to reuse software; multiple inheritance can facilitate reuse by allowing mixing of different class hierarchies. Remember that the inheritance relationship is just another way to say "is-a-kind-of." It is entirely possible for this relationship to hold within more than one class hierarchy. See Figure 1-9.

As Ellis [3] points out, the characteristics of a helicopter and a fixed-wing propeller airplane are significantly different. So how do you classify the Osprey V-22? It is a helicopter that has two propellers that can be oriented vertically as in a helicopter, or rotated in-flight to the orientation of propellers on a fixed wing airplane. Both "Rotary Wing Vehicle" and "Fixed Wing Vehicle" applies, so which do you choose?

Figure 1-10 shows another instance of multiple inheritance, adapted from [4]. Here are two important hierarchies for a university—employees and students. Employees have attributes such as:

- Rate of pay
- Tax deductions
- Medical plan options
- Social Security payments made this year

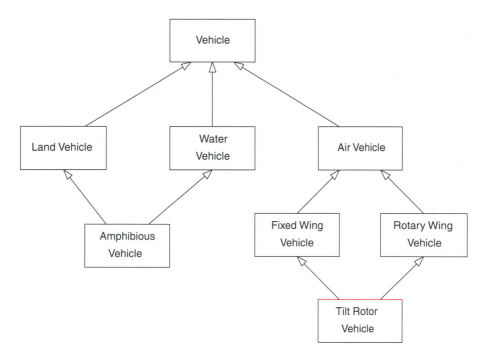

Figure 1-9: *Multiple Inheritance*

Students have an entirely orthogonal set of attributes such as:

- Current class load
- Grade point average
- Advisor
- Major
- Minor
- Year
- Unpaid tuition amount due University

These are both rich types containing important information. Which hierarchy do you select as most important for a graduate teaching assistant?

One solution to both these problems is to inherit from both hierarchies. This solution is problematic if the two hierarchies have a common point anywhere above the direct parents of the class. Remember that an object inherits all characteristics of its parent. If the School Member has the characteristics shown in Table 1-7, then the definition of Student and Faculty might be that in Tables 1-8 and 1-9, respectively.

So, the Graduate Teaching Assistant would then have the class definition described in Table 1-10.

Oops! Since the class Graduate Teaching Assistant inherits from two hierarchies (that just so happen to be joined at the hip), it has two of all characteristics from the School Member class. So if a class updates an *address*, which one is modified? Both?

C++ addresses this by providing the facility to mark a base class as *virtual*. A virtual base class will only be represented once in a multiply-

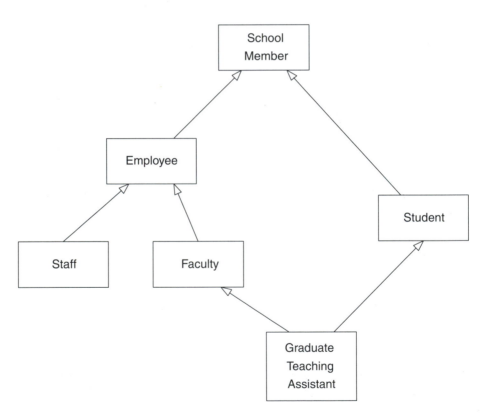

Figure 1-10: *Multiple Inheritance of School Membership*

Table 1-7: *School Member*

Attributes	Name Address
Behaviors	Accept school mailer

Table 1-8: *Student*

Attributes	Name (inherited from School Member) Address (inherited from School Member) Student number GPA Current class load Tuition owed
Behaviors	Accept school mailer (inherited from School Member) Send tuition bill Compute GPA

Table 1-9: *Faculty*

Attributes	Name (inherited from School Member) Address (inherited from School Member) Employee number Pay rate Pay period Deductions Social Security Number Medical benefits plan
Behaviors	Accept school mailer (inherited from School Member) Send paycheck Change deductions

inherited child class. If you forget to do this, though, you have two copies of all base class attributes. References to the base class members are now ambiguous unless they are fully qualified using the scope resolution operator ::, as in student::Name and Faculty::Name.

Inheritance is a mechanism to represent generalization-specialization.

Table 1-10: *Graduate Teaching Assistant*

Attributes	Name (inherited from School Member)
	Address (inherited from School Member)
	Student number
	GPA
	Current class load
	Tuition owed
	Name (inherited from School Member)
	Address (inherited from School Member)
	Employee number
	Pay rate
	Pay period
	Deductions
	Social Security Number
	Medical benefits plan
Behaviors	Accept school mailer (inherited from School Member)
	Send tuition bill
	Compute GPA
	Accept school mailer (inherited from School Member)
	Send paycheck
	Change deductions
	Accept school mailer (inherited from School Member)
	Send tuition bill
	Compute GPA

That is, the parent class is a generalized version of the child class. One of the important principles of generalization is the Liskov Substitution Principle (LSP). LSP states that a subclass must be freely substitutable for its superclass. This means that a subclass must continue to act as though it also is an instance of its superclass. A dog may be a specialized, extended form of mammal, but an instance of dog is still a mammal and has all the properties of mammals. LSP requires that subclasses do not constrain superclass behavior, such as by blocking or selectively inheriting some properties.

Almost always, a single inheritance hierarchy is specialized along a single characteristic or a small set of closely related characteristics. Multiple inheritance usually makes sense only if the sets of inheritance hierarchies are specialized along *orthogonal characteristics* (properties with nothing in common). Otherwise, another solution probably will be more appropriate.

Refinement (Templates)

The refinement relationship takes an incompletely specified entity and adds the previously unspecified aspects. The UML notational guide identifies the following types of refinement:

- Relation between a type and a class that realizes it (realization)
- Relation between an analysis class and a design class (design trace)
- Relation between a high-level construct at a coarse granularity and a lower-level construct at a finer granularity
- Relation between a construct and its implementation at a lower virtual layer, such as the implementation of a type as a collaboration of lower-level objects (implementation)
- Relation between a straightforward implementation of a construct and a more efficient but obscure implementation that accomplishes the same effect (optimization)

Normally, the only use of refinement you'll see is taking a generic, but incomplete, class specification and creating from it an instantiable class. A generic (*template* in C++-speak) is not, strictly speaking, a class. It is a template from which classes may be constructed by adding the missing details. You cannot construct an object from a generic directly—a class must be instantiated first.

Refinement is similar to generalization in that it also creates more specialized classes. At first glance, the distinction seems subtle indeed—in either case you are specializing some entity to get a class. Inheritance is used when you want to specialize how some behavior is performed or how some class is constructed. Generic instantiation is used when you want exactly the same behavior or structure, but applied on a novel component type.

Collection or container classes are a common application of the refinement relationship. A collection class is one that aggregates many component objects. These component objects are usually homogenous (of the same class), or at least from a single inheritance hierarchy. Exactly the same behavior applies regardless of the class being collected. Things you want to be able to do with a collection of classes might be:

- Get the first object in the collection
- Get the next object in the collection
- Add an object to the collection
- Remove an object from the collection

These behaviors are exactly the same regardless of whether you are dealing with a group of bank accounts, photodiode sensors, or automobiles. The behaviors of the objects themselves are vastly different, but the collection itself should behave in the same way nevertheless.

This is difficult to implement using inheritance, but straightforward using generic instantiation. Figure 1-11 shows how generics are represented. They use a dashed line with a closed arrowhead, similar to a generalization. The refining parameters are shown either on the association with a «bind» stereotype[11] or with the parameters shown in the class box between angled brackets. The classes created as a result of

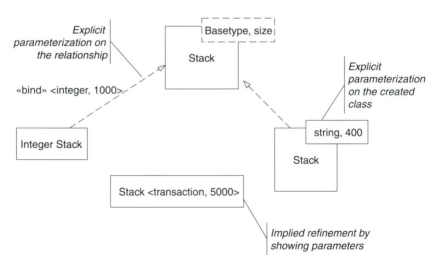

Figure 1-11: *Refinement Relationship*

---

[11] A *stereotype* is the class of an entity in the UML metamodel. Stereotypes are discussed in more detail in the next section.

the refinement look the same except that the base type is defined, and the base type appears inside a box with a solid line. This example declares a generic stack, and then instantiates three different stack classes—one for integers, one for strings, and one for transaction objects.

Note that in Figure 1-11, one of the refined classes has no refinement relationship shown with the generic. It is implied by the use of the generic's name and the inclusion of the replacing parameters enclosed by angled brackets.

1.5 UML Diagrams and Notation

UML has a rich set of notations and semantics. This richness makes it applicable to a wide set of modeling applications and domains. In this chapter we have only scratched the surface. In the coming chapters, new notations within UML will be presented when the context requires them. A concise overview of the notation is provided in the Appendix. Some notational elements we wish to present here include the text note, the constraint, and the stereotype because they will be used in a variety of places throughout the book.

A text note is a diagrammatic element with no semantic impact. It is visually represented as a rectangle with the upper right-hand corner folded down. Text notes are used to provide textual annotations to diagrams in order to improve understanding.

A constraint is some additional condition applied against a modeling element. Timing constraints can be shown on sequence diagrams (discussed in some detail in the next chapter) specifying the time between messages, for example. Constraints are always shown inside curly braces, and may appear inside of text notes.

Figure 1-12 shows text notes and constraints used together. At the top, the class model for a doubly-linked list is shown as a single class with constrained associations. At the bottom, the associations between classes Worker and Team Member are constrained, in that the Manager_of association is a subset of the Member_of association.

A *stereotype* is the class of an entity in the UML metamodel. The UML metamodel is the model of UML itself, expressed in UML. Stereotypes provide an important extension mechanism to UML, allowing

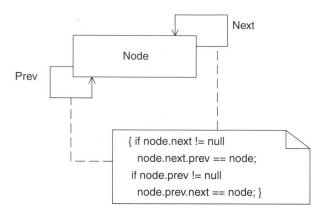

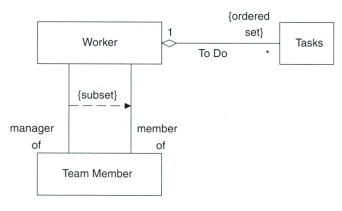

Figure 1-12: *Constraints in Action*

users to extend the modeling language to better address their needs. Each modeling element in UML is represented as a metaclass. A stereotyped metaclass is ultimately derived from an existing UML metaclass. For example, it is possible to create a new (meta)class of the UML *class* construct, which is just like the normal UML class but is extended or specialized. A class that represents the type (interface) of a class is just such a stereotyped class.

The usual notation for stereotypes is to enclose the stereotype in guillemets[12] preceding the name of the entity; for example "«type» stack," which is the name of a class providing a stack interface for another implementation. Special icons can be used instead of guillemets for common stereotypes. UML defines a number of common stereotype icons; feel free to add your own application domain specific icons (at the risk of introducing some nonportability, of course).

Figure 1-13 illustrates a few common UML stereotype icons. The "lollipop" is the icon for an «type» stereotype, which is a class that provides an interface for another. The stick figure is the icon for an «actor» stereotype, which refers to an external object that interacts with the system. The parallelogram icon is the stereotype for an «active» class, whose instances are the roots of threads.

All modeling entities in the UML can be stereotyped. For example, messages can be stereotyped. Some common stereotypes are shown in Figure 1-14. The coming chapters will introduce more stereotypes as needed.

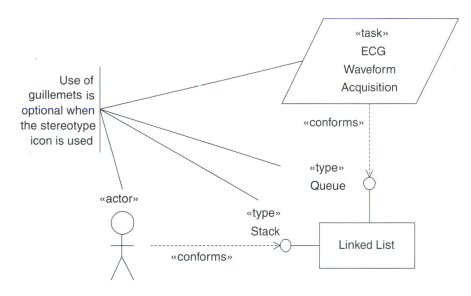

Figure 1-13: *UML Class Stereotypes*

---

[12] If guillemets are unavailable, then double angled brackets are an acceptable alternative. For example, <<type>> may be substituted for «type».

Stereotype	Icon	Applies to
«interface»	 ○—	class
«control»	 ↺	class
«active object»	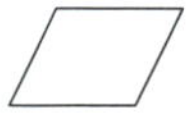 ▱	class
«utility»		class
«actor»	 ⚟	class
«bind»		refinement relation
«imports»		dependency relation
«calls»		dependency relation
«friend»		dependency relation
«instantiates»		dependency relation
«extends»		use case relation
«uses»		use case relation
«self»		association role
«local»		association role
«parameter»		association role
«global»		association role
«signal»		event
«becomes»		node dependency relation

Figure 1-14: *Some Common UML Stereotypes*

1.6 A Look Ahead

So far, we have only touched on the defining characteristics of real-time systems and the fundamental aspects of the object-oriented perspective. In the subsequent chapters of this book, we'll apply these ideas to the process of creating real-time embedded applications. The process is broken into the overall process steps of analysis and design. Analysis is subdivided into specification of external requirements and the identification of inherent classes and objects. Design is divided into three parts—architectural, mechanistic, and detailed levels of abstraction. Architectural design specifies the strategic decisions for the overall organization of the system, such as the design of the processor and concurrency models. Mechanistic design is concerned with the medium level of organization—the collaboration of objects to achieve common goals. Detailed design defines the internal algorithms and primitive data structures within classes. All the process steps are required to create efficient, correct designs that meet the system requirements.

1.7 References

[1] Leveson, Nancy G., *Safeware: System Safety and Computers.* Reading, MA: Addison Wesley Longman, 1995.

[2] Neumann, Peter G., *Computer Related Risks.* Reading, MA: Addison Wesley Longman, 1995.

[3] Ellis, John R., *Objectifying Real-Time Systems.* New York: SIGS Books, 1994.

[4] Rumbaugh, James, Michael Blaha, William Premerlani, Frederick Eddy, and William Lorensen, *Object-Oriented Modeling and Design.* Englewood Cliffs, NJ: Prentice Hall, 1991.

Chapter 2

Requirements Analysis of Real-Time Systems

Real-time systems interact with their external environment. The set of external objects of significance and their interactions with the system form the basis for the requirements analysis of the system. This is expressed in two forms—an external event context and the use case model. The external event context is expressed as an object model in which the system itself is treated as a single black-box composite object sending and receiving messages to external actor objects. The use case and scenario models decompose the primary functionality of the system and the protocols necessary to meet these functional requirements.

Notation and Concepts Discussed

Actors	Context diagram
Events	Use case diagram
Scenarios	

2.1 External Events

The *system context* is a map of the world of interest to the system. In the structured analysis world, the context diagram represents this world view. The context diagram from traditional structured methods can be used directly in an object-oriented context because it really shows objects rather than functional processes.

Since our concern is the development of real-time object-oriented systems, the term *system* includes the conceptual whole consisting of software, electrical hardware, and mechanical hardware under development. The context diagram shows the system as a single entity surrounded by other objects in the real world.

The UML does not explicitly support a context diagram, such as that found in structured analysis (for example, see [1], [2], and [3]). However, the UML object diagram,[1] along with appropriate stereotypes on messages and objects, serves this purpose nicely. It is this idiomatic usage of the UML object diagram that we shall refer to as a *context diagram* in this book.

The benefit of creating the context diagram is that it captures the environment of the system, including the actors with which the system must interact. Just as important, it captures and allows you to characterize the messages and events flowing between the system and its environment. A detailed understanding of the message and event characteristics is crucial early in the selection of processors, bus architectures, languages, and tools.

2.1.1 Context-Level Objects

A context diagram shows the system object interacting with one or more external objects. The system object includes any sensors and actuators internal to the system. The external objects are devices monitored, controlled, or interacting with the system that are outside its boundaries.

Ellis [4] provides some guidance with the categorization of internal

---

[1] The UML object diagram is identical to the class diagram except that it shows class instances rather than classes. As discussed in the previous chapter, standard objects are shown as rectangles with underlined names to distinguish them from classes.

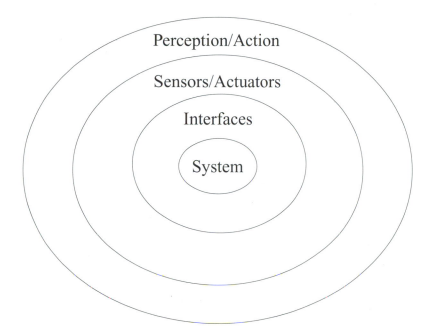

Figure 2-1: *Ellis' Onion Skin Analogy (From* Objectifying Real-Time Systems, *by John R. Ellis, copyright 1994 by SIGS Books, Inc. All rights reserved. Used by permission.)*

versus external objects. He models the world as an onion; that is, one composed of a set of successive layers with the system at the heart, as you can see in Figure 2-1. Regardless of any gustatory predilections, this analogy can provide a useful guide.

At the outer skin of the onion, user perception and actuation occur. At this layer, the user sees the data on the monitor or can observe the action taking place. For example, an elevator floor indicator displays the location of the floor. Actuators also exist in this layer, moving wings, inserting control rods into the reactor core, pacing the heart, etc.

The next layer contains the physical interfaces (sensors and actuators that monitor the world or produce the effects in the outermost layer). In our elevator example, the door pressure and optical sensors reside in this layer. These devices have interfaces to the system that reside in the third layer. Finally, in the center the system makes decisions and processes data.

Table 2-1: *Some Elevator Context Objects*

Perception/Action	Sensor/ Actuator	Interface	System
Passenger disembarks, obstructing door	Door Door Sensors	Ethernet LAN linking sensors and processors	Elevator System
Potential passenger requests elevator	Elevator Request Button	Ethernet LAN	Elevator System
Passenger requests floor	Floor Request Button	Ethernet LAN	Elevator System
Passenger holds the door open with the Open Button	Door	LAN	Elevator System
Passenger watches elevator position	(Elevator) Floor Indicator	LAN	Elevator System

For example, as seen in Table 2-1, some of the objects in the elevator can be classified within the onion schema (for the purposes of discussion, some low-level design decisions are presumed here).

Typically, the middle two columns of the table contain objects that may be internal or external to the system. The first column represents various use cases[2] specified in the problem statement.

Objects identified in the middle two columns of the table are external when any of the following conditions apply:

- The problem statement explicitly calls out the object, as when the system must interface with existing devices
- The object is already present in the problem domain environment; i.e., it will not be developed as part of the system
- The object supplies or receives information or commands from the system but is not supplied with the system

---

[2] A function point or a primary capability provided by the system. Use cases are described in more detail in Section 2.3.

- The object is a person monitoring the system output, entering information or commands, or directly affected by the system actions

If none of these apply, but the object is important in the context of the system, it must be part of the system *per se*. Figure 2-2 illustrates the decomposition of an elevator system overlaid on the onion analogy.

Using the context diagram view, the system object is treated as a composite, containing all its internal system "innards." Most often, the context diagram shows the system object as a black box, as in Figure 2-3. Note the use of the actor stereotype icons in that figure to show the external objects.

The context diagram can show the "onion" layers using UML packages to group the interfaces as shown in Figure 2-4. The dependency re-

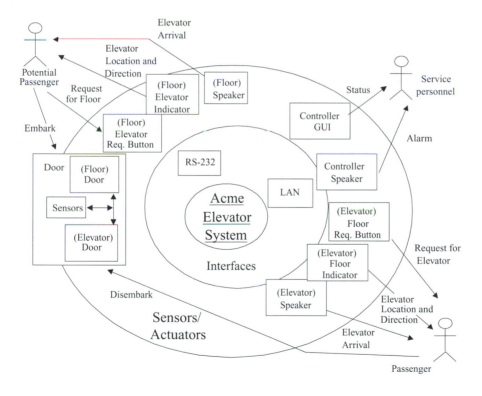

Figure 2-2: *Elevator Onion Skin*

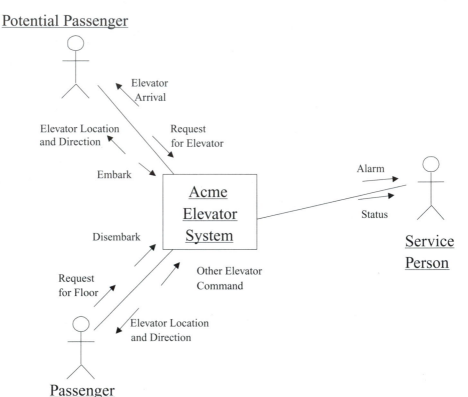

Figure 2-3: *Elevator Context Diagram*

lationships among the packages indirectly depict the external visibility of the packages. (Packages are groups of classes and objects related by subject matter and topic; see Chapter 5 for more details.)

2.1.2 Context-Level Flows

UML defines the *message* as the fundamental unit of object communication. Later in design, we'll decide whether this message is implemented in terms of a direction invocation of an object behavior, an RTOS message, or a message across a communications bus. At this point in the development process, it is more important to capture the

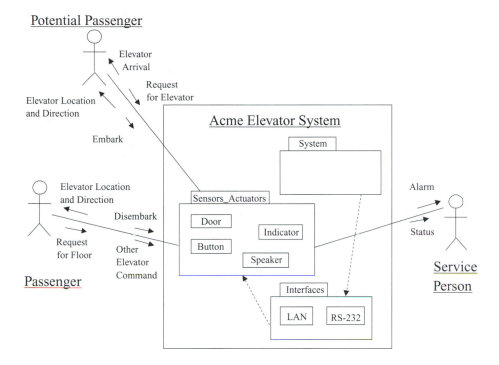

Figure 2-4: *Elevator Context with System Packages*

essential properties of the messages that are exchanged between the system and the actors interacting with it. Subsequent design will define the implementation of each message.

Message Properties

The essential properties of messages are their data content, arrival pattern, and synchronization pattern. An event is a message signifying an important occurrence. Events are classes, and just like other classes, event classes optionally contain data. The UML calls named events *signals,* which is why event classes carry the stereotype «signal». For example, a control knob can send an event when it is turned. One approach would send out an event for each click of the knob. A more robust approach is to band-limit the rate at which these events are sent.

The event message then conveys not only the fact that the event occurred but also the number of clicks that occurred. We will use the terms *event* and *message* synonymously in this text.

The arrival pattern of the message describes the timing behavior of the message group. UML does not describe these directly, but the definition of arrival patterns is crucial for analysis of schedulability and deadlines. This is important to define early because often the very feasibility of a cost-sensitive product is determined by the component and development costs. By understanding the message and event characteristics, it is possible to perform early performance analysis of different processor architecture choices and make good business decisions about whether or not the product can be delivered within an acceptable cost window.

Message arrivals can be *episodic* or *periodic*. An episodic arrival pattern is inherently unpredictable, but it may still be *bounded*. Episodic messages may have a *minimum interarrival time*—a minimum time that must occur between message arrivals. Episodic messages may also have an *average rate*—a computed average frequency, even though the message arrivals may vary greatly from message to message. Episodic messages may be *bursty*, meaning that they tend to arrive in clumps. Episodic messages may be *random*, in which case the arrival of one messages does not affect the probability of the arrival of the next (except for the minimum interarrival time). Formally speaking, this is called a *renewal process.*

Periodic messages are characterized by a *period* with which the messages arrive, and by *jitter*, which is the variation around the period with which messages actually arrive. Jitter is normally modeled as a uniform random process but always totally within the jitter interval.

Synchronization patterns are explicitly, if somewhat weakly, supported by the UML standard. Synchronization defines the characteristics of the rendezvous of two objects that occurs during the exchange of a message. The synchronization patterns explicitly defined by UML are *call, asynchronous,* and *waiting.*

The call and waiting synchronization patterns are similar in that the sender is blocked from continuing until the target completes its processing of the message. The call synchronization pattern models the yielding of control during a function or method call that occurs within a single thread of control. The waiting synchronization pattern models the yielding of control to another thread until the message processing is complete. Remote Procedure Calls (RPCs) are normally implemented with just this synchronization pattern. The asynchronous synchronization pattern is inherently multithreaded, because it models a message being passed to another object without the yielding of control.

Booch [5] also defines *balking* and *timeout* synchronization patterns, which are an extension to the core UML model. The balking synchronization pattern models the behavior of one object aborting the message transfer if the other is not immediately available. The timeout pattern models the balking pattern, except that a fixed waiting time is defined for the receiver object to accept the message. The Ada programming language tasking constructs explicitly support balking and timeout synchronization.

Taken together, we can build a class metamodel of UML messages as in Figure 2-5. This model uses the *and-generalization* relationship of UML. And-generalization allows a class to be specialized along orthogonal dimensions independently. In this case, *message* is specialized along both the arrival and synchronization pattern dimensions. An in-

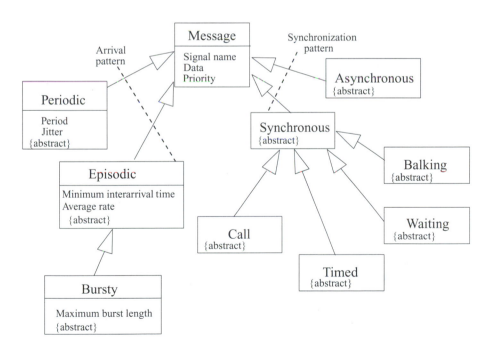

Figure 2-5: *UML Message Class Model*

stantiable class must inherit from all orthogonal dimensions in the hierarchy. For example, creating a class by inheriting from *periodic* and *asynchronous* creates the instantiable class «*periodic-asynchronous*» *message*.[3]

The metaclass model in Figure 2-5 extends core UML. The primary extension mechanism for extending UML is the *stereotype,* mentioned in the previous chapter. We will use stereotypes to indicate the instantiable message subclass, as in «periodic-asynchronous». If desired, iconic representations can be used instead of the subtypes.

Figure 2-6 shows the iconic stereotypes that I use for the orthogonal subclasses in Figure 2-5. These icons may be combined to form instantiable stereotypes, as shown in Figure 2-6. Both the standard guillemet notation or the iconic representation may be used. Naturally, if you are not concerned with the message arrival and synchronization types, the message stereotype may be omitted from the diagram.

Since most real-time systems must explicitly support concurrency, it is usually necessary to capture the mechanism of thread synchronization. The arrival and synchronization patterns allow the analyst to specify more precisely the message passing semantics. These annotations may be added to any diagram that shows messaging and events. This includes context, sequence, object message, and state diagrams.

As mentioned, events indicate significant occurrences, but other than that, they may be treated as ordinary messages. Events can be due to:

- Receipt of an explicit signal from another object
- Expiration of a timeout
- Receipt of a call of an operation by another object (a.k.a., a triggered operation)
- A condition coming true

Events in state diagrams normally trigger state transitions (see Chapter 4). Events may themselves be structured into a class hierarchy. This has impact on state behavior because a trigger may be on an event (which includes any of its subclasses) or only on a specific subclass.

---

[3] In early analysis, only the arrival pattern may be known. Synchronization patterns can be added later.

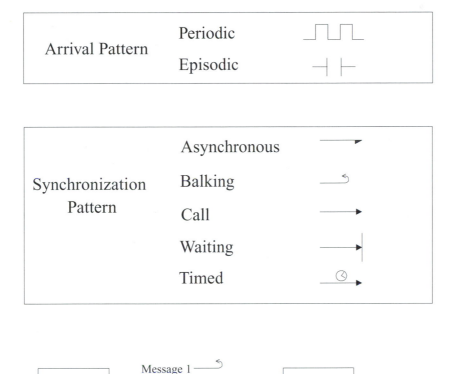

Figure 2-6: *Message Stereotypes*

Event hierarchies allow the development of general and specific event handlers at various levels of nesting and abstraction. Figure 2-7 shows an event hierarchy from an elevator system.

2.2 Specifying External Events

In real-time systems, external events play an important role in constraining and defining the system behavior. On the elevator context diagram (Figure 2-3), the message flow "Other Elevator Command"

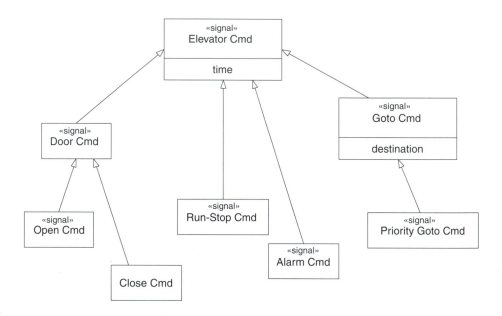

Figure 2-7: *Event Hierarchy*

includes event instances such as toggling the Stop-Run switch or pushing an alarm button. The flow supports a potentially rich set of actual events that may be decomposed into an event hierarchy.

Events by themselves provide insufficient information for the development of a system. The expected system response to each event must be specified in terms of what the system should do and the timing requirements for this response.

2.2.1 External Event List

The external event list is a detailed list of the environmental events that are of interest to the system. The list defines not only the events, but also the expected system response, their arrival patterns, and the event source. Table 2-2 shows an external event list for an elevator system.

As you can see, the external event list provides a number of attributes to capture the essential properties of events.

Reactive systems, by definition, primarily respond to external events. In such systems, most or all the events listed will be IN. The

Table 2-2: *Elevator External Event List*

	Event	System Response	Direction Pattern	Arrival Pattern	Synchronization Performance	Response
1	Potential passenger requests Elevator	a. Backlight button b. Select elevator c. Send selected elevator to floor	IN	Episodic	Asynchronous	a. Backlight 0.5 s b. 5 s c. ASAP
2	Passenger requests floor	a. Backlight button b. Send elevator to floor	IN	Episodic	Asynchronous	Backlight 0.5 s
3	Passenger sets Stop-Run switch to Stop	Stop elevator	IN	Episodic	Asynchronous	2.0 s
4	Passenger sets Stop-Run switch to Run	Continue elevator to handle pending requests	IN	Episodic	Asynchronous	2.0 s
5	Passenger obstructs door during closure	Door reopens and restarts timer	IN	Episodic	Asynchronous	Detect 0.5 s
6	Passenger presses Open button	Door stays open, door closure timer reset	IN	Episodic	Asynchronous	0.5 s
7	Passenger presses Close button	Door closure cycle begins	IN	Episodic	Asynchronous	0.5 s
8	Door closure time elapsed	Door closure cycle begins	IN	Episodic	Asynchronous	0.5 s
9	Passenger presses Emergency Call button	Notify the central station operator	IN	Episodic	Asynchronous	1 s
10	Elevator arrives at floor	a. Remove button backlight b. Announce arrival via speakers c. Begin door open cycle	IN	Episodic	Asynchronous	a. 1 s b. 1 s c. 2 s
11	Elevator leaves floor	Elevator goes to nearest destination on its destination list	IN	Episodic	Asynchronous	1 s
12	Operator command clamp release	Elevator goes to nearest destination on its destination list	IN	Episodic	Asynchronous	1 s
13	Cable tension fails	a. Engage locking clamps b. Notify central station via alarm	<internal> OUT	Episodic	Asynchronous	a. 0.25 s latency 0.5 s service b. 1 s

control responses issued from the system are directed OUT to external objects. At the context level, more flows will have an asynchronous synchronization pattern.

2.2.2 Response Time

In the realm of real-time systems, defining the external timing requirements is crucial to understanding the problem. An otherwise correct result delivered past its deadline is a system failure in a hard real-time environment. The key is to extend the external event table to include reactive timing.

A number of parameters are required to specify the timing requirements for real-time systems. Naturally, incoming messages must have their timing characterized. If they are periodic, then their periods and jitter must be identified. If they are episodic, then their minimum inter-arrival times and average rates must be defined. The system response timing must be defined in terms of deadlines. If the response has a hard deadline, then missing the deadline constitutes a systems failure. In a soft deadline system, the average throughput must be specified. Soft systems are permitted to lag in their response but are expected to maintain an average throughput or system response. Firm deadlines have both a hard deadline as well as an average throughput.

Response performance may be further specified into a worst-case hard deadline and an average response time when appropriate. Some performance requirements must be met only in the long run, and occasionally missing a deadline creates no difficulties. These soft deadlines must be identified as average response time requirements. Firm deadlines have both a hard deadline and a shorter average response time. Unless otherwise specified, the numbers listed in the Response Performance column are hard deadlines. To indicate soft deadlines reflecting average throughput, precede the number with a tilde (~) to indicate that this number is approximate.

More complex timing behavior requires more complex modeling. In some cases, scalars cannot specify the timing of behavioral responses adequately. Many actions require relatively long periods of time to perform and intermediate responses may be important. For example, an emergency shutdown of a nuclear reactor is implemented by insertion of control rods into the core. This may be initiated by an event such as a coolant leak or an explosive temperature and pressure build up. This takes some period of time. To avert an incident, it is preferable to insert the rods 90% of the way as soon as possible even if the remaining 10% takes much longer. Control loops are another example. Quick, if incomplete, responses stabilize PID control loops, even if the system response asymptotically converges much later.

These issues are domain- and system-specific. For many situations, the only concerns are service time and latency. Modeling 50% or 80% response times may be important in some special applications. In other applications, several points from a stimulus-response curve may be required to adequately characterize nonlinear performance requirements.

In most real-time systems, the time-response requirements are crucial because they define a performance budget for the system. As objects and classes are defined, this performance budget propagates through the analysis and design phases. Ultimately, they define a performance (sub)budget for each and every operation and function call in the thread of execution responding to the event. The sum of the (sub)budgets must meet the overall system performance requirement specified here. For example, a message and the completion of its reaction may require 500 ms. The overall reaction may be implemented via a chain of six operations. Each of these operations must be allocated some portion of the overall performance budget.

2.3 Use Cases

External event lists show single events clearly. They do not fare so well when the events cause an extended dialog between the actors and the system to begin, resulting in a flurry of messages. In early analysis, the *use case diagram* is similar to the context diagram. It shows the general cases of interaction among the system and the external objects. The use case diagram relies on the underlying event flows from the context diagram. The use case diagram provides a separate means of verification of the context diagram or may be used to help construct it.

Use case diagrams capture a broad view of the primary functionality of the system in a manner easily grasped by nontechnical users. The use case diagrams can become a centralized roadmap of the system usage scenarios for people specifying the requirements of the system. Use

cases themselves can be decomposed into other uses cases and ultimately into scenarios that show detailed sequences of object interaction. Because they are at a high conceptual level and use the problem
domain vocabulary, many people find the use case diagram the single
most important tool for communicating with the users. The use case diagram can feed into a more rigorous textual specification and assist the
process of requirements definition. The use case diagram allows this to
occur in a collaborative fashion since all participants can understand
the notation and semantics.

Scenarios are instances of a use case, just as objects are instances of
classes. In this way, use case diagrams are like class diagrams—they
show the logical static structure of scenarios. Scenarios may define
elaborate protocols consisting of many messages sent in particular sequences. Scenarios are more elaborate than single messages and rely on
many external object interactions to achieve the required system function points. Scenarios are a powerful means for communicating detailed requirements because implementation and computer science
concerns are effectively abstracted away. The scenarios can be directly
associated with a number of detailed requirements so that their characteristics and implications are clear.

The relationship between use case and protocols is shown in Figure
2-8. The use case uses the protocols (and their contained event and data
flows) to fulfill the system responsibilities. The event and data flows
must be sufficiently rich to support the required uses of the system.

The top-level use case diagram is another view of the system context. It provides an overview of the system, not of classes and objects,
but of function points. A function point is a broad scope area of functionality of the system and is isomorphic to a use case. These function
points and use cases can relate to vertical partitioning of the system
(logical organization of the system is discussed in the next chapter).
Note that external objects may participate in some use cases but not
others.

Figure 2-8 shows the system boundary as a rectangle with the external objects outside the system. These external objects connect to use
cases within the system via protocols. Additionally, some use cases depend on others—this is shown with an arrowed line connecting the use
cases.

Use cases are generic transactions typically involving potentially
many external objects and many messages. Use cases are important be-

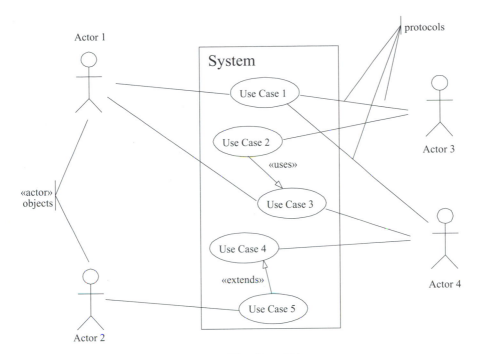

Figure 2-8: *Use Case Diagram*

cause they provide a valuable tool for capturing system requirements. Figure 2-9 shows the context diagram for an ECG monitor. For simplicity, many normal functions of an ECG monitor have been omitted, such as monitoring blood oxygen saturation (SpO_2) and invasive and noninvasive blood pressure. Five external objects are identified. The most important of these are clearly the patient (the primary data source) and the physician (the primary recipient of processed data and events). The other external objects of interest in this example are a remote display for the surgeon, a chart recorder for producing hardcopy recordings of waveforms, and the service representative who maintains the equipment. Message stereotypes are shown using both standard stereotype and iconic notations.

What are some ECG monitor use cases? Some candidates are:

• Configure Remote Display
• Autoconfigure
• Display Waveforms

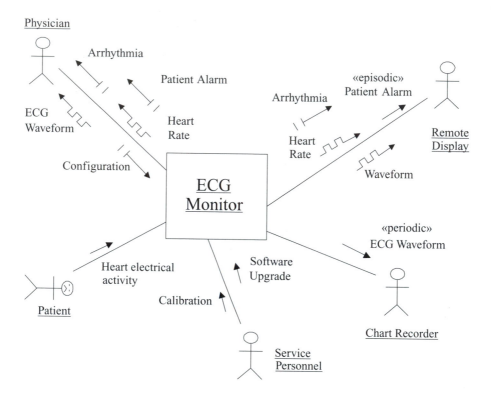

Figure 2-9: *ECG Monitor Context Diagram*

- Capture Waveforms
- Process Alarms
- Calibrate Sensors
- Update software

A little thought shows that these use cases are not merely simple data flows. Consider the Display Waveforms use case. This involves the physician:

- Connecting up to 12 electrical leads
- Configuring from one to six separate waveforms, including for each:
    - ▼ The electrical axes desired
    - ▼ Time base (sweep speed)

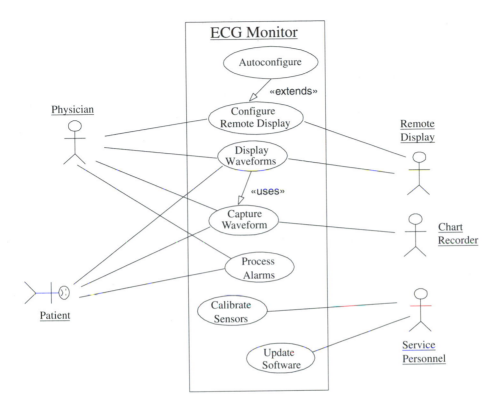

Figure 2-10: *ECG Monitor Use Case Diagram*

- ▾ Erase bar or scrolling waveform style
- ▾ Amplitude scale
- ▾ Screen position
- Setting alarm limits
- Setting overall display configuration

This lengthy and involved process can take multiple paths, depending on the leads selected, the number and selections of desired waveforms, etc. Each separate sequence of events is a different scenario. The totality of all such scenarios comprises the use case for Display Waveforms.

Updating the software is another example. Many scenarios are possible:

- Different things can be upgraded
  - ▼ The update is for the BIOS only
  - ▼ The main software is updated
  - ▼ A new type of sensor is added so the upgrade is software and hardware
  - ▼ An optional feature is added without modifying existing software
- The process can proceed differently
  - ▼ The update goes well (no errors)
  - ▼ The hardware is incompatible with the upgrade, so the software must detect the incompatibility and do the right thing
  - ▼ Electrical noise in the environment prohibits the proper completion of the upgrade
  - ▼ The disk containing the upgrade contains a disk error

These are all different scenarios that are instances of a single use case.

A couple of relationships are defined within the UML among use cases. The first is the «extends» relationship, which is a stereotyped generalization in which both the parent and the child must be use cases. The second is the «uses» relationship, a stereotyped form of generalization in which one use case depends on the functionality provided by another. The Autoconfigure use case is an example of the former in which the child use case is specialized from the Configure Remote Display. The relationship between the Capture Waveforms use case and the Display Waveforms use case is an example of the latter.

Acme elevator has a number of easily identifiable use cases, as shown in Figure 2-11.

An elevator is a fairly simple device, but even a use case as simple as "Take a ride" can produce many scenarios:

- A suitable elevator is already on the floor
- An elevator is available but must travel to the floor
- A suitable elevator exists, but has a pending request
  - ▼ Pending request must be handled first
  - ▼ Pending request should be handled after picking up passenger

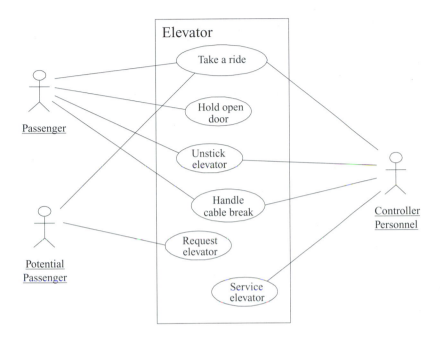

Figure 2-11: *Elevator Use Case Diagram*

- No suitable elevator exists, request must pend, waiting for next available elevator
- Passenger engages Stop on the Stop-Run switch as elevator is on the way to pick up the passenger
- Picked up passenger engages Stop en route to selected floor
- Passenger selects floor not in the direction originally selected (request must be serviced last)

and so on.

2.3.1 Identifying Use Cases

How does the analyst extract typical and nontypical uses of the system? Although some domain experts may think in abstract terms, the vast majority will be more comfortable identifying specific scenarios rather than use cases. The analyst must identify the dozens (or hundreds) of scenarios that map the important system aspects, and deduce the use cases from these. A number of approaches to identifying the scenarios are possible.

The analyst can sit with the customer and ask probing questions, such as:

- What are the primary functions of the system?
- What are the secondary functions of the system?
- Why is this system being built? What is it replacing and why?

The analyst must then identify for each use case:

- The role the external objects and system play in each scenario
- The interactions (flows) necessary to complete the scenario
- The sequences of events and data to realize the scenario
- What variations on the scenario are possible (other related scenarios)

For example, the primary functions of the ECG monitor are to display waveforms for the physician, provide discrete patient numeric values (such as heart rate), and alarm when the patient is at risk. Secondary functions might be to provide a remote display for the surgeon, provide a permanent patient record, supply billing information to the hospital network, and so on. Why is the system being built? Perhaps it provides better arrhythmia detection, color displays for better differentiation of lead configurations, faster response times, or it interfaces to the hospital network and the operating room anesthesia machines.

Another approach works well with a small team. Each object in the context diagram is written on a 3x5 card (which can evolve into Class-Responsibility-Collaboration [CRC] cards for use a little later in the analysis phase), including the system as one of the objects. Each team member takes a card and assumes the identity of the object. The team members role play the scenario by passing written messages to each other. As each team member receives a message, the member must identify different responses that he or she can reasonably make at this point. Each unique thread of responses is a scenario. The possible paths of these branch points define a decision tree. From this tree, a list of separate scenarios can be deduced.

A simple example is shown in Table 2-3. The last three columns are the objects being simulated by the team members during the role playing exercise. The descriptions shown inside square brackets [ ] are not messages, but just annotations to help describe activities not explicitly represented in the scenario.

What are some branch points? Passenger 2 could have requested the elevator when it was actually passing the third floor. Would that be a different scenario? Clearly not because the thread of the scenario would be the same—the elevator would continue going up to pick up passenger 1 and all subsequent actions would be the same. However, what if Passenger 2 requested an elevator going up before the elevator was even at floor 2? In this case, a different scenario would have resulted: the elevator would have stopped and picked up Passenger 2 since a) it could, and b) the request was in the same direction as the elevator's current direction. This latter alternative does present a scenario branch point.

The number of scenarios can quickly grow very large, and will require pruning. All scenarios that invoke identical system responses at each opportunity constitute a single scenario. Primary scenarios elaborate the major ways the use case is realized in practice. Secondary scenarios are relatively minor variants of the primary scenarios to explore exception handling, safety issues, and other important (but at this stage, peripheral) issues. Booch suggests that a moderate project will have a few dozen use cases, an order of magnitude more primary scenarios, and an order magnitude more secondary scenarios [6].

2.3.2 Using Use Cases

Use cases can provide a unifying strategy for the entire project development. They are an embodiment of what the customer wants and expects to see when the dust settles[4] and the product ships. Use cases group together functionally related scenarios and provide valuable information to all phases, as shown in Table 2-4.

---

[4] That is, the customer finally stops changing his or her mind long enough for you actually to *build* the darned thing.

Table 2-3: *Role Playing Scenario*

Step	Message	Action	Doug Passenger 1	Lauren Passenger 2	Wayne Elevator
	[Elevator idle at ground floor]				
1	Requests elevator at floor 6 going up	Elevator starts going to floor 6	Source		Target
2	[Elevator passes floor 2]				
3	Requests elevator at floor 2 going down	Elevator pends request		Source	Target
4	Elevator arrives at floor 6		Target		Source
5	Passenger 1 gets in and selects floor 8	Elevator closes door and begins going to floor 8			
6	Elevator arrives at floor 8 and opens door		Target		Source
7	Passenger 1 disembarks				
8	Door closure timer times out	Elevator closes door and begins going to floor 2			
9	Elevator arrives at floor 2 and opens door			Target	Source
10	Passenger 2 gets in and requests floor 1	Elevator closes door and begins going to floor 1		Source	Target
11	Elevator arrives at floor 1 and opens door	Passenger 2 disembarks		Target	Source
12	Elevator closes door and goes idle				

Table 2-4: *Use Cases*

Phase	Application of Use Cases
Analysis	Suggest large scale partitioning of the domain
	Provide structuring of analysis objects
	Clarify system and object responsibilities
	Capture and clarify new features as they are added during development
	Validate analysis model
Design	Validate the elaboration of analysis models in the presence of design objects
Coding	Clarify purpose and role of classes for coders
	Focus coding efforts
Testing	Provide primary and secondary test scenarios for system validation
Deployment	Suggest iterative prototypes for spiral development

2.4 Scenarios

As mentioned previously, scenarios are specific instances of use cases. Scenarios model order-dependent message sequences among objects collaborating to produce system behavior. Different scenarios within a given use case show permutations of object interactions. Even early in analysis, the advantage of scenarios is that domain experts and users usually can quite easily walk the analyst through dozens of typical system usage scenarios. The domain expert can explain why each step is taken, who initiates it, what the appropriate responses are, and what kinds of things can go awry. In going through this process, the analyst will uncover many important facets of the system behavior not mentioned within the problem statement. Scenarios provide an invaluable tool for validating the problem statement against the user's expectations, as well as uncovering the less obvious requirements. Late in analysis, they can be used to test the object structure by ensuring the appropriate participation by each object in each scenario.

Early in analysis, the objects available for scenarios are the system and the external objects identified in the context and use case diagrams. Later analysis decomposes the system into objects, and the scenario process can be applied to them as well. Ultimately, internal scenarios must map to the identified use cases. In fact, the identified objects decompose into multiple objects, and the messages are decomposed into protocols consisting of many messages. Just as iterative refinement of the object model identifies more classes, refinement of the scenarios adds more detail to the interactions.

It is important to stress that building and analyzing scenarios is a creative process of discovery. It is not simply a matter of starting with postulates and applying mathematical deduction to derive all possible behavior paths. Deep within the crevices of the domain experts' minds are hidden requirements that, if left to their own devices, will never be explicitly identified (at least not until the product is delivered!). These cannot be deduced from the problem statement *per se.* The process of scenario modeling brings these hidden requirements to the surface where they can be added to the system features.

Two primary scenario models exist: sequence and collaboration diagrams. Sequence diagrams are the most commonly used and emphasize messages and their sequence. Collaboration diagrams are also popular and tend to stress the system object structure. Both diagrams show scenarios but differ in what they emphasize. Although most people tend to stick to one or the other, some people find it useful to use sequence diagrams early and switch to collaboration diagrams once the object and class structure has stabilized.

2.4.1 Sequence Diagrams

Sequence diagrams show the sequence of messages between objects. The graphical syntax for sequence diagrams is shown in Figure 2-12. This figure shows all the elements used in most sequence diagrams. The vertical lines represent objects, with the name of the object written above or below the line. The horizontal directed lines are messages. Each message line starts at the *originator object* and ends at the *target object* and has a message name on the line. This name might, in later phases, specify an operation with a parameter list and a return value.

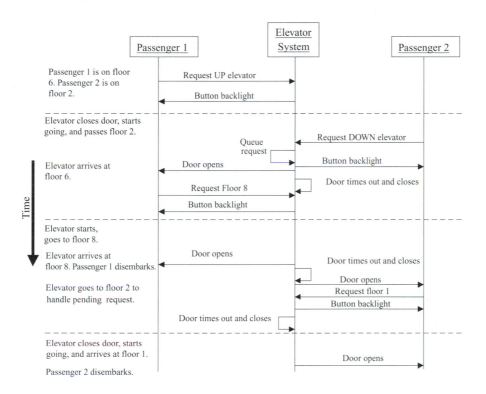

Figure 2-12: *Example Sequence Diagram*

Time flows from the top of the page downwards so that "Request UP elevator" is sent before "Button backlight," and so on. The time axis shows only sequence; the scale is not linear nor is a scale provided.

Note the textual annotation along the left side of the diagram. This descriptive text identifies initial conditions, actions, and activities not shown by the message sequence itself. Some of the messages are internal to the object; that is, with the same originator and target object. This means that the message is sent internally from one method to another within the same object. It is not strictly necessary to identify such messages, but it can be illuminating to do so. For example, the internal message "Door times out and closes" helps to set off the preceding "Door opens" (on floor 8) and the subsequent "Door opens" (on floor 2) messages.

Most sequence diagrams contain only the elements identified in Figure 2-12: objects, messages, (implicit) inactive periods, and scenario annotations. Sequence diagrams can contain a great deal more information when necessary, however. The full graphical syntax of message diagrams is shown in Figure 2-13.

The additional features shown in this figure are:

- Event identifiers
- Timing marks
- Broadcast messages
- State marks

Each message in Figure 2-13 has an optional identifier to the left or right of it; in this case, a letter from a to f. These are *event identifiers,* and can be provided when it is necessary to reference the event giving rise to the message. Additionally, they can be included in timing mark expressions to indicate relative time between events.

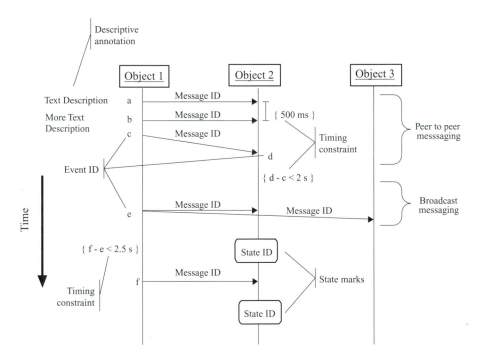

Figure 2-13: *Sequence Diagram Syntax*

Timing marks are indicated in two different fashions. The first is to use a marker bar with a time value between the two ends. This kind of time mark is shown between events a and b. It defines the time between the two events as 500 ms in this example. Relational expressions can also indicate timing constraints. These are to one side of the relevant messages and are delineated by curly braces. Event IDs are used in time expressions, as in

$$\{\, d - e <= 5\, s \,\}$$

which means simply that the time between events e and d must be less than or equal to five seconds.

Timing mark expressions need not be only for adjacent events. Imagine two constraints:

- The sum of the time among five events; a through e must be less than 10 seconds
- The time between c and d must be less than or equal to 500 ms.

It is perfectly reasonable to write

$$\{\, e - a < 10\, s \\ d - c <= 500\ ms \;\}$$

Thus, it is possible to provide multiple timing constraints within the same timing mark. It is even possible to provide more elaborate constraints. Suppose a series of six messages recurs every 30 seconds, and the series of six has a hard constraint of five seconds, with an average time constraint of three seconds. This can be indicated as shown in Figure 2-14.

UML does not define the language used to specify constraints—although its own definition includes one (OCL)—so we are free to add constraint notations as the need arises. The period is shown in two ways on the figure, although normally only one would be used at a time. An enclosing rectangle encapsulates the periodic message sequence. The sequence begins with an initial event ID of a and the last event ID of b. The notation

$$\underline{ab}\ = 30\ s$$

means *the period of the sequence begun by a and ended with b is 30 seconds long.* An alternative is to use the expression

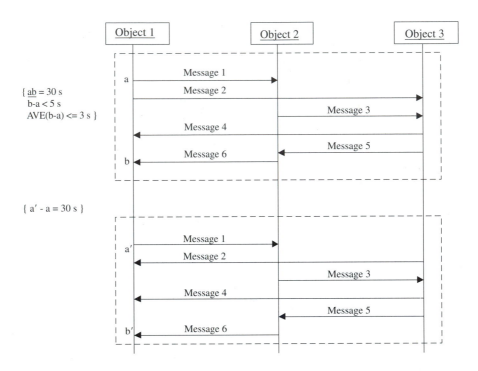

Figure 2-14: *Elaborate Constraints for Timing Marks*

$$\{ a' - a = 30 \text{ s} \}$$

which says exactly the same thing. If preferred, the expression can just be written out as

$$\{ \text{PERIOD}(ab) = 30 \text{ s} \}$$

The hard time constraint of five seconds between events b and a is denoted by the expression

$$\{ b - a <= 5 \text{ s} \}$$

The soft constraint that the average time must be less than or equal to three seconds uses the AVE operator to indicate average:

$$\{ \text{AVE}(b - a) <= 3 \text{ s} \}$$

Note that it is perfectly permissible to have multiple constraints on the same events, but they must be mutually consistent.

The vast majority of sequence diagram messages are *peer-to-peer*. That is, one object transmits a specific message and one object receives it. *Broadcast messages* are messages that are sent by a single object but received by more than one. Broadcast messages imply concurrency (otherwise multiple messages would have to be sent). They apply both to uniprocessor systems running multiple threads of execution and to multiprocessor systems. Events must often be sent to multiple threads within a single processor. This is common when a resource becomes available. RTOSs support this using event queues. Multidrop buses are common in multiprocessor systems. These are buses that multiple devices use to communicate among themselves. Such systems usually have some messaging to which all devices must listen.

Broadcast messages originate from the source object at the same point in time, but arrive at different objects at potentially different times. Arrows terminate on all objects that receive the message. Even though the messages are broadcast, not all objects in the scenario must receive the message. The terminating arrows indicate those objects that receive the message.

State marks are an extension to core UML that bridge the gap between sequence and state diagrams. State marks are rounded rectangles (the standard UML notation for a state on a state diagram) placed on the vertical object line. This allows the scenario to follow the state as it changes due to incoming events. The sequence diagram in Figure 2-15 illustrates the use of state marks. States and statecharts are discussed in detail in Chapter 4.

More specialized forms of sequence diagrams show detailed focus of control. These are discussed later, in the chapters on design.

2.4.2 Collaboration Diagrams

The other popular technique for showing scenarios is the collaboration diagram. Collaboration diagrams show the same basic information as the sequence diagrams. The difference is that sequence diagrams focus on the sequence of messages, but collaboration diagrams focus on the static structure of the collaborating objects. A simple collaboration diagram is shown in Figure 2-16.

This figure shows exactly the same scenario as in the sequence diagram of Figure 2-12. The object structure is clearer than in the sequence diagram, but finding the sequence can require some hunting. Some

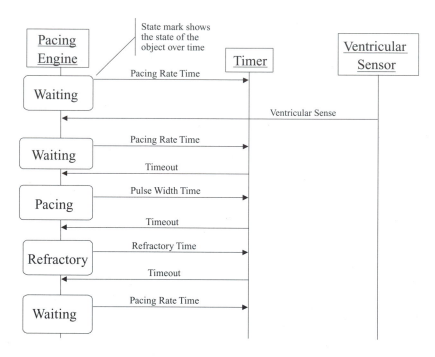

Figure 2-15: *Use of State Marks in Sequence Diagrams*

CASE tools support collaboration diagrams, but not all provide automatic message numbering. Thus, if the analyst adds a missing message, he or she must manually renumber all subsequent messages in the diagram. The other downside of collaboration diagrams is that if the structure of collaboration changes, they require more work to maintain than sequence diagrams. Nevertheless, they are valuable in their depicting of the structure of collaboration and map directly to the class diagram.

The components of collaboration diagrams are:

- Named objects
- Relationships joining the objects that exchange messages
- Messages with
  - ▼ Sequence numbers
  - ▼ Identifiers
  - ▼ Message direction

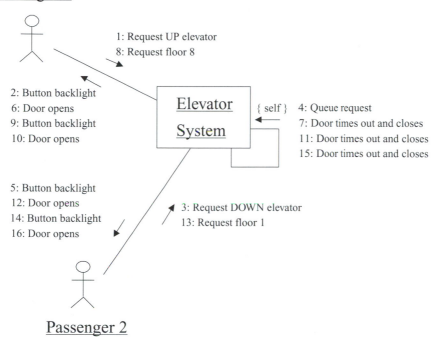

Figure 2-16: *Elevator Collaboration Diagram*

Figure 2-17 shows the basic form of a collaboration diagram with these basic elements.

The object names identify which objects are participating, and the association links[5] show which objects collaborate. An association link between two objects must exist for one object to send a message to another. The messages themselves are named with message identifiers. A sequence number precedes the identifier to define the flow of messages in the scenario, just as in sequence diagrams. Broadcast messages use the same source, message name, and sequence number. Finally, the direction of the message defines the sender and the receiver of the message.

---

[5] UML defines a *link* to be an instance of an association. Thus, an association on a class diagram gives rise to an association link on an object or collaboration diagram.

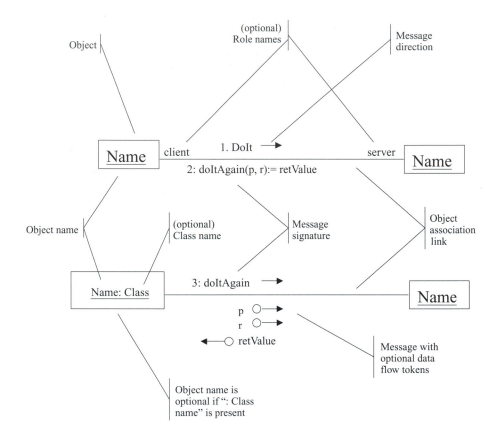

Figure 2-17: *Collaboration Diagram Syntax*

Collaboration diagrams support a much richer syntax than this minimum set, and can support the wider range of semantics shown in Figure 2-18. The syntactic elements include

- Preconditions
- Role names
- Message qualifiers
    - ▼ Iteration expressions
    - ▼ Parameters
    - ▼ Return values
    - ▼ Guard

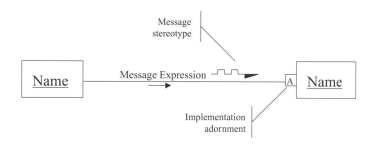

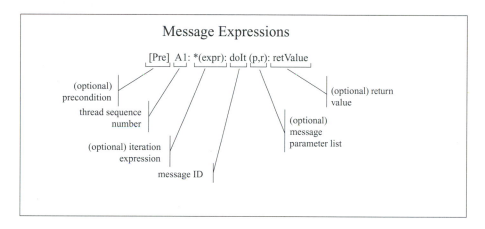

Figure 2-18: *Additional Collaboration Diagram Syntax*

- ▼ Message stereotype
- • Concurrent thread sequencing
- • Thread dependencies

These features are optional and should be included only when they add important information to the scenario.

Preconditions

In multithreaded scenarios, the delivery of some set of messages may form a precondition for a specific message to be sent. Such a precondition is a kind of guard and is enclosed within square brackets that precede the message name. The precondition is specified as a comma-separated list of message sequence numbers that must refer to messages appearing elsewhere in the diagram. The precondition list clarifies the thread synchronization requirements in the presence of multiple threads.

Role Names

A *role name* identifies the participatory role an object plays in an association. Role names are optional but should be included when they clarify the association. It is rarely necessary to name both roles because one role is always the conjugate of the other. For example, if one role is Owns, the other is necessarily something like Owned by. An object may have more than one association, including multiple associations with the same object. Just remember that each association has an impact on implementation. For sequential messages with the «call» stereotype, these associations will be implemented using pointers or references. CASE tools that automatically generate executable code from object models (as opposed to code frames) may use the role name as the names of pointers or references in the generated code and will provide default role names when they are omitted.

Roles may have implementation stereotypes. UML defines the implementation stereotypes for roles as shown in Table 2-5.

Iteration Expressions

The iteration expression defines a set of similar messages sent along the link. They are denoted by the preceding asterisk and the parenthesis around the expression. Iteration variables may be included if desired.

Table 2-5: *Role Implementation Stereotypes*

Stereotype	Description
«association»	Redundant; this is the default
«parameter»	Procedural parameter
«local»	Local variable
«global»	Global variable
«self»	Link to the same instance (object can send itself a message)

For example, the following two iteration expressions are equivalent:

>   *(j=1..n)
>   *(1..n)

The asterisk alone specifies an unknown number of iterations.

Since iterated messages are part of the same message flow, they must all have the same message stereotype.

Parameter Lists and Return Values

Later in design, the object behaviors evolve into defined operations with parameters and return values. The collaboration diagram can model these details. The return value may be indicated either by following the parameter list with a colon and the return value, or with an assignment statement using the := operator. For example:

>   DoIt(a,b,c): status
>   status := DoIt(a,b,c)

The analyst may use his or her discretion as to which form is preferred.

Guard

A *guard* is a Boolean condition that must evaluate to TRUE before the message can be sent. It provides a simple way of showing conditional message transmission on a single scenario. The UML does not specify the precise language for guard expressions, so you are free to use source code, structured English, or mathematical expressions in your guard expressions. For example,

>   DoIt[x>0]
>   DoItAgain[isOk( )]

are messages with guards.

Message Stereotype

Earlier in this chapter, we defined a number of *message stereotypes* that defined the arrival and synchronization patterns for the messages. This stereotype may be included in the standard guillemet form preceding the message identifier or may be indicated using an iconic message arrow. The two forms are equivalent, and which one you use is a matter of individual preference.

Thread Sequence Numbers

Sequence numbers identify the order in which messages occur in the scenario. Simple scalar sequence numbers indicate sequence when only a single thread is active. In concurrent object systems, the order of events between synchronization points is not known. In concurrent models, the sequence number may be preceded by a thread indicator. This is normally a letter to distinguish it from message sequence numbers, but can be a thread name. Within a given thread, the normal sequence number rules apply.

Including a preconditional guard expression explicitly shows the synchronization dependencies among threads. For example, the message

$$[B6, A3]C13: DoIt[x + y < z]$$

has a thread ID of C and a sequence number within that thread of 13. It must be preceded by message instances B6 (thread B, message instance 6) and A3 (thread A, message instance 3) and the guard expression x+y<z must evaluate to TRUE. Preconditions are needed only in the case of concurrent object models.

2.4.3 Concurrent Collaboration Diagrams

Active objects are often implemented as composites whose components inherit their owner's thread. Elaborate multithreaded collaborations can be shown easily on UML collaboration diagrams using composites and thread-specific messages.

The scenario shown in Figure 2-19 depicts the execution of a robot assembly system containing a Console Controller, Robot Worker, and Robot Stand. The Master Task Plan object downloads relevant portions of the plan to the active composites *Robot Worker 1* and *Robot Stand*. These objects proceed independently using threads A and B, respectively. The *Robot Stand* passes a command to the *Arm* object to grab the work item. The *Arm* is itself decomposed into four objects: *Controller, Joint 1, Joint 2,* and the *Manipulator.* The command to grab the work item results in multiple messages, one to each of the other objects within the arm. After the *Stand* grabs the work item, it orders the *Moving Work Surface* to move to Station 1 so that *Robot Worker 1* can perform

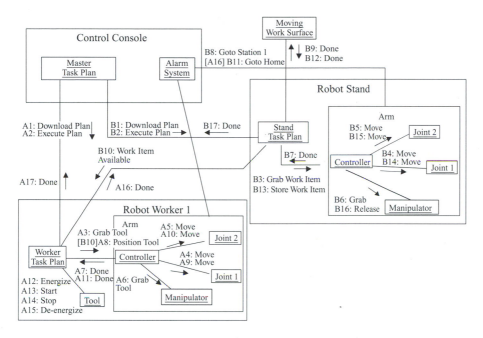

Figure 2-19: *Concurrent Collaboration Diagram*

its task. Once completed, the *Stand* sends a message to the *Robot Arm* that the work item is ready (B10).

The *Robot Worker 1*, meanwhile, has not been idle. Working within thread A, it has grabbed the appropriate tool by moving its joints and grabbing the tool. However, prior to positioning or energizing the tool, it waits for the tool to be in position. That is why message A8 depends on B10.

2.5 Context Diagrams and Use Cases in Real-Time Systems

In this chapter we have explored the importance of capturing the system's environment in order to understand and characterize system behavior in a variety of circumstances. Context and use case diagrams capture different aspects of the environment. Context diagrams treat the system as a composite object and identify the events and messages that transpire between the external actors and the system object. These messages can then be refined to include their arrival and synchronization patterns.

Use cases capture the information about the system's environment in a different way. Use cases are a functional decomposition of the system's systemic behavior without regard to the system's internal structure. Use cases emphasize the behavior of the system rather than the incoming and outgoing events.

Use cases group together functionally related scenarios. Scenarios, in turn, group functionally related messages together into *protocols* as they pass among objects. The complete set of interesting scenarios define the external behavior of the system. Scenarios are modeled using sequence and collaboration diagrams.

The information gathered during the construction of both these diagrams is required before any object decomposition of the system can occur. The characterization of the external events and the integration of these events into the system use cases complete the external view of the system.

The next two chapters will drill down into the systems and define the key objects, classes, and their relationships. Chapter 3 provides a number of different strategies for the identification of objects and classes, and Chapter 4 focuses on the specification of object behavior using state machines and operations.

2.6 References

[1] Laplante, Philip A., *Real-Time Systems Design and Analysis: An Engineer's Handbook.* New York: IEEE Computer Society Press, 1992.
[2] Gomaa, Hassan, *Software Design Methods for Concurrent and Real-Time Systems.* SEI Series in Software Engineering, ed. by Nico Habermann. Reading, MA: Addison Wesley Longman, 1993.
[3] Ward, Paul and Steve Mellor, *Structured Development for Real-Time Systems.* 4 vols. Englewood Cliffs, NJ: Prentice Hall, 1985.
[4] Ellis, John R., *Objectifying Real-Time Systems.* New York: SIGS Books, 1994.
[5] Booch, Grady, *Object-Oriented Analysis and Design with Applications.* 2nd ed. Redwood City, CA: Benjamin/Cummings, 1994.
[6] Booch, Grady, *Object Solutions: Managing the Object-Oriented Project.* Menlo Park, CA: Addison Wesley Longman, 1996.

Chapter 3

Analysis: Defining the Object Structure

Once the system's external environment is defined, the analyst must identify the key objects and classes and their relationships within the system itself. This chapter presents several strategies that have proven effective in real-time systems development for the identification of the key objects and classes. These strategies may be used alone or in combination. Relationships and associations among classes and objects enable their collaboration to produce higher-level behaviors. This chapter goes on to identify some rules of thumb for uncovering and testing these relationships.

Notation and Concepts Discussed

Object identification strategies   Class diagrams

Object associations   Sequence diagrams

Class relationships

3.1 The Object Discovery Process

In this chapter, we'll discuss object and class identification and how to infer relationships and associations among them. The next chapter will deal with the definition and elaboration of object behavior and state. The topics covered in this and the next chapter form the basis of all object-oriented analysis.

The use case and context diagrams constructed in the previous step provide a starting point for object-oriented analysis *per se.* The end result will be a structural model of the system that includes the objects and classes identified within the system, their relationships, and generalization hierarchies. This structural model will be complemented by the behavioral model (see Chapter 4) and the entire analysis model will be elaborated in design.

Figure 3-1 shows the steps of object-oriented analysis. The order of these steps is not particularly significant. Object oriented analysis is a process of discovery that proceeds as much by free association as by se-

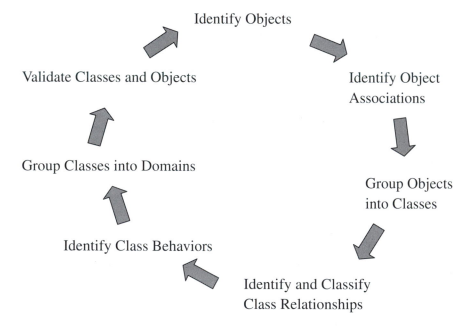

Figure 3-1: *Steps in Core Object-Oriented Analysis*

quential processes. Performing the steps in a different order may be better for some problems or some analysts. For example, sometimes it may be more profitable to identify the object behaviors first and then the class relationships, rather than the other way around.

3.2 Key Strategies for Object Identification

Over the years, I've consulted in an extremely varied set of problem domains, from medical systems to factory automation to avionics and fire control. The *good* part about consulting in such a broad range of fields is that it is extraordinarily interesting and I get to learn daily.[1] The *bad* part about that is that I am expected to sound intelligent about the problem almost immediately (good looks and charm get you only so far when they actually want to *fly* the thing!). For any consultant to be successful in that kind of environment, he or she must have some effective strategies for working with engineers and managers who understand their problem domain very well but are often neophyte object newbes. Table 3-1 outlines what I have found to be the most effective of these object-identification strategies.

This chapter will discuss all these strategies, but note that the analyst need not use them all. These approaches are not orthogonal and the objects they will find will overlap to a significant degree. In fact, many different subsets of the strategies will find exactly the same set of objects. Some methods will fit some analysts' approaches better than others. As with all modeling strategies, use those that work well for you and discard the rest.

3.2.1 Underline the Noun Strategy

The first strategy works directly with the problem or mission statement from the concept phase. Underline each noun or noun phrase in the statement and treat it as a potential object. Objects identified in this way can be put into three categories:

---

[1] Which has dropped me square in the middle of what I call the *knowledge paradox*: the more I *learn*, the less I *know*. I figure by the time I'm 60, I'll have learned so much that I will actually *know* nothing whatsoever!

Table 3-1: *Object Discovery Strategies*

Strategy	Description
Underline the noun	Used to gain a first-cut object list, the analyst underlines each noun in the problem statement and evaluates it as a potential object.
Identify active objects	Identify the sources of actions, events, and messages; includes the coordinators of actions.
Identify services (passive contributors)	Identify the targets of actions, events, and messages as well as entities that passively provide services when requested.
Identify real world items	Real world items are entities that exist in the real world, but are not necessarily electronic devices. Examples include objects such as respiratory gases, air pressures, forces, anatomical organs, chemicals, vats, etc.
Identify physical devices	Physical devices include the sensors and actuators provided by the system as well as the electronic devices they monitor or control. In the internal architecture, they are processors or ancillary electronic widgets.
Identify key concepts	Key concepts may be modeled as objects. Bank accounts exist only conceptually, but are important objects in a banking domain. Frequency bins for an on-line autocorrelator may also be objects.
Identify transactions	Transactions are finite instances of associations between objects that persist for some significant period of time. Examples include bus messages and queued data.
Identify persistent information	Information that must persist for significant periods of time may be objects or attributes. This persistence may extend beyond the power cycling of the device.
Identify visual elements	User interface elements that display data are objects within the user interface domain such as windows, buttons, scroll bars, menus, histograms, waveforms, icons, bitmaps, and fonts.
Identify control elements	Control elements are objects that provide the interface for the user (or some external device) to control system behavior.
Apply scenarios	Walk through scenarios using the identified objects. Missing objects will become apparent when required actions cannot be achieved with existing objects.

- Objects of interest
- Uninteresting objects
- Attributes of objects

The point of the exercise is to find objects within the first category—objects of interest. Uninteresting objects are objects that have no direct relevance to your system. Attributes also show up as nouns in the problem statement. Sometimes an attribute is clearly just a property of an object. When in doubt, tentatively classify the noun as an object. If subsequent analysis shows the object is insufficiently interesting, it can be included as an attribute of some other object.

An elevator is a real-time system familiar to everyone. Following is a problem statement for an elevator system with the noun phrases underlined.

> A software <u>system</u> must control a <u>set</u> of 8 <u>Acme elevators</u> for a <u>building</u> with 20 <u>floors</u>. Each <u>elevator</u> contains a <u>set of buttons</u>, each corresponding to a desired <u>floor</u>. These are called <u>floor request buttons</u>, since they indicate a <u>request</u> to go to a specific <u>floor</u>. Each <u>elevator</u> as well has a <u>current floor indicator</u> above the <u>door</u>. Each <u>floor</u> has two <u>buttons</u> for requesting <u>elevators</u> called <u>elevator request buttons</u>, because <u>they</u> request an <u>elevator.</u>
>
> Each <u>floor</u> has a sliding <u>door</u> for each <u>shaft</u> arranged so that two <u>door halves</u> meet in the center when closed. When the <u>elevator</u> arrives at the <u>floor</u>, the <u>door</u> opens at the same time the <u>door</u> on the <u>elevator</u> opens. The <u>floor</u> does have both <u>pressure and optical sensors</u> to prevent closing when an <u>obstacle</u> is between the two <u>door halves</u>. If an <u>obstruction</u> is detected by either <u>sensor</u>, the <u>door</u> shall open. The <u>door</u> shall automatically close after a <u>timeout period</u> of five seconds after the <u>door</u> opens. The detection of an <u>obstruction</u> shall restart the <u>door closure time</u> after an <u>obstruction</u> is removed. There is a <u>speaker</u> on each <u>floor</u> that pings in response to the arrival of an <u>elevator</u>.
>
> On each <u>floor</u>, there are two <u>elevator request buttons</u>, <u>one for UP</u> and <u>one for DOWN</u>. On each <u>floor</u>, above each <u>elevator door</u>, there is an <u>indicator</u> specify-

ing the current <u>floor</u> of the <u>elevator</u> and another <u>indicator</u> for its current <u>direction</u>. The <u>system</u> shall respond to an <u>elevator request</u> by sending the <u>nearest elevator</u> that is either idle or already going in the requested <u>direction</u>. If no <u>elevators</u> are currently available, the <u>request</u> shall pend until an <u>elevator</u> meets the previously mentioned <u>criterion</u>. Once pressed, the <u>request buttons</u> are backlit to indicate that a <u>request</u> is pending. Pressing an <u>elevator request button</u> when a <u>request</u> for that <u>direction</u> is already pending shall have no <u>effect</u>. When an <u>elevator</u> arrives to handle the <u>request</u>, the <u>backlight</u> shall be removed. If the <u>button</u> is pressed when an <u>elevator</u> is on the <u>floor</u> to handle the <u>request</u> (i.e., <u>it</u> is slated to go in the selected <u>direction</u>), then the <u>door</u> shall stop closing and the <u>door closure timer</u> shall be reset.

To enhance safety, a <u>cable tension sensor</u> monitors the <u>tension</u> on the <u>cable</u> controlling the <u>elevator</u>. In the event of a <u>failure,</u> in which the <u>measured tension</u> falls below a <u>critical value</u>, then four external <u>locking clamps</u> connected to running <u>tracks</u> in the <u>shaft</u> stop the <u>elevator</u> and hold <u>it</u> in place.

The result of this process to the problem statement is a list of the following nouns and noun phrases:

system	elevator	building
floor	set of 8 Acme elevators	button
floor request button	request	current floor indicator
door	elevator request button	they
pressure sensor	optical sensor	obstruction
door half	speaker	one for UP
internal door set	floor door	secondary pressure sensor

elevator control panel	Open button	Close button
Emergency Call button	alarm	central station
one for DOWN	elevator door	indicator
direction	elevator request	effect
backlight	it	door closure timer
compartment	telephone	elevator occupants
Stop-Run Switch	guidelines	message
state	switch	status
alarming status	elevator location	increments
elevator direction	cable	cable tension sensor
emergency locks	alarm area	mechanical locking clamp
pressure sensor	tracks	electrical power source
failure	measured tension	critical value
set of buttons	nearest elevator	

Many of these are clearly redundant references to the same object. Others are not of interest. The elevator *cable*, for example, is not nearly as interesting to the safety system as the *cable tension sensor*.[2] Likewise, the *passengers* are not as interesting as the *buttons* they push and the *indicators* they read. Other objects clearly need not be modeled at all.

This list can be reduced by this kind of analysis. The result is a smaller list of proposed objects for the domain model. The following list shows object quantities, where specified, with parentheses:

---

[2] That is, it need not be modeled within the system. The cable tension sensor, however, must be modeled.

system (1)	elevator (8)	building (1)
floor (20)	request	button
floor request button (8*20)	elevator request button (20*2)	current floor indicator (8)
door (20*8 + 8)	optical sensor	obstruction
pressure sensor	speaker	UP button
door half	elevator door	indicator
DOWN button	floor door	secondary pressure sensor
internal door set	Open button	Close button
elevator control panel	alarm	central station
Emergency Call button	elevator request	door closure timer
electrical power	telephone	elevator occupants
Stop-Run Switch	switch	message
emergency locks	alarm area	mechanical locking clamp
pressure sensor	tracks	electrical power source

The result also includes a couple of attributes, as shown in Table 3-2. You can see that this strategy quickly identified many objects but also identified nouns that are clearly not interesting to the analyst.

3.2.2 Identify the Active Objects

Once the potential objects are identified, look for the most fundamental ones. These are objects which:

• Produce or control actions

• Produce or analyze data

• Provide interfaces to people or devices

Table 3-2: *Model Objects and Attributes*

Object	Attribute
Elevator	Direction Status Location
Button	Backlight
Alarm	Status
Cable Tension Sensor	Cable tension Critical value

- Store information
- Provide services to people or devices
- Contain other types of fundamental objects
- Are transactions of device or person interaction

The first two categories are commonly lumped together as *active objects*. An active object is an object that autonomously performs actions, coordinates the activities of component objects, or generates events. Active objects are normally implemented as the root composite object of a thread. Their components execute within the context of the thread of the owner composite.

Clearly, the most fundamental elevator objects are few in number:

Floor
Elevator
Door
Button
Request
Indicator
Cable tension sensor
Mechanical locking clamp

3.2.3 Identify Services (Passive Contributors)

Passive objects are less obvious than active objects. They may provide passive control, data storage, or both. A simple switch is a passive control object. It provides a service to the active objects (it turns the light on or off upon request), but does not initiate actions by itself. Passive objects are also known as servers because they provide services to client objects.

Simple sensors are passive data objects. An A/D converter might acquire data on command and return it to an actor, or as the result of an event initiated by an active object. Printers and chart recorders are common passive service providers as they print text and graphics on command. A hardware passive service provider might be a chip that performs a cyclic redundancy check computation over a block of data.

3.2.4 Identify Real-World Items

Object-oriented systems often need to model the information or behavior of real-world objects even though they are not part of the system *per se*. A bank account system must model the relevant properties of customers, even though customers are clearly outside the accounting system. Typical customer objects will contain attributes such as:

- Name
- Social Security Number
- Address
- Phone number
- List of owned accounts

An ECG monitor might model a heart as containing:

- Heart rate
- Frequency of preventricular contractions
- Electrical axis

In anesthesia systems, modeling organs as "sinks" for anesthetic agent uptake can aid in closed loop control of agent delivery and prevent toxemia.

This strategy looks at things in the real world that interact in the system. If the system manipulates information about these things, then the system should model them as objects.

3.2.5 Identify Physical Devices

Real-time systems interact with their environment using sensors and actuators. These devices in turn must communicate through other devices called interfaces. The system controls and monitors physical devices inside and outside the system. Devices providing information used by the system are typically modeled as objects. Devices themselves must be configured, calibrated, enabled, and controlled so that they can provide services to the system. For example, deep within the inner workings of the system, processors typically perform initial Power On Self Tests (POSTs) and periodic (or continuous) Built-In Tests (BITs). Devices frequently have nontrivial state machines and must provide status information on command. When device information and state must be maintained, the devices may be modeled as objects to hold the information about their operational status.

For example, a stepper motor is a physical device that can be modeled as an object with the attributes and behaviors shown in Table 3-3.

3.2.6 Identify Key Concepts

Key concepts are important abstractions within the domain that have interesting attributes and behaviors. These abstractions often do not have physical realizations, but must nevertheless be modeled by the system. Within the User Interface (UI) domain, a *window* is a key concept. In the banking domain, an *account* is a key concept. In an autonomous manufacturing robot, a *task plan* is the set of steps required to implement the desired manufacturing process. In the design of a C compiler, *functions*, *data types*, and *pointers* are key concepts. Each of these objects have no physical manifestation. They exist only as abstractions modeled within the appropriate domains as objects.

Table 3-3: *Stepper Motor Object*

Attributes	Behaviors
Operations	Step(nSteps) GetPos Zero

Table 3-4: *Example Transaction Objects*

Object 1	Object 2	Association	Transaction Object
Woman	Man	Marriage	Marriage object: Wedding date Wedding location Prenuptial agreement Witnesses Divorce object: Filing date Decree date Maintenance schedule Amount paid to lawyers
Controller	Actuator	Controls	Control message over bus
Customer	Account	Owns	Deposit Withdrawal Open account Close account
Customer	Store	Buys things at	Order Return
Display system	Sensor	Displays values for	Alarm Error
Elevator request button	Elevator	Issues request to	Request for elevator
Floor request button	Elevator	Issues request to	Request for floor
Task plan	Robot arm	Controls	Command

3.2.7 Identify Transactions

Transactions are objects arising from the interactions of other objects. Some example transaction objects are outlined in Table 3-4.

    In the elevator case study, an elevator request is clearly a transaction. It has a relatively short life span, either:

- Beginning when the (future) passenger pushes the elevator request button and ending when the elevator arrives and opens its doors, or

- Beginning when the passenger pushes the floor request button and ending when the elevator arrives at its destination and opens its doors

Other examples of transactions are alarms and (reliable) bus messages. Alarms must persist as long as the dangerous condition is true or until explicitly handled, depending on the system. Alarms typically will have attributes such as:

- Alarm condition
- Alarm priority
- Alarm severity[3]
- Time of occurrence
- Duration of condition

Reliable message transfer requires that a message persists at the site of the sender until an explicit acknowledgment is received. This allows the sender to retransmit if the original message is lost. Bus messages typically have attributes such as:

- Message type
- Priority
- Source address
- Target address
- Message data
- Cyclic redundancy check

3.2.8 Identify Persistent Information

Persistent information typically is held within passive objects such as stacks, queues, trees, or databases. Either volatile memory (RAM or SRAM) or long-term storage (FLASH, EPROM, EEPROM, or disk) may store persistent data.

---

[3] Priority and severity are orthogonal concepts. *Priority* refers to the timeliness requirements of the alarm, and the *severity* refers to how bad the outcome of the fault condition may be if unhandled. These concepts are discussed in more detail in [5].

Table 3-5: *Possible Persistent Information Objects*

Information	Storage Period	Description
Task plans	Unlimited	Programs for the robotic system must be constructed, stored, recalled for editing, and recalled for execution.
Errors	Between service calls	Error log holding the error identifier, severity, location, and time/date of occurrence. This will facilitate maintenance of the system.
Alarms	Until next service call	Alarms indicate conditions that must be brought to the attention of the user, even though they may not be errors. Tracking them between service calls allows analysis of the reliability of the system.
Hours of operation	Between service calls	Hours of operation aid in tracking costs and scheduling service calls.
Security access	Unlimited	Stores valid users, their identifiers, and passwords to permit different levels of access.
Service information	Unlimited	Tracks service calls and updates performed: when, what, and by whom.

A robot must store and recall task plans. Subsequent analysis of the system may reveal other persistent data. For example, the information, in Table 3-5 may be persistent.

Such data can be used for scheduling equipment maintenance, and may appear in monthly or yearly reports.

3.2.9 Identify Visual Elements

Many real-time systems interact directly or indirectly with human users. Real-time system displays may be as simple as a single blinking LED to indicate power status, or as elaborate as a full Windows-like

GUI with buttons, windows, scroll bars, icons, and text.[4] Visual elements used to convey information to the user are objects within the user interface domain.

In many environments, user interface (UI) designers specialize in the construction of visual interaction models or prototypes that the developers implement.

For example, consider the sample screens for the elevator central control station shown in Figures 3-2 through 3-4.

We see a number of common visual elements:

- Window
- Rectangle
- Rounded panel
- Horizontal scroll bar
- Scroll button (left, right, up, down)
- Button
- Menu bar
- Menu selection
- Drop-down menu
- Menu item
- List box
- Text
- Icon (for alarm silence)

Each of these is an object within the UI domain for the elevator central station. These UI objects are depicted in an object message diagram later in this chapter.

3.2.10 Identify Control Elements

Control elements are entities that control other objects. These are specific types of active objects. Some objects, called *composites*, often orchestrate

---

[4] No doubt you've all heard this one: "How many Microsoft engineers does it take to change a light bulb? Answer: None. Bill Gates just declares 'Darkness at your Fingertips' to be the new standard graphical user interface."

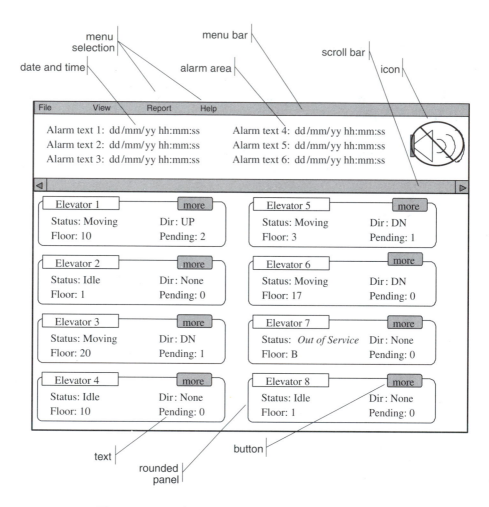

Figure 3-2: *Elevator Central Station: Main View*

the behaviors of their component objects. These may be simple objects or may be elaborate control systems, such as:

- PID control loops
- Fuzzy logic inference engines
- Expert system inference engines
- Neural network simulators

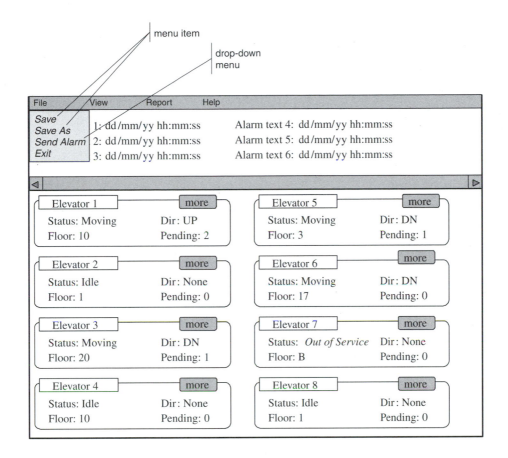

Figure 3-3: *Elevator Central Station: Menu View*

Some control elements are physical interface devices that allow users to enter commands. The elevator case study has only a few:

- Button (elevator and floor)
- Switch (elevator and floor)
- Keyboard (central station only)
- Mouse (central station only)

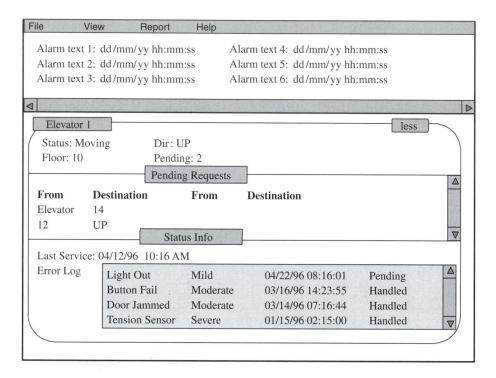

Figure 3-4: *Elevator Central Station: Zoom View*

3.2.11 Apply Scenarios

The application of use case scenarios is another strategy to identify missing objects. Using only known objects, step through the messages to implement the scenario. When "you can't get there from here" occurs, often it identifies one or more missing objects.

Consider the scenario involving the request and response of an elevator, as shown in Figure 3-5.

Step 4 is of the "then a miracle occurs" variety. Somehow the message Elevator Request from the button on the floor ends up selecting one particular elevator from eight possibilities.

One approach to solve the problem is to have the button be responsible for selecting the elevator. Perhaps only a single elevator can ever be summoned to a particular floor in a particular direction. That approach has the advantage of being simple, but it is an inefficient use of

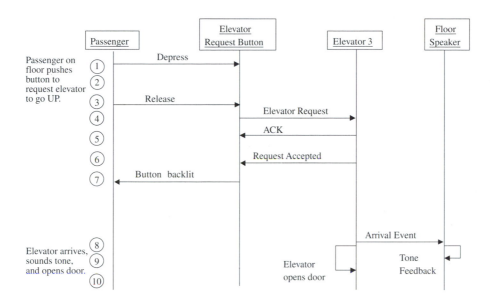

Figure 3-5: *Elevator Request Event Sequence*

available resources. Another solution would send the message to all elevators, and the first one to arrive wins. As with the previous approach, this solution is easy to implement but far from optimal. One could even have the elevators debate which of them should go to the floor and decide by consensus.

A simpler solution would postulate the existence of an elevator controller,[5] responsible for determining which is the most appropriate elevator and passing that request on to only that elevator. With such a scheme, it is easy to implement efficient use of all elevators. A variety of algorithms could be used to determine elevator selection, based on elevator status information, such as the following:

1. The selected elevator should be close to the desired floor, moving in the selected direction, and not yet past the floor.

---

[5] The astute reader will note that this is actually an architectural design decision, since it is not inherent in the problem domain. However, such strategic decisions are often made in analysis when the choice seems clear. Architectural design is discussed in more detail in Chapter 5.

2. If no elevator is sufficiently close to meeting criterion 1, send the nearest idle elevator.

3. If no elevator is idle, and criterion 1 is not met, then send the nearest elevator going in the correct direction.

4. If no elevator is idle, criterion 1 is not met, and no elevators are going in the correct direction, then queue the request until an elevator becomes idle or begins traveling in the correct direction.

5. In a fire alarm situation, send all elevators to the ground floor.

The addition of the elevator controller gives us Figure 3-6. The elevator controller is the "Elevator Gnome" shown in the scenario. The description uses the term *gnome* for a couple of reasons. The first definition of gnome is "One of a fabled race of dwarf-like creatures who live underground and guard treasure hoards." The second definition is "thought, judgment, intelligence."[6] Our elevator gnome clearly meets both the need for programmers to anthropomorphize their designs as

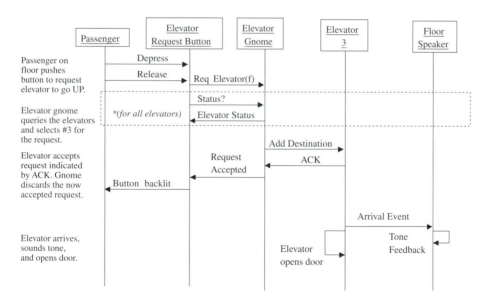

Figure 3-6: *Elevator Request Event Sequence Revisited*

---

[6] *Webster's New World Dictionary Second College Edition, 1980.*

well as the requirement for intelligence in the controlling object. We can imagine a small dwarfish creature living at the bottom of the elevator shaft passing notes in tubes that whisk the requests off to the elevators (at least *I can;* see [1] for thoughts on related topics).

The gnome receives and arbitrates requests for elevators according to some set of rules. Once it receives the request from the button, it queries all the elevators for their current status: their location (e.g., floor 5), direction (e.g., UP), and state (e.g., MOVING). In this example, the gnome determines that Elevator 3 is the best choice and forwards the request to that elevator via the *Add Destination* message. The elevator receives and queues the request and issues an ACK to the gnome. At this point, the gnome may discard the request (since it has been dispatched to an elevator) and signal the button to backlight.

3.3 Identifying Object Associations

Early in the analysis, some objects seem to relate to others even though it is not always clear exactly how. The first step is to identify the existence of such associations. We will discuss the characterization of associations later in this chapter.

There are a few strategies for the identification of object relationships. Each relies on the fact that objects send messages to other objects and every message implies an association, as shown in Table 3-6.

In our elevator example, there are a number of associations, shown in Table 3-7.

Class and object diagrams capture these associations. A line drawn between two objects represents a link (instance of an association) between those objects supporting the transmission of a message from one to the other.

The object diagram in Figure 3-7 shows the general structure of the identified objects and their neighbors. The system consists of 38 high-level objects: 8 shafts, 8 elevators, 20 floors, and one central station and one elevator gnome. The numbers at the upper left-hand corner of the object represents the instance count, that is, the number of instances of the object in the enclosing context. The shaft, elevator, and floor are all

Table 3-6: *Object Assocation Strategies*

Strategy	Description
Identify messages	Each message implies an association between the participating objects.
Identify message sources	The sensors that detect information or events and the creators of information or events are all *message sources*. They pass information on to other objects for handling and storage.
Identify message storage depots	Message storage depots store information for archival purposes or provide a central repository of information for other objects. The depots have associations with the message sources as well as the users of that information.
Identify message handlers	Some objects centralize message dispatching and handling. They will form connections to either or both message sources and message storage depots.
Apply scenarios	Walk through scenarios using the identified objects. The scenarios explicitly show how the messages are sent between objects.

composites that strongly aggregate their components. The instance counts of their components are per instance of their context. That is, each *Elevator* has 20 instances of *Floor Request Button*.

3.4 Object Attributes

The UML defines an attribute to be "a named property of a type." In this sense, they are smaller than objects. In some abstract sense, attributes are equivalent to mandatory unidirectional aggregations because you can navigate from the object to its properties. Practically speaking, attributes are the data portion of an object. A sensor object might include attributes such as a calibration constant and a measured value.

Table 3-7: *Elevator Object Associations*

Message Source	Message Target	Message
Elevator request button	Elevator gnome	Request an elevator
Elevator gnome	Elevator	Request status
Elevator gnome	Elevator	Add destination for elevator
Elevator	Elevator gnome	Accept destination
Elevator	Floor speaker	Arrival event beep
Elevator floor sensor	Elevator	Location
Cable tension sensor	Locking clamps	Engage
Central station	Locking clamps	Release
Cable tension sensor	Central station	Alarm condition
Elevator	Central station	Status
Floor request button	Elevator	Add destination
Run-stop switch	Elevator	Stop/Run
Run-stop switch	Central station	Stop/Run
Alarm button	Central station	Alarm condition
Elevator	Door	Open/Close

Attributes are almost always primitive and cannot be broken down into subproperties productively. If you find attributes to be nonprimitive, then they should be modeled as component objects owned by the original object. For example, if a sensor had a table of calibration constants rather than a simple scalar, the calibration table should be modeled as an object aggregrated unidirectionally by the sensor object.

Sometimes the primary attributes of an object are obvious, but not always. Developers can ask themselves some key questions to identify the most important attributes of objects:

- What information defines the object?
- What information do the object's operations act upon?
- From the object's viewpoint, "What do I know?"

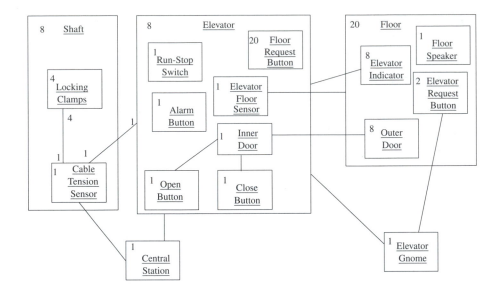

Figure 3-7: *First-Cut Elevator Object Diagram*

- Are the identified attributes rich in either structure or behavior? If so, they are probably objects rather than attributes.
- What are the responsibilities of the object? What information is necessary to fulfill these responsibilities?

The *Elevator* class provides a good example of a real-time class with attributes. Let's ask these questions about this class:

- What information defines the object?
  The *Elevator* is a physical thing that must be controlled. To fulfill its function it must know where it is, where it is going (destination list), and its current direction.
- What information do the object's operations act upon?
  It has a goto() operation that must act on where it is, its current direction, and its state (moving, stopped, etc.).
- From the object's viewpoint, "What do I know?"
  I know where I am, where I am going, and what I am doing right now (stopped, idle, moving, etc.).

- Are the identified attributes rich in either structure or behavior? If so, they are probably objects rather than attributes.
  The *Elevator* has a *door* that has state (open, closed, opening, closing), interlocks with the floor door, and has operations. It is probably an object.

- What are the responsibilities of the object? What information is necessary to fulfill these responsibilities?
  The *Elevator*'s primary responsibility is to transport passengers from one floor to another. It needs the attributes of where it is, in which direction it is traveling, a list of current destinations, and its current state.

There are cases in which an object with no attributes is valid within the domain. A button is a reasonable class, but what attributes does it have? Not many, other than perhaps some implementation attributes to store its current state. Some composite objects are only aggregates of many objects with no data specific in and of themselves. Other objects contain only functions and so are often called functoids or (in UML-speak) class utilities. These are discussed next.

3.5 Class Utilities

Occasionally, an identified object has no attributes. This can be because of faulty analysis—the proposed object is merely a function wrapper rather than a true object. However, sometimes such a wrapper makes sense. For example, the C++ and Ada 95 languages support both objects and functions. The UML calls traditional functions and procedures *class utilities* and shows them on the class diagram as contained within a class with the stereotype «utility».

In other cases, the function truly does belong to an object, but the object has yet to be identified. The pertinent question is: On what data does the function operate? If an object encapsulates this data, then put the function within the same object.

For example, consider a function that computes a cyclic redundancy check (CRC) over a block of data. Communicating systems commonly use CRCs on bus message contents to provide feedback error detection. The CRC function can be modeled as a class utility, as in

```
unsigned int CRC(byte *block, int length);
```

The receiver can reapply the CRC function and compare the result with the transmitted CRC code, thus detecting a corrupted message.

An alternative is to encapsulate the CRC operation within the message object. Using C++ class syntax, this could be something such as

```
class message {
    unsigned CRC;
public:
    ...
    void makeCRC(void);
    boolean checkCRC(void);
};
```

The trouble with this approach is that CRCs are useful for checking validity of lots of things—executable code, messages, and safety-relevant data. For example, Power On Self Tests (POSTs) and ongoing Built-In Tests (BITs) frequently use CRCs to ensure code and data integrity. Insertion of the CRC function directly into each class that uses it requires writing the code several times. If the code must be modified (fixed or improved) then each instance must be tracked down and modified. We want to write this only once and use it where it is needed.

Alternatively, a base class called checkedData can be created that knows how to compute a CRC. This base class can be subclassed to construct classes that know how to validate themselves. For example,

```
#include <stdlib.h>
class checkedClass {
    unsigned CRC;
    char *cPtr;
    int nChars;
public:
    checkedClass(void): CRC(0), cPtr(NULL), nChars(0)
    { };
    // actually computes CRC
    virtual unsigned computeCRC(void);
    // assigns local CRC attribute
    void makeCRC(void) {
        CRC = computeCRC();
```

```
        };
    bool checkCRC(void) {  // checks local CRC attribute
        return (CRC == computeCRC());
        };
};

class checkedIntArray: public checkedClass {
    int a[100];
public:
    checkedIntArray(void) { // constructor
        for (int j=0;j<100;j++)
        a[j] = 0;
        };

    int get(index) {

        if (index < 0 || index >= 100)
            throw("Index out of range");
        if (checkCRC())
            return a[index];
        else
            throw("CRC ERROR ON READ");
    };

    void put(index, value) {
        if (checkCRC()) {
            a[index] = value;
            makeCRC();
            }
        else
            throw("CRC ERROR ON WRITE");
    };

    void computeCRC(void) {
        cPtr = (char *)a; // treat array as a char stream
        nChars = sizeof(a) / sizeof(a[0]);
        checkedClass::makeCRC( ); // use base class
                                  // operation
    };
}; // end class checkedIntArray

void main(void) {
    checkedIntArray myArray;
    for (int j=0; j<100; j++)
        put(j, rand());

    // do a check and raise an exception on failure
    int temp = get(16);
}; // end main
```

Another solution is to encapsulate the function in a class utility and form associations with client classes, such as the protectedIntArray, as follows.

```
class protectionUtility {
    unsigned CRC;
    char *cPtr;
    int nChars;
public:
    protectionUtility(void *dataPtr, int size): CRC(0),
    nChars(size) {
            cPtr = (char *)dataPtr;
            computeCRC();
            };
        // actually computes CRC
        unsigned computeCRC(void);
        // assigns local CRC attribute
        void makeCRC(void) {
            CRC = computeCRC();
            };
        // checks local CRC attribute
        bool checkCRC(void) {
            return (CRC == computeCRC());
            };
};

    class protectedIntArray {
    int a[100];
    protectionUtility *p;
public:
    protectedIntArray(void): {
        p = new protectionUtilty((void)a, sizeof(a) /
        sizeof(a[0]));
        };
    int get(index) {
        if (index < 0 || index >= 100)
            throw("Index out of range");
        if (p->checkCRC())
            return a[index];
        else
            throw("CRC ERROR ON READ");
        };
    int put(index, value) {
        if (index < 0 || index >= 100)
            throw("Index out of range");
        if (p->checkCRC()) {
```

```
        a[index] = value;
        p->makeCRC();
        }
     else
        throw("CRC ERROR ON READ");
     };
  }; // end class protectedIntArray

void main(void) {
   protectedIntArray myArray;
   for (int j=0; j<100; j++)
      put(j, rand());
   // do a check and raise an exception on failure
   int temp = get(16);
}; // end main
```

Implementing the protected class using C++ templates is straight-forward and is left as an exercise to the reader.

3.6 Verifying the Problem Statement

Problem statements are the best place from which to start object-oriented analysis. They are (or should be) written by people who really understand the domain and the market requirements. However, problem statements are usually incomplete, inconsistent, and ambiguous. Most people who write problem statements are not trained in the formal or rigorous thinking required to engineer systems. The sheer scope of many systems can hide subtle problems that can prove literally fatal when deployed in the field.[7] There are a number of questions that can be addressed to the problem statement (or the domain expert) to elaborate the problem statement, such as:

- What is the purpose for each object in the environment? How does it interact with the system? Does it act alone or must it work closely with other objects?

---

[7] Such as the F-16 bug, which caused the plane to *turn upside-down* when it crossed the equator. In another case, the F-16 flew upside down because it was unable to decide in which direction to roll [6]. Fortunately, these problems were detected in the flight simulator before actual deployment.

- How does the system interact with the user?
- What are the performance constraints on the system?
- What functionality does the system provide?
- Must the system maintain any persistent information?
- Must the system react to any external events? What are the performance requirements of such reactions?

Just as the system itself has a set of responsibilities to fulfill, so do its component objects. In fact, objects often have multiple responsibilities. The primitive things that it can do are its *behavior*. Both an object's behavior and its attributes must work together to support its responsibilities, but behaviors themselves are more primitive and less abstract than responsibilities. The question of collaboration often yields important insights into the problem domain dynamics. In the case of the elevator, both the floor and the elevator contain doors. These doors must act in concert to fulfill their responsibilities. This implies associations between the doors that otherwise might not be obvious. Some implementation mechanism must ultimately provide the means for this coordinated behavior, such as a mechanical or electronic interlock.

3.7 Discovering Candidate Classes

Of the objects identified in the problem statement, many of them are structurally identical. In the elevator case study, for example, there are eight elevators, all the same. Similarly, there are scads of buttons (*scad: a technical term meaning a lot; antonym: scootch*), but they all appear to be structurally identical. Each is activated by depression, acknowledges with a backlight, etc. Objects that are identical in structure and behavior are said to be of the same *class*. The next analysis activity is to propose candidate classes for the identified objects.

Classes are abstractions of objects. Objects that are identical in type (even if different in value) are abstracted into a class. In the elevator example, buttons differ as to their purpose. Floor request buttons reside within the elevator and request a destination for that specific elevator. Elevator request buttons reside on the floor and request any elevator to come to the floor and take passengers in a specific direction. Each button is structurally identical and differs only in its context. It depresses when pushed and issues a message when released. When the message is accepted, the button is backlit. The *button* appears to be a good choice for a candidate class.

Similarly, other objects can be abstracted into candidate classes:

- Elevator
- Door
- Floor
- Speaker
- Floor indicator
- Elevator indicator

and so on. From these classes, specific objects, such as "Elevator #2 Request Button for Floor #8" may be instantiated.

3.8 Class Diagrams

Class diagrams are the single most important diagrams in object-oriented analysis and design. They show the structure of the system in terms of classes and objects, including how the objects and classes relate to each other. Class diagrams are the primary road map of the system and its object-oriented decomposition. They are similar to object diagrams except they show primarily classes rather than instances.

Figure 3-8 shows a class diagram for a banking application. The 0,1 - * multiplicity between the ATM Card class and the Checking Account class shows that the ATM Card object is optional, and that, at most, a single ATM Card object may participate. At the other role of the association, a single ATM Card object may reference multiple Checking Account objects. This can occur when a single bank customer has multiple checking accounts, all of which may be accessed via a single ATM Card and PIN (PIN is a qualifier and will end up as an attribute within the ATM Card class).

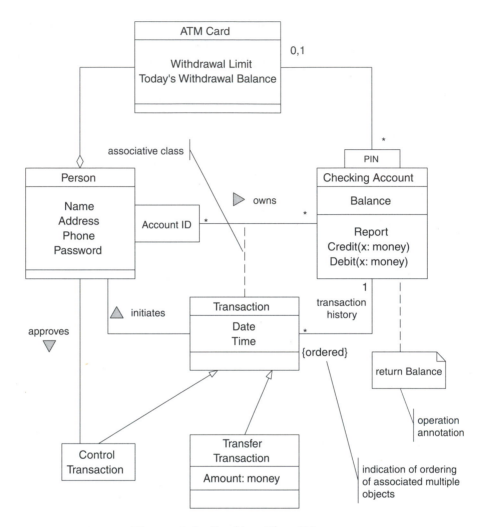

Figure 3-8: *Banking Class Diagram*

Similarly, an * - * association exists between the Person class and the Checking Account class. This is because a person may have more than one checking account (hence the * at the Checking Account role end) and a checking account may be owned by more than one person (hence the * at the Person role end). Although * - * associations are relatively rare, they do pop up from time to time. Note also that the association is bidirectional, so that given a client you can get to their accounts, and given an account you can find its owner clients.

Three new features appear on this figure: an associative class, an annotation, and an ordering constraint. As noted in Chapter 1, associations themselves may have interesting attributes and behaviors. In this case, the Transaction class captures the interesting parts of the relationship between the Person and the Checking Account classes. Transactions may be things like transferring money (as in debits and credits) or may control checking account behavior (such as Open and Close).

Just to complicate things, these transactions persist in the form of a transaction history. The relationship between the Checking Account and Transaction classes is 1 - *. A single checking account object maintains a list (zero or more) of transactions. The checking account *report* operation prints a list of the transactions periodically. This 1-* relationship is maintained as an ordered list, as indicated by the {ordered} constraint. This is normally a design detail, but it may be added whenever the requirement for the constraint becomes clear.

Annotations may be added for a variety of purposes. In this case, the annotation shows the return type of the checking account's Debit operation. Other information of interest may be added freely.

Figure 3-9 shows some special types of associations. In Microsoft Windows, various controls, such as list boxes and buttons, are themselves windows. The owner window contains these controls and manipulates them via *handles*. This characteristic is an instance of a general method of accessing objects called *access keys*. When appropriate, access keys may be indicated on the relationship to indicate how this relationship is managed. Relationships with access keys are called *qualified relationships*. Access keys, known as *qualifiers*, are special attributes of a class used to manage access.

This figure also shows two recursive relationships. The first, explained previously, accounts for the fact that a window may contain controls, and that controls are windows themselves. The second, from the MDI (Multiple Document Interface) Window subclass, indicates links to different objects, which also happen to be of class Window. This figure demonstrates that multiple relationships between a pair of classes can exist and do so for one of two reasons:

- Different associations with the same objects
- Associations with different objects

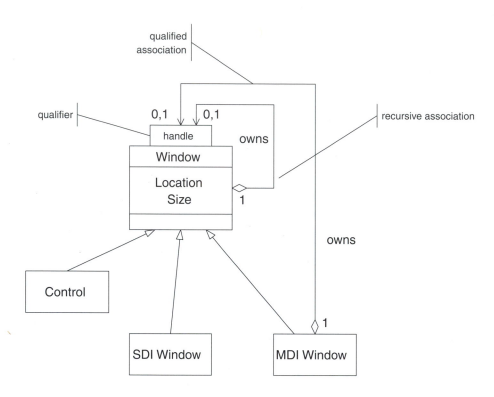

Figure 3-9: *Special Associations*

3.8.1 Elevator Class Diagram Example

Figure 3-10 shows the class diagram for an elevator system. It contains the fundamental classes, their (unrefined) associations, and the multiplicity of their associations. The multiplicity implies, but does not strictly define, the number of objects to be instantiated from a class. For example, the 1-1 association between the Elevator and its Run-Stop switch component indicates that there is a single switch for each elevator. The 1-8 relationship between the Elevator and the Elevator Gnome indicates that there are eight elevators for each gnome, but not the total number of gnomes. A large elevator system might have several banks of elevators, each with its own gnome controller. There is only a single instance of the Central Station class, so it includes the stereotype «singleton».

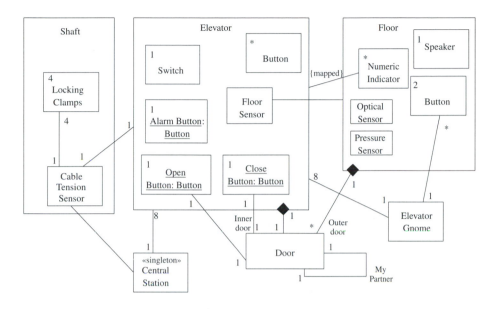

Figure 3-10: *First-Cut Elevator Case Study Class Diagram*

Some of the associations deserve additional explanation. Two different notations for composition are used in the diagram. In one case, a filled diamond is used, and in the other simple class nesting implies the composition association but without the association line. In this latter case, the multiplicity is shown as an *instance multiplicity* in the class or object. The Elevator has two associations to the class button. The first is shown as the <u>Alarm Button: Button</u> object instance. The role name that would be used on the association line is used as the instance name. The second is the composition relation to the Floor request buttons.[8] Additionally, Open and Close buttons define two more associations between the Elevator and Button classes.

The 1-* association between the Elevator and the Numeric Indicator is due to the fact that each floor has an indicator dedicated to each elevator. Therefore, there are 20 indicators for each elevator, one for each

---

[8] *Floor Request Button* is the name of the object, instantiated from the class *Button* within the class *Elevator*, that requests the elevator go to a specific floor. Remember that all the buttons are structurally the same so *Floor Request Button* is of the same class as *Elevator Request Button*.

floor, monitoring each elevator. From the perspective of the floor, each floor has one elevator indicator for each of the eight elevators, hence the 1-* relationship between Floor and Elevator Indicator. The {*mapped*} constraint notes the fact that there must be a 1:1 map between these sets of objects.

3.9 Defining Class Relationships and Associations

The first part of this chapter presented strategies for identifying objects, grouping them into classes, and the initial identification of the associations among the objects and classes. This section will provide a taxonomy of object and class associations and strategies for their classification. This will aid in the identification of associations and how they can be used effectively to assist the required collaborations.

3.9.1 Message Passing in Analysis

The abstraction for object communication is *message passing*. Objects communicate by sending each other messages. This is important because prior to design, the analyst does not know the tasking and processor details. The message passing schema allows analysts to consider object communication in terms of its semantic content without having to deal with the details of whether the message is passed by a synchronous function call, sending mail to a task, rendezvousing with a semaphore, or sending a bus message to another processor. The analysis model for these different communication implementations looks the same. It is the job of the design phase to detail how the communication among objects will ultimately manifest itself.

Figure 3-11 is a collaboration diagram (an object diagram that shows individual messages) with three objects; a Sensor, Controller, and Actuator. The relationships support the messages that pass between the Sensor and the Controller, and between the Controller and the Actuator. The message passing can be implemented in a number of ways.

As a simple function call:

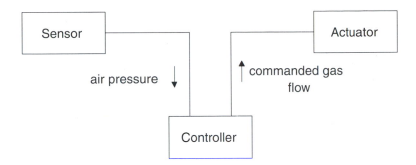

Figure 3-11: *Object Communication*

```
class Controller {
    Sensor *pSensor;
    Actuator *pActuator;
public:
    void controlPressure(void) {
        int x, y;
        x = pSensor->AirPressure();
        y = magicFunction(x);
        pActuator->SetGasFlow(y);
        };
};
```

These are synchronous messages with the «call» stereotype. The caller (Controller object) and the callee (Sensor and Actuator objects) synchronize for the duration of the function call. The caller suspends operation until the callee returns control. This is the simplest form of message passing, but other implementation strategies are possible.

If the objects each run in their own thread on an RTOS, sending messages to the thread mailbox might be the trick:

```
void Controller::controlPressure(void) {
    int x,y, j, status;
    int timeout = 10;
    thread_msg msg;

    // send request for data
    post(Sensor_thread, GET_REQUEST);

    j = 0;
    do {  // wait for sensor value
        status = pend(Sensor_thread, x, timeout);
```

```
        j++;
        } while ((status != OK)&&(j<10));

    y = magicFunction(x);

    msg.type = ACTION_TYPE;
    msg.value = y;
        // send cmd to actuator
    post(Actuator_thread, msg);

    j = 0;
    do {  // wait for acceptance by actuator
        status = pend(Sensor_thread, x, timeout);
        j++;
        } while ((status != OK)&&(j<10));
};
```

This is still synchronous message passing since the caller waits for the response before continuing. However, the technique is more general because the caller could issue the request and do other work while waiting. The Sensor and the Controller objects could even agree to have the Sensor send data periodically or when the value changes, in which case the Controller can be *reactive* to sensor data. The following code illustrates how this might be done in Ada.

```
task body Sensor is
var
    x: integer;
begin
    loop
        delay 2.0;
        x := readAD;
        Controller.SensorData(x);
    end loop;
end Sensor;

    task Controller is
    entry Sensor_Data(x: in integer);
    entry Other_Stuff;
end Controller;
task body Controller is
begin
    loop
        select
            accept Sensor_Data(x: in integer) do
                y:= MagicFunction(x);
                Actuator.Cmd(y);
```

```
        end Sensor_Data;
    or
        accept Other_Stuff do
            - other interesting things
        end OtherStuff;
    end select;
  end loop;
end Controller;

task Actuator is
    entry Cmd(setPt: in integer);
end Actuator;

task body Actuator is
begin
    loop
        accept Cmd(setPt: in integer) do
            setValue(setPt);
        end Cmd;
    end loop;
end Actuator;
```

This Ada code actually runs the objects as tasks and uses the Ada rendezvous task communications model. The Controller task loops waiting for an entry to be called. If the entry is Sensor_Data, then the Controller transforms the data and calls the Actuator task. If the called entry is Other_Stuff, then it processes that message instead. The Controller task is reactive in that it reacts to different entry calls made by other tasks but initiates no actions by itself.

The objects need not even run on the same processor. The normal mechanism for distributed computing is to send bus messages. Other mechanisms can be envisioned for this, including using an Object Request Broker (ORB) to arbitrate the call. The call to the ORB is synchronous, but may result in a local synchronous call, a thread rendezvous, or a bus message transaction depending on the location of the message target. The ORB maintains information about registered communicating objects so that the callers need not rely on their location or communications media. The ORB encapsulates this information (the Broker Pattern is discussed in Chapter 5).

Many different implementation mechanisms exist for object communication. Analysis ignores these details, focusing instead on the intrinsic abstractions of the domain and their interactions. Subsequent design work details the implementation of the message passing process.

3.9.2 Relationship Taxonomy

Object-oriented systems provide several important types of relationships:

- Association
- Aggregation
- Composition
- Generalization

A fifth type of relationship, *refinement,* is usually identified during design. For this reason its discussion is deferred until later.

The existence of an association between objects means that one or both objects send messages to the other. Associations are *structural,* meaning that they must be part of the class from which the objects are instantiated. For that reason, analysis considers association as belonging to classes, rather than objects. Instances of associations, called *links,* occur between objects.

Generalization is fundamentally a relationship between classes (rather than objects), because it defines a set of attributes, behaviors, and interfaces for the descendent classes. It is not implemented as messages sent to a parent class to invoke inherited behavior—subclasses already *have* these attributes and behaviors.

For example, Figure 3-12 shows a class diagram with the primary objects of a controller, sensor, and actuator. This figure has all four types of relationships. Compare this to the object message diagram shown in Figure 3-11. Figure 3-12 shows the structural arrangement of classes, and Figure 3-11 shows specific objects sending specific messages. Naturally, these diagrams must be consistent with each other.

3.10 Associations

Associations are logically bidirectional unless explicitly constrained. The association between a *dog owner* and his *dog* can be expressed in either direction indicating this bidirectionality.

> *He owns the dog.*
> *The dog belongs to him.*

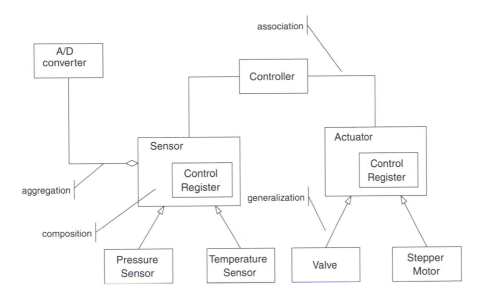

Figure 3-12: *Class Relationships*

or

> *The Floor Request button sends requests to the Elevator.*
> *The Elevator receives requests from the Floor Request button.*

It is rare that a relationship is actually implemented bidirectionally. In practice, such relationships are usually navigated only in a single direction. For example, the message would usually be sent as

> *Dog.Send(Tail->Wag)*

rather than

> *Tail.Send(Dog->Wag)*

Associations are most often implemented as pointers or references to objects. Navigating in a single direction implies that one object may navigate to the other (via an operation in the latter), but not vice versa. For example,

```
class Dog {
    Tail* pT;
public:
```

```
    void BeHappy(void) { pT->Wag(20); );
    void BeSad(void) { pT->Wag(2); };
    void BeExcited(void) { pT->Wag(50); };
    void BeMelancholy(void) { pT->Wag(5); };
};
```

It may not be possible, given just a tail, to identify which dog is emoting. It is a question of navigability.

Associations navigable in a single direction are known as *client-server associations*. The client is the object with the reference, and the server is the object with the data or operation invoked by the client. Servers are mostly passive or reactive objects, responding to requests on the part of the client. Clients must know about the servers to be able to invoke services from them. Servers should not know about their clients because this induces pathological coupling and makes the addition of new clients more difficult.

An embedded patient monitor might have a single display but might be able to monitor multiple patient parameters. The display and printer devices provide services to the other processors. Some subsystems acquire data and send it off to the display server for viewing. Another may print an alarm log to the printer. The servers (Display and Printer) in this case know nothing of the clients.

Figure 3-13 shows four classes and three associations. The patient parameters are modeled as client classes, and the display is modeled as a server. The display system must somehow be able to cope with up to four ECG waveforms, an oxygen saturation value (SpO2), and up to two arterial blood pressures. The parameter classes contain associations to navigate their data to the display server class. The display need not know anything about the sources of information. It responds passively upon receipt of data from the active parameter classes.

An alternative is shown in Figure 3-14. In this figure, the roles are reversed. The display is the active object (client) that solicits information to display from the passive (server) parameter classes.

Either architecture is feasible and reasonable. In both cases, the information flow is from the patient parameters to the display. The difference lies in which objects initiate the actions and which passively provide services.

An alternative to client-server association is a *peer-to-peer* association. Although much less common than client-server, it does occur

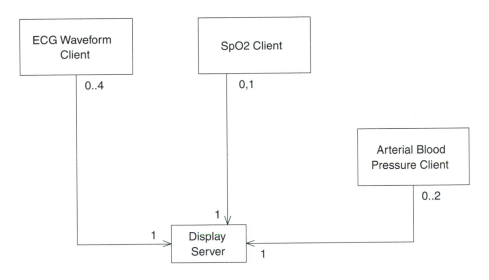

Figure 3-13: *Client-Server Association*

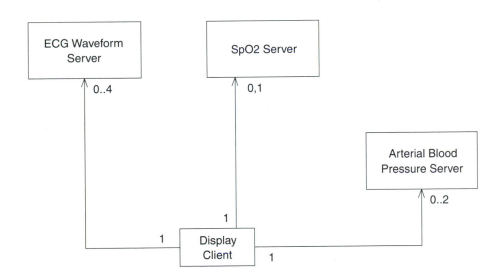

Figure 3-14: *Clients and Servers Revisited*

from time to time. A peer-to-peer association implies bidirectional message passing. Each object must know about the other. Generally, this is implemented as two independent client-server relationships, one in each direction.

3.11 Aggregation and Composition

An *aggregation* is a special type of association that imples logical or physical containment. Some authors prefer the term *aggregation* for this type of relationship, and still others prefer the term *whole/part*.

Aggregation is further subtyped into *physical* and *catalog aggregation*. The term *physical aggregation* is used when the multiplicity on the part end is "1". Note, however, that although the name suggests a physical relationship, the meaning is only that the whole directly accesses the part.

When the multiplicity of the part is either optional or greater than one, then the relationship is *catalog aggregation*. The name implies that the same relationship accesses a group of similar objects via a pointer or reference. The relationship must provide some means of navigating among the multiple parts.

Both physical and catalog aggregation support sharing of the same parts among different owners. This is shown adding the constraint of {*shared*} on an aggregate from a single class with the multiplicity of greater than one. If two different classes share a part, then the {*shared*} constraint must be applied to both aggregations. This syntax is shown in Figure 3-15.

Composition is a strong form of aggregation, similar to Booch's *aggregation by value* [2]. Composition means that part objects (called *components*) are solely the responsibility of the composite class. Composites must create and destroy their components. Components cannot be shared among composites. Composition is shown by graphical inclusions of the components within the composite or with a filled-in aggregation diamond. When inclusion is used, the multiplicity of the component is provided at its upper left-hand corner.

Aggregation may be *recursive*. That is, an aggregate may contain parts that may themselves contain classes of the original whole (al-

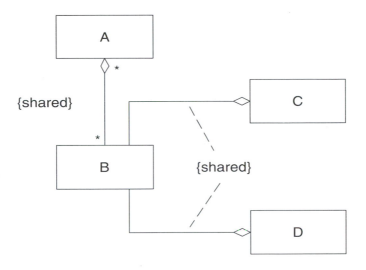

Figure 3-15: *Two Ways of Sharing Aggregates*

though with different instances). Mathematical expression parsing provides a simple example of recursive aggregation. The general rules of parsing are:

- *Expressions* are constructed of *terms,* linked together with *term operators,* + and – (binary operators).
- *Terms* are constructed of factors, linked together with *factor operators,* * and /.
- *Factors* are either primitives, with optional *unary operators* + and –, or *expressions* grouped by parentheses (and).

Using *expression* as a recursive aggregate (see Figure 3-16), mathematical formulae of arbitrary complexity may be constructed,[9] such as

    1 + 2*3
    –2 * +4 /(a+6*b–2)

In terms of implementation, aggregation is normally implemented as a pointer or reference (just as associations can be implemented) although declaration within the class scope is also possible for composi-

---

[9] You are encouraged to write the object diagrams for these expressions as an exercise.

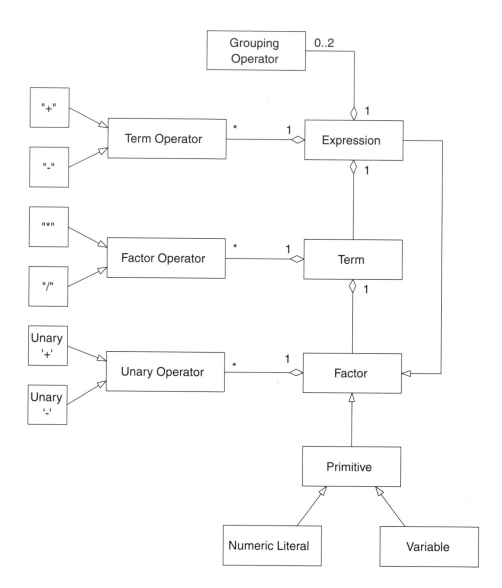

Figure 3-16: *Recursive Aggregates*

tion. For borderline cases, it may be difficult to decide if the two classes are related by association or aggregation. In these cases, just plan on implementing the association with a pointer.

3.11.1 RTOS Example

Figure 3-17 shows a real-time example of association and aggregation. This figure depicts the portion of a real-time operating system that manages tasks. The RTOS Kernel contains a number of fixed-sized

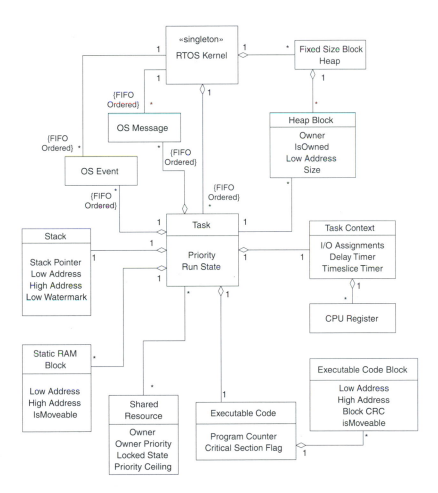

Figure 3-17: *RTOS Task Example*

heaps and tasks. Additionally, it provides services to post multiple events and messages to a task. RTOS kernels normally provide FIFO (first-in-first-out) queues to the task for this purpose. However, the actual structure of these message depots is a job for design, rather than analysis. Therefore, the relationship is shown as catalog aggregation. During design, classes to manage the events and messages must be added. For the purpose of analysis, however, it does not matter whether these components are arranged in a linear list, a binary tree, or some more exotic organizational structure. It *is* important in the problem domain to order the components. In this case, the problem statement (supposedly) specifies a FIFO ordering, but ordering by task priority could have been specified as well.

The *task* is clearly the central class in the figure. The RTOS must maintain a great deal of information about the tasks in order to properly schedule and manage their execution. From the RTOS perspective, tasks contain a number of critical components:

- Task stack
- Task context
- Executable code
- Static RAM blocks
- OS Event collection
- OS Message collection

A task also has some important attributes:

- Priority
- Run state

When multiple tasks are ready to run, a priority-driven scheduler will select the task with the highest priority to run. In fact, it will preempt currently executing tasks to run a ready higher priority task.

The *task context* class contains information for internal use of the OS. It contains an image of CPU registers, so the RTOS can restore the task state exactly as it was prior to preemption.

The *executable code* class contains information about the task code. The program counter marks exactly where the program was preempted so that it can resume (note that this could be stored with the CPU registers as well, but this model is somewhat more general). This particular RTOS does not constrain tasks to exist within contiguous memory. Tasks contain one or more *executable code blocks*, each of which has:

- Its memory block defined
- Defined whether the block can be moved by the OS
- A CRC over the block

The CRC allows the OS to run a background watchdog task to check for executable code corruption. The allowance for multiple code blocks allows for some portions of executable memory to be in ROM with other portions in RAM. Similarly, a task may contain multiple static RAM blocks for global memory as well.

Each task has a separate stack. The stack pointer attribute could be stored with the CPU registers, but again this model is somewhat more general. In particular, it allows for the simulation and execution of tasks at a level much higher than the underlying CPU hardware. The low water mark is an address an RTOS watchdog could check. Some RTOSs fill stack memory with a specific byte. The definition of a *low water mark* allows for a watchdog task to check for a low stack condition.

The *isMoveable* attribute on static RAM and executable code blocks implies that some design work is ahead. For RAM access, it indicates the need for multiple levels of indirection for static memory access. If the OS moves the location of the static RAM, then the task code must reference into an RTOS table that references the actual memory. When the memory is moved, the task references need not be modified. It is sufficient to change only the second reference within the RTOS itself. Executable code references must be indirect and the code position-independent.

Tasks have a couple of associations as well. Notably, they use *heap blocks* from the heap and they share *shared resources*. The heap blocks allow the task to allocate memory dynamically. Fixed sized heap blocks mitigate the common memory fragmentation problem.[10]

Shared resources are a thorny issue for real-time systems. A task may require a resource in order to continue. Another client locking a re-

---

[10] Repeated allocation from the memory free store can result in memory being fragmented into small noncontiguous chunks. This can lead to memory allocation failure when no fragment is large enough to satisfy a request even though the total available amount of memory is adequate.

source required by a task blocks it from continuing. When this occurs, the RTOS sets the task's run state attribute to *blocked*. The RTOS kernel typically moves the task from the ready queue to the blocked queue until the OS posts an event indicating that the resource is available for the task. Resources can have a *priority ceiling*[11] attribute as well. See Chapter 5 for more details on modeling shared resources.

3.12 Associative Classes

In distributed systems, the classic example of an associative class is a message class. In addition to the information being sent from one object to another, the message object may contain additional information specific to the relationship, and even to the link instance. For example:

- Message priority
- Message route
- Session identifiers
- Sequence numbers
- Flow control information
- Data format information
- Data packaging information
- Time-to-live information for the message
- Protocol revision number
- Data integrity check information

In a transaction-oriented system, associative classes also contain information specific to the transaction.

An associative class is used when information does not seem to belong to either object in the association or belongs to both equally. Marriage is an association between two people objects. Where do the following attributes belong?

---

[11] Priority ceiling is used in priority ceiling scheduling algorithms. Such algorithms elevate task priorities dynamically when resources are locked to bound priority inversion.

- Date of marriage
- Location of marriage
- Prenuptial agreement

Clearly, these are attributes of the marriage and not the participants. Figure 3-18 shows a case of an associative class. In this distributed system model, one subsystem contains the sensor class and acts as a

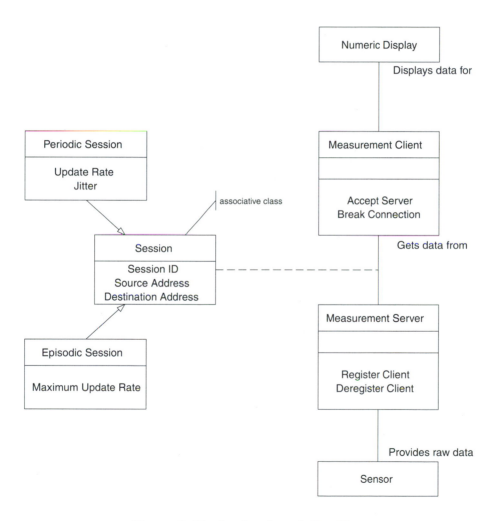

Figure 3-18: *Session Associative Class*

server for the data from the sensors. The client subsystem displays this data to the user. The association between the measurement server and measurement client is of interest here.

One way to implement the association is to have the client explicitly ask whenever it wants data to display. Another is to have the server provide the data whenever it becomes available. However, neither option may be the best use of a finite-bandwidth bus. Additionally, what if another client wants to be added to the recipient list for the data? Some buses provide the ability to broadcast such data, but most target a specific recipient.

The associative class solution provided here uses a *session*. A session is a negotiated agreement between two communicating objects. Sessions save bandwidth because they negotiate some information up front so that it need not be passed within each message. Nonsessioned communications (called *connectionless*) are similar to postcards. Each and every time a postcard is mailed, it must contain the complete destination and source addresses. A session is more like a phone call. Once the destination is dialed and the connection established, communication of arbitrary length and complexity can be performed without resending the phone number or reconnecting.

In this case, the session contains two important pieces of information: the source and target addresses. Two different session subtypes are defined based on the update policy. The update policy can be either *episodic* or *periodic*. Episodic, in this context, means that the server sends data when it changes—that is, when an episode occurs. Periodic means that the server must send the data at a fixed interval. Episodic sessions in this example have a maximum update rate to make sure that a bursty system does not overload the bus. Periodic sessions have a defined update rate. (It is possible to use multiple inheritance to create an epiperiodic class that has both episodic and periodic behavior.)

The measurement server contains two operations to assist in session management. The first is Register Client. This operation accepts the registration of a new client and participates in the negotiated construction of a session object. The Deregister Client operation removes a registered client.

The measurement client contains two operations to support its role in negotiating the session: Accept Server and Break Connection.

Who owns the session? Arguments can be made for both the server and the client. The server must track information about the session so that it knows when and how to issue updates. The client initiates the session and must also know about update policy and rates. The solution shown in Figure 3-18 is that the session is an associative class and contains attributes about the relationship between the two primary classes. Because this is a distributed system, the implementation would involve creating two coordinating session objects (or a single *distributed object*), one on each processor node, providing session information to the local client or server.

3.13 Generalization Relationships

Generalization is a taxonomic relationship between classes. The class higher in the taxonomic hierarchy can be called the parent, generalized, base, or superclass. The class inheriting properties from the base class can be called the child, specialized, derived, or subclass. Derived classes have all the properties of their parents, but may extend and specialize them. Most commonly, all of the classes derived from any given base class are specialized along a single characteristic only.[12]

Using Aristotelian logic and standard set theory, generalizing along a single characteristic guarantees that the classes are *disjoint*.[13] When the set of subclasses enumerates all possible subclasses along the characteristic, the subclassing is said to be *complete.*

The button subclasses in Figure 3-19 are specialized along the lines of behavior. Simple buttons issue an event message when pressed, but have no state memory. Toggle buttons jump back and forth between two states on sequential depressions. Multistate buttons run through a (possibly elaborate) state machine upon each depression. Group buttons deselect all other buttons within the group when pressed.

---

[12] This kind of relationship is called *or-generalization.* The UML also defines an *and-generalization* relationship in which specialization takes place along multiple dimensions simultaneously. Because this feature of UML has little applicability to real-time systems, we won't examine it in detail in this book.

[13] By *disjoint* it is meant that the classes represent nonoverlapping or orthogonal alternatives. Male versus female, for example, are disjoint sets. Fuzzy sets are inherently nondisjoint and allow partial membership. Object subclasses are assumed to be crisp sets (all-or-none membership) rather than fuzzy.

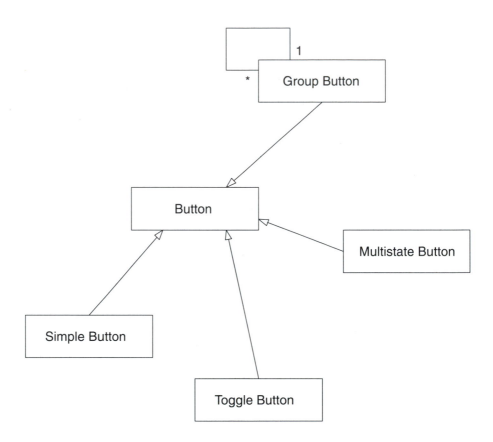

Figure 3-19: *Button Subclasses*

The principal rule for good subclassing is the *Liskov Substitution Principle* (LSP) [3]. It states that a subclass must obey polymorphic rules in exactly the same manner as its superclass. In terms of implementation, it means that a pointer or reference to a base class can use subclasses derived from it. For example,

```
class Animal {
public:
    virtual void speak(void) = 0; // virtual base class
};

class dog: public Animal {
public:
```

```
      void speak(void) { cout << "Arf!" << endl; };
};

class fish: public Animal {
public:
   void speak(void) { cout << "Blub!" << endl; };
};

class cat: public Animal {
public:
   void speak(void) { cout << "<Aloof disdain>" <<
   endl; };
};

void main(void) {
   Animal *A;
   dog d;
   fish f;
   cat c;

   A = &d;
   A->speak();
   A = &c;
   A->speak();
   A = &f;
   A->speak();
};
```

The base class (Animal) accesses the three subtypes through a pointer (A). Nonetheless, the access to the speak() method for each is identical, satisfying the LSP.

For the LSP to work, the relationship between the superclass and subclass must be one of specialization or extension. Whatever is true of the superclass must also be true of the subclass because the subclass *is* a type of its superclass. A dog *is* an animal, so all of the things true about animals are also true about dogs. All of the behaviors of animals can also be performed by dogs. If the animal has an attribute or behavior that is not true of dogs (such as being able to produce free oxygen via photosynthesis), a dog would not be "a type of" animal.

That being said, a subclass is free to specialize the behavior of a superclass. The speak() method defined within animal is an example. Each subclass does a different thing while still meeting the requirement of supporting the behavior speak(). Locomote() is another example. Dogs, cats, fish, and birds all locomote, but they implement it differently. This is what is meant by specialization.

Subclasses are also free to extend their inherited structure by adding new behaviors or attributes. We can add some new behaviors to the dog and cat classes that are not true of animals in general.

```
class dog: public Animal {
public:
    void speak(void) { cout << "Arf!" << endl; };
    void slobber(float slobberIndex);
    void AttackJogger(int fearLevel);
};

class cat: public Animal {
public:
    void speak(void) { cout << "<Aloof disdain>" <<
    endl; };
    void ClawFurniture(long ClawLength);
    void IgnoreOwner(void);
};
```

Now dogs can slobber() and AttackJogger(), and cats can ClawFurniture() and IgnoreOwner(). Animals (such as fish) can, in general, perform none of these charming behaviors.

Frequently, base classes cannot be instantiated without first being specialized. Animal doesn't do anything interesting, but dogs, cats, and fish do. When a class is not directly instantiable, it is called an *abstract class*. C++ classes are made abstract by the inclusion of a *pure virtual function*. A C++ virtual function is a class method that is denoted by the keyword *virtual*. It need only be so indicated in one class in the inheritance tree, and it will be virtual for all derived classes. A virtual function is made *pure virtual* with the peculiar syntax of assigning the function declaration the value zero. For example,

```
class widget {
public:
    virtual void doSomething() = 0;
};
```

Note that in C++, constructors and destructors cannot be made pure virtual. Furthermore, if a C++ class contains a virtual function, it is a logical error not to define the destructor as virtual (just one of many such opportunities provided by the C++ language). C++ does not allow virtual constructors.

3.13.1 Positioning Attributes in the Inheritance Tree

Generalization relationships form class hierarchies with the most general classes at the top and the most specialized classes at the bottom. Structuring these hierarchies is done by using three complementary approaches:

- Derived classes that extend the capabilities of the parent (top-down)
- Derived classes that specialize the capabilities of a parent (top-down)
- Bubbling up attributes and behaviors that are common in peer children (bottom-up)[14]

The first strategy, extension, means that a subclass can add behaviors and attributes to those it inherits from its parents. This is an example of the Open-Closed Principle (OCP) [4]. The OCP states that for maximum reusability, a class should be open for extension but not modification. The focus of the OCP is that changes in a well-designed class hierarchy should be made by subclassing rather than modifying the hierarchy itself. Another name for this concept is *programming by difference.* The developer finds a class in the hierarchy that is close to what is needed, subclasses it, and extends the subclass to meet the particular needs. The OCP focuses on reuse, but it applies equally well to the construction of class hierarchies. Subclasses may extend the capabilities of their parents without modifying the parents.

Figure 3-20 shows a simple example of extending a subclass. The *queue* superclass provides three methods: insert(), remove(), and clear(). It is subclassed by the *persistent queue* class. This child class acts exactly like its parent for the defined methods—in fact, it does not redefine them but reuses them as is from the parent. However, it adds two new methods: save() and restore(). The child class extends the functionality of the parent by providing only new behaviors.

Specializing a subclass redefines some of the class' (virtual) behaviors. The redefinition of the methods inherited from a parent special-

---

[14] Note that restriction of the parent class is not included. All popular object-oriented languages allow the *augmentation* or *extension* of a class, but not *restriction* (removal of a behavior or attribute). To do so breaks the fundamental tenet of inheritance—that the child *is a type of* its parent—and therefore violates the LSP.

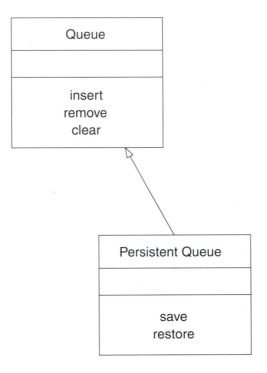

Figure 3-20: *Extending Parent Classes*

izes a subclass for an application. For example, Figure 3-21 shows a specialization of the class *queue*.

The subclass *Cached Queue* implements exactly the same methods as its parent, but it does so in a different way. The parent class stores all of its queue elements in normal memory. However, real-time systems often provide multiple read/write storage—dynamic RAM, static RAM, dual-ported RAM, FLASH memory, EEPROMs, disk storage, etc. The simple queue is limited to available memory for storing queue elements, but in some circumstances it may be necessary to queue more data than can be held in main memory.

The *Cached Queue* class provides one solution to this problem. It provides the same insert() and remove() operations as queue, but internally the methods work differently. A straightforward implementation for *Cached Queue* would maintain three areas: incoming, outgoing, and long-term blocks. The incoming and outgoing blocks in normal memory store the newest and oldest data, respectively. The long-term block

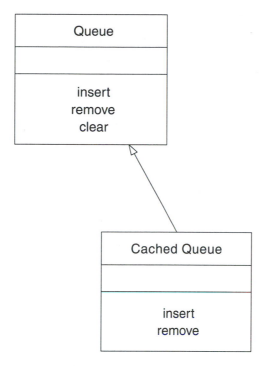

Figure 3-21: *Specializing Parent Classes*

in the slower memory stores the bulk of the queued data. Calls to insert() would put the inserted data into the incoming block. When this fills, insert would flush the incoming block to the long-term storage. The overhead for slower memory is often the same whether the access is for a single byte or for a larger block. This makes caching the data more efficient than writing to the slower memory on each insert() call. Saving up data in higher speed memory and writing to slower memory in blocks reduces the average performance hit per insertion.

The remove() method works in reverse. If the outgoing block is not empty, remove() simply dequeues there. When a remove() call finds the outgoing block empty, it reads in the next block of values from the long-term storage area, and then dequeues the oldest item. If the long-term storage area is also empty, then it must move data from the incoming block directly into the outgoing block for maximum efficiency.

Clearly, this behavior is more elaborate than one would expect for a simple *Queue*. The cached queue must redefine the existing access methods to provide this more complex implementation. Note, however, that LSP is still maintained. The client doesn't know whether it has a reference to a *Queue* or *Cached Queue* since the effect is the same from its perspective. In other words, *Queue* and *Cached Queue* have the same *type* but are of a different class.

The last strategy for constructing generalization hierarchies works from the leaves of the inheritance tree. After structuring the hierarchy, siblings subclassed from the same parent are examined for attributes and behaviors in common. If all siblings have the same property, it belongs to the parent rather than being replicated in each sibling. If the characteristic is common to some, but not all, of the siblings, then it may indicate a class is needed between the parent and the similar siblings.

Figure 3-22 shows an inheritance tree for bus messages. Each child class inherits the attributes *Priority, Source Address,* and *Destination Ad-*

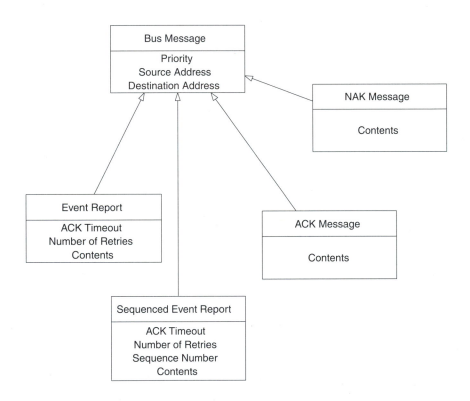

Figure 3-22: *Positioning Attributes in the Generalization Hierarchy*

dress. We see, however, that each message has a *Contents* attribute. *Event Report* and *Sequenced Event Report* messages must identify the event in their *contents* field. ACKs and NAKs must identify the message to which they are responding in their *contents* field. Since all siblings have the contents attribute, it can be moved up into the parent class *Bus Message.*

Event Report and *Sequenced Event Report* messages share ACK Timeout and Number of Retries attributes. These do not appear in the ACK and NAK messages. Therefore, these may be abstracted into a class between *Event Report* and *Bus Message* and *Sequenced Event Report* and *Bus Message.* This is called *Reliable Message* because protocol mechanisms exist to support retransmission if no response to them is received. Figure 3-23 shows the resulting reorganization.

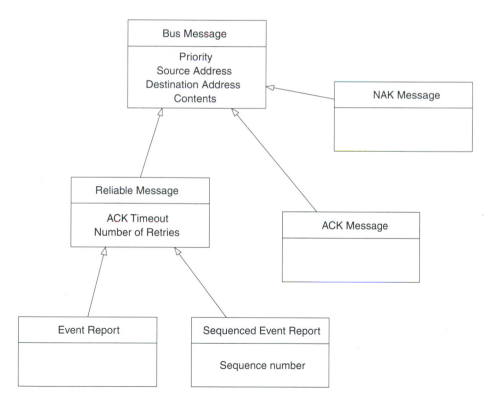

Figure 3-23: *Repositioned Attributes*

Of course, the astute analyst may mix all three strategies. It is possible to extend, specialize, and bubble up all at the same time.

3.14 Summary

This chapter has discussed the first half of analysis—identification of objects, classes and relationships. Many strategies can be used to identify objects and classes—underlining the nouns, identifying the physical devices, looking for persistent data, and so on. These objects have attributes and behaviors that allow them to fulfill their responsibilities. Classes are abstractions of objects so that all objects instantiated from a particular class are structurally identical.

To support collaboration of objects, classes have relationships to each other. These may be associations among class instances, such as aggregation, or they may be relationships between classes, such as generalization. Objects use these associations to communicate by sending messages to each other.

The other half of analysis is concerned with defining the behavior of the classes. As we shall see in the next chapter, class behaviors may be classified in three different ways—simple, state, and continuous. The dynamic properties of these classes allows them to use their structure to meet the system responsibilities in real-time.

3.15 References

[1] Cook, Rick, *The Wizardry Compiled*. Riverdale, NY: Baen Books, 1990.
[2] Booch, Grady, *Object-Oriented Analysis and Design with Applications*. 2nd ed. Redwood City, CA: Benjamin/Cummings, 1994.
[3] Liskov, Barbara, "Data Abstraction and Hierarchy," *SIGPLAN Notices 23*, no. 5 (May, 1988).
[4] Martin, Robert, "The Open-Closed Principle," *C++ Report 8*, no. 1 (1996).
[5] Douglass, Bruce Powel, *Doing Hard Time: Objects and Patterns in Real-Time Software Development*. Reading, MA: Addison Wesley Longman, 1998.
[6] Neumann, Peter G., *Computer Related Risks*. Reading, MA: Addison Wesley Longman, 1995.

Chapter 4

Analysis: Defining Object Behavior

The previous chapter showed how to define the system structure by identifying the fundamental objects and classes and their relationships. In this chapter, we define and refine operations and behaviors. There are a number of means for specifying overall object behavior; the most important of these is modeling the object as a finite state machine. Scenario modeling helps you test your behavioral models to ensure that the objects can collaborate together to achieve the system responsibilities. The state and scenario models lead to the definitions of class operations required to process the incoming messages and events.

Notation and Concepts Discussed

Simple behavior	Event
Continuous behavior	Transition
State behavior	Statechart
State	Operations

4.1 Object Behavior

Chapter 3 presented the analysis and decomposition of systems into their object structure and relationships. The other key pillar of object-oriented analysis is the specification of *dynamic behavior*. Behavior binds the structure of objects with their attributes and relationships so that objects can meet their responsibilities. Ultimately, an object's operations implement its behavior. This chapter will discuss these concepts in some detail.

4.1.1 Simple Behavior

We define three types of behavior: *simple, state,* and *continuous.* The object with *simple* behavior performs services on request and keeps no memory of previous services. A simple object always responds to a given input in exactly the same way regardless of its history. Some examples of simple behaviors are:

- Simple mathematical functions, such as cosine or square root
- A search operation of a static data structure that always starts from the same point, such as the search of a static binary tree
- Sort operations
- A knob that returns the number of clicks for a given user action

For example, $\cos\frac{\pi}{2} = 0$ regardless of what value was passed to the cos() function. In other cases, the distinction is not as clear. Is the search of a binary tree simple or state-driven? If the behavior changes due to previous input, then it cannot by definition be simple. If the binary tree provides methods like next() and previous(), then it must maintain an internal state between calls.[1] If the tree provides only calls such as find(), then at least to its clients it exhibits stateless behavior.

4.1.2 State Behavior

The second type of object behavior is called *state, state-driven,* or *reactive.* Our definition of a state is as follows:

---

[1] The caller can maintain this state as well. This is the basis for the Container Pattern discussed in Chapter 6.

A state is an ontological condition that persists for a significant period of time, is distinguishable from other such conditions, and is disjoint with them. A distinguishable state means that it differs from other states in the events it accepts, the transitions it takes as a result of accepting those events, or the actions it performs. A transition is a response to an event that causes a change in state.

Modeling an object as a *finite state machine* (FSM) attempts to reduce the behavioral complexity by making some simplifying assumption. Specifically, it assumes:

- The system being modeled can assume only a finite number of existence conditions, called *states*
- The system behavior within a given state is essentially identical and is defined by:

  ▾ The messages and events accepted

  ▾ The actions associated with each incoming event

  ▾ The state's reachability graph

  ▾ The complete set of (event, transition, target state) triads:

  - The ongoing activities within the state

  - The actions done entering or leaving the state

- The system resides in states for significant periods of time
- The system may change these conditions only in a finite number of well-defined ways, called *transitions*
- Transitions take (approximately) zero time

To explore state machines just a little bit, let's build a state machine to parse a string of parentheses to see if they are balanced; that is, the number and order of left- and right-parentheses is correct and equal. For example, see Table 4-1.

This turns out to be hard to model as a FSM (hard, as in *impossible*). By our previous definition of states, each of the following is a different state (at the last parenthesis in the expression):

Table 4-1: *Balancing Parentheses*

Expression	Description
( ) ( )	Balanced
((( ) ( )))	Balanced
(( ) ( )	Unbalanced: +1
( ) ( ))	Unbalanced: -1
) (	Unbalanced due to order
( ))(( ) ( )	Unbalanced due to order

```
(
( (
( ( (
)
( )
) (
```

Because it is possible to be unbalanced infinitely to the left or right, in principle a finite set of states cannot model a parser of this grammar. If we limit the string length to a finite value, then it is possible. Just for grins ☺, let's limit the string length to four characters, and the only characters in the grammar are (and). Such a state machine looks something like Figure 4-1.

Figure 4-1 shows the state space for an expression parser for this simple grammar.[2] The valid balanced states are shown using heavy lines. The transitions are not named to simplify the diagram.

Only four of the 31 states shown represent valid balanced expressions. Many of the expressions are simply unbalanced, such as)))(, but others have an incorrect sequence, such as)(. The resulting statechart is unsatisfying because it seems like it *ought* to be simple, and because a more parsimonious graph that contains a complete enumeration of all possible expressions *ought* to be possible. The implication is that while

---

[2] Error transitions for illegal tokens (e.g., w) are not shown as these would complicate the diagram further.

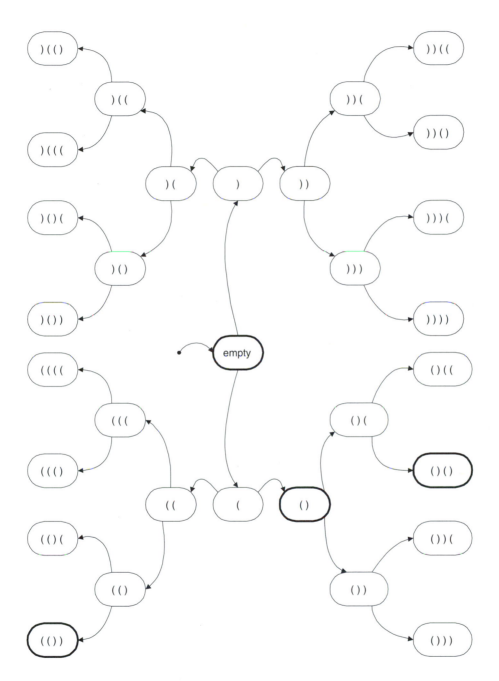

Figure 4-1: *Finite Parenthetical Expression Parser*

FSMs are theoretically helpful, in many applications their state spaces will grow unmanagably large and complex for even simple problems (and then you die).

A modified approach, however, can simplify the problem. You may note that three conditions are met by all valid expressions states:

1. The number of characters is even (0, 2, or 4)

2. The number of left parentheses equals the number of right parentheses

3. The next token received when the state corresponds to a balanced expression must be a left parenthesis.

Figure 4-2 shows a greatly simplified FSM that does exactly the same thing as the FSM in Figure 4-1. The exact syntax for statecharts is defined in Section 4.3, but briefly, this FSM consists of three states and eight transitions. Transitions are labelled with the incoming token optionally followed by a / character, and an action expression, such as balance++. This action expression is executed when the transition is taken. The diamond is a *conditional connector,* which allows different transitions to be taken when an event occurs based on some boolean expression called a guard (shown in square brackets).

The reason that the FSM in Figure 4-2 is simplified so greatly is because we use memory (the variable *balance*) to track the balance state for the expression. This is a great asset in this case because all the left unbalanced states can be represented with a single state, all the balanced states with another, and all the invalid expressions (incorrect sequence and right unbalanced) with a third. Pure FSMs have no memory and must represent the automaton using only states. However, we can cheat and combine FSMs with memory and other kinds of machines (such as push-down stacks, queues, or more elaborate machines) with the resulting net simplification. Throughout the remainder of this book, when we refer to an FSM, we mean one augmented with memory as necessary. State machines will be the major focus of this chapter and will be discussed in more detail in Section 4.2.

4.1.3 Continuous Behavior

The third kind of object behavior is called *continuous.* Many objects show continuous behavior, including digital filters and pseudorandom

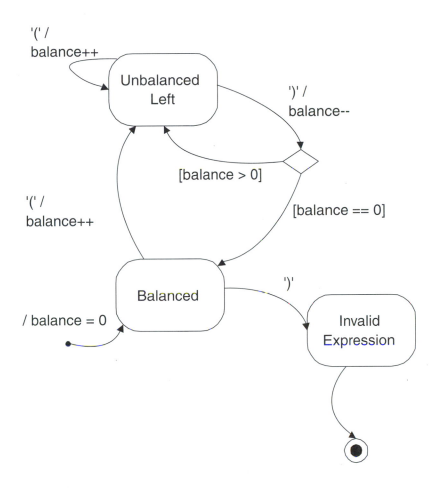

Figure 4-2: *Simplified Finite Parenthetical Expression Parser*

functions. All that is required is that the current output depend on the previous history in a smooth way. An object with continuous behavior is one with an infinite, or at least unbounded, set of existence conditions. PID control systems, fuzzy sets, and neural networks all display continuous behavior.

State machines fundamentally rely on Aristotelian logic and indirectly on the Law of the Excluded Middle (LEM). The LEM states that existence conditions can be divided into two mutually exclusive groups.

If the first is called *A,* then the second can be called *Not A* or *~A.* Classical set theory, on which finite state analysis is based, is firmly rooted in the basic notion that states have hard, crisp boundaries and that an object must be either in the set *A* or in the set *~A.* It cannot be in both, but it must be in one. States are essentially nothing more than disjoint sets of the object's behavior space. A simple FSM must be in one and only one state at a time. In fact, FSMs follow the same LEM as do sets.

Objects with continuous behaviors do not follow the LEM, either because the concept of states doesn't apply or because states are not disjoint. If a value is a real number between 0 and 1, it cannot be modeled by an FSM because it can assume any of an infinite set of values. Even when continuous systems have states, these states are not disjoint—and this is the very basis for fuzzy set and control theory. Before we get into FSMs in more detail, let's examine a system with continuous behavior—in this case a fuzzy logic system.

A fuzzy automobile braking control system is a relatively simple example. Such a system would have the responsibility of slowing down the car smoothly as it approaches its destination. The amount of braking to be applied depends on two independent variables: automobile speed and distance from destination. When the car is moving fast and is close, the brakes must be applied more vigorously than when the car is either {moving fast and is far away} or {moving slowly and is close}.

The fuzzy car braking system can be codified by defining the membership functions (inputs) and the rules applied to set members (outputs to the brake). A diagrammatic representation of the fuzzy sets used in the definition of an automobile braking system is given in Figure 4-3.

In conventional terms, the speed of the automobile constitutes one state (set) variable, and the distance another. Since these concerns are fundamentally orthogonal, it makes sense to consider each separately in separate state machines.[3] The state values for speed are *stopped, slow, sauntering,* and *galloping.* The state values for distance are *at, close, near, removed, and far.*

The output of the control system is the braking pressure. It has four states: *none, light, medium,* and *hard.* Brakes should not be applied when

---

[3] More specifically, they are orthogonal components of a single (although fuzzy) state machine. Orthogonal components are discussed in detail later in this chapter.

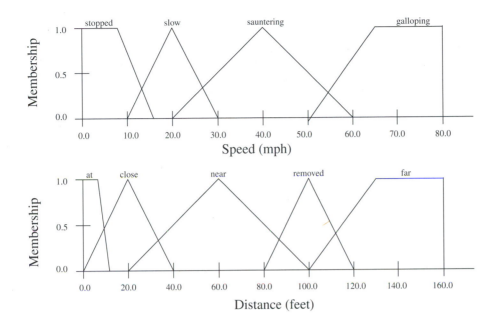

Figure 4-3: *Fuzzy Automobile Brakes*

trying to accelerate or maintain speed, but only when trying to slow down. The other states are of various strengths related to the desired amount of instantaneous deceleration.

The rule set is defined in Table 4-2.

In a fuzzy state machine, the system is in all states simultaneously, so *all* rules are applied *all* the time. The degree to which they are applied depends directly on the degree of membership within the particular state. For example, if the current speed is 25 miles per hour then *slow* is half true (0.5) and *sauntering* is also partially true (0.25). If the distance is 85 feet, then *near* is true 0.3 and *removed* is true 0.2. Therefore, the following rules have nonzero outputs:

- Slow and Near → Light
- Slow and Removed → None
- Sauntering and Near → Medium
- Sauntering and Removed → Light

Table 4-2: *Fuzzy Automobile Braking Rules*

Speed State	Distance State	Output Rule (Braking pressure applied)
Stopped	Any	None
Slow	At	Medium
Slow	Close	Light
Slow	Near	Light
Slow	Removed	None
Slow	Far	None
Sauntering	At	Hard
Sauntering	Close	Medium
Sauntering	Near	Medium
Sauntering	Removed	Light
Sauntering	Far	None
Galloping	At	Hard
Galloping	Close	Hard
Galloping	Near	Medium
Galloping	Removed	Light
Galloping	Far	None

You can also see that the logical statement *slow and near* is more true than the statement *sauntering and removed*. The resulting outputs are combined (using what is called a *defuzzifier*) to produce an output that is a weighted sum of the inputs, called the *centroid*.

It is clear that fuzzy sets are more general than crisp sets because crisp sets can be defined as constrained fuzzy sets. In this same sense, continuous behavior is more general than state behavior. With this increased generality, however, comes more complexity. Constraining the object behavior to crisp sets simplifies the system design. For this reason, we will focus the next section on crisp state machine behavior applied to objects.

4.2 Defining Object State Behavior

In state machines designed by traditional structured methods, the portion of the system exhibiting the state behavior is not clearly defined. Some set of functions and data collaborate together in a way that lends itself to finite state modeling, but generally this set is only vaguely defined. In object-oriented methods, the programmatic unit exhibiting state behavior is clear—only classes define state models and only objects execute state machines.[4]

Consider a simple retriggerable one-shot timer. Such a timer is generally in one of two possible states: idle and counting down. When the timer has counted down, it then issues an event (such as causing an interrupt leading to some system action), resets the timer, and returns to the counting down state. This model is shown in Figure 4-4.

States are shown as rounded rectangles. Transitions are directed lines beginning at the starting state and finishing at the target state. Transitions have names optionally followed by actions (i.e., functions or operations), which are executed when the transition is taken.

The example state machine shown in Figure 4-4 consists of two states and three transitions. In the Idle state, the timer isn't counting down—it sits patiently waiting for the Start Cmd. Once the Start Cmd event occurs, it enters the Counting Down state. As a result of the transition, two actions are performed: The count value of the timer is set and the timer mechanism itself is started. Actions are shown in an action list, which is separated from the transition label with a slash (/). The model assumes that these actions take approximately zero time. The solid circle indicates the starting state when the system first begins.

Once in the Counting Down state, the timer can respond to two events: a Timeout and a Stop Cmd. In the former case, the timer raises an interrupt, resets the time, and resumes the Counting Down state from the reset value. In the latter case, the timer performs the *stop timer* action and enters the Idle state.

Using only pure FSMs, a countdown timer, such as that shown here, which counts down using a 16-bit counter, would have 65,537 states

---

[4] We use the term *state model* to mean the definition of a state machine, which must be defined within a class. The term *state machine* is an instance of a state model and therefore must belong to an object.

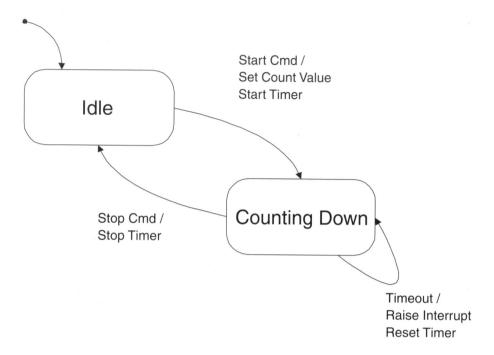

Figure 4-4: *Retriggerable One-Shot Timer*

(2^{16} + 1) in the state model (drawing this diagram is an exercise left for you). However theoretically pure such a definition might be, it isn't useful. The actions performed by the timer are the same (i.e., decrementing the count value) within the Counting Down state, and it receives the same transitions. By our (impure) definition of state, all conditions in which the timer is counting down are identical and therefore constitute a single state. The behavior of the counter can most profitably be decomposed into two sets of conditions—*counting down* and *idle.* Therefore, we will opt for the more parsimonious and useful definition and use two states rather than tens of thousands.

Another example of object state behavior is provided by a message transaction object within a reliable communication scheme. When one object (the sender) sends a bus message to a remote object (the receiver) using a reliable communication protocol, a transaction object is created temporarily until it can be verified that the receiver has received the message properly. If a timeout period elapses without the receipt of an explicit acknowledgement from the receiver, the message is retransmitted. Once an acknowledgement is received, the transaction object can be destroyed. In addition, the transaction object should be limited to a finite number of retries before giving up, informing the sender of the communications failure, and being destroyed. This behavior can be captured in a simple state diagram (see Figure 4-5).

The diamond symbol represents a *conditional connector* that allows branching transitions based on some guarding condition. Guards are shown inside square brackets, such as [Trans Count <= Limit]. If the event occurs and the guard evaluates to TRUE, then the transition branch is taken. If an event occurs that leads to a conditional connector and none of the exiting guard conditions evaluates to TRUE, then the

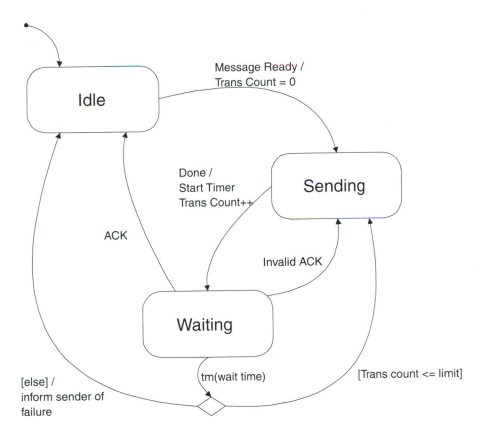

Figure 4-5: *Message Transaction State Diagram*

event is discarded and the transition is not taken. The simple state diagram in Figure 4-5 represents the behavioral states of the message transaction object simply and clearly.

4.3 UML State Diagrams

Harel statecharts [1] form the basis of UML state diagrams; we shall use the terms statechart and state diagram interchangeably. Statecharts overcome the limitations of traditional FSMs while retaining benefits of finite state modeling. Statecharts include both the notions of nested hierarchical states and concurrency while extending the notion of actions.

4.3.1 Basic State Diagrams

The essential syntax of statecharts is similar to traditional state diagrams in the simple case. In fact, Mealy-Moore state diagrams (M&Ms)[5] can be redrawn directly using statechart notation. The important basic features of statecharts are shown in Figure 4-6.

The most noticeable departure from traditional state diagrams is the nesting of states within states. The outer enclosing state is called a *superstate*. The inner states are called *substates*. For example, state S2 contains two substates, U1 and U2. While the system is in state S2, it must be in *exactly* one of the nested substates. The nested states may be shown physically within the superstate, or the superstate may be depicted on another diagram altogether. This is an extremely powerful concept, as we will see later.

Transitions may be drawn to the specific substate, such as transition T5, or may be drawn to the containing superstate, such as transition T1. In the latter case, some rules must be applied to determine which sub-

---

[5] Mealy FSMs allow actions only when a transition is taken; Moore state models allow actions only upon state entry. In addition, M&Ms do not allow state nesting or othogonal components, topics that are discussed in more detail later in this chapter.

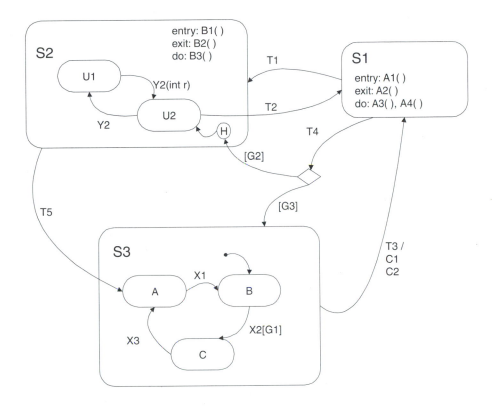

Figure 4-6: *Basic Statecharts*

state is entered. When there is ambiguity, an initial or default state must be identified using a filled circle and an arrow, just as in traditional FSMs. Additionally, a *history connector* may be included, as in state S2. When present, it points to the default state with an arrow just as the normal default transition does. This is the initial state when there is no history. When the superstate has been active before (i.e., when there is history), the last active substate becomes the next default. If the last substate was U1 and transition T5 was taken, when S2 is subsequently reentered the default will be substate U1.

Transitions may be made to and from either a superstate or a substate. When a transition is indicated *to* a superstate, then the default substate is entered. When a transition is indicated *from* a superstate, it means that the transition applies to *all contained substates.* This is a great help in simplifying diagrams since a single transition from a superstate represents transitions from each of its contained substates. In the figure, Transition T3 can be taken from any substate of S3. In traditional M&M diagrams, a separate transition activated by the same event for each of the substates A, B, and C would have to be drawn to represent the same behavior.

Statechart behavior may be more elaborate than in traditional FSMs. Both states and transitions can have actions associated with them. States may have both *entry* and *exit actions* as well as *activities.* Entry actions are operations that are performed when the state is entered, and exit actions are performed when the state exits. Activities are performed as long as the state is active. Activities are indicated in the state activity list by the word "do:". Actions still are assumed to take an insignificant amount of time, and activities are performed as long as the state is active. This rich behavioral modeling allows efficient representation of a wide set of behaviors.

Entry actions are executed in the same order as the nesting when entering a nested substate from outside its enclosing superstate. See Figure 4-7. When transition t1 is taken, the sequence of actions is w, then x, y, then z. When transition t2 is taken, the reverse order applies (innermost → out), so the sequence of exit actions is p, then n, then m. When transitioning between states, as with the transition t3, the exit actions of the source state are taken, followed by the transition actions, followed by the destination state's entry actions. In the case of transition t3, the sequence is p, then n, then g, then s. States may be nested arbitrarily deeply and these rules apply recursively.

Transitions may have parameters and guards as well as actions. The syntax for transitions is

event-name(parameters) [guard] / action list ^ event list

All of the fields in Table 4-3 are optional. Even the name may be omitted in the case of an anonymous transition to be taken when a state completes its activities.

A common transition in real-time systems is the timeout transition. It is denoted by the event name *tm(interval).* This avoids the necessity of building explicit timer objects with propagate transitions to the other objects that use them.

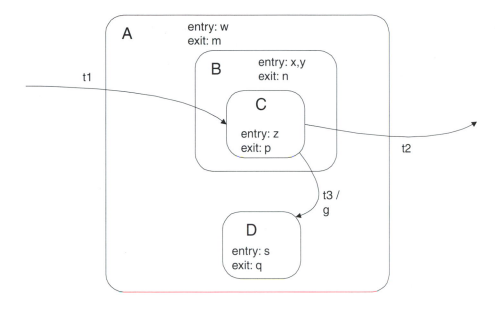

Figure 4-7: *Actions and Nested States*

Table 4-3: *Transition Fields*

Field	Description
Event-name	The name of the event triggering the transition.
Parameters	A comma-separated list containing the names of data parameters passed with the event signal.
Guard	A boolean expression that must evaluate to TRUE for the transition to be taken, often used in conjunction with the conditional connector.
Action list	A comma-separated list of operations executed as a result of the transition being taken. These operations may be of this or another object.
Event list	A comma-separated list of events generated as a result of this transition being taken. This allows events to be propagated to other (concurrent) state machines.

4.3.2 Orthogonal Components and Concurrency

One of the weaknesses of M&Ms is that unrelated components of objects result in combinatorial numbers of states. A simple class illustrates this problem:

```
enum tColor {eRed, eBlue, eGreen};
enum tMode {eNormal, eStartup, eDemo};
class orthoClass {
public:
    tColor Color;
    bool ErrorStatus;
    tMode Mode;
    void setColor(tColor c);
    void setES(bool es);
    void setMode(tMode m);
};
```

What are the states for this class? In the traditional view, each combination of values of the class attributes constitutes a different state of an object of this class. Figure 4-8 shows a list of the states. Note that we didn't even try to show all the transitions caused by the acceptance of the SetColor, setES, and setMode operations because it would render the diagram completely unreadable (something for you to do on those cold Minnesota nights when your favorite web server is overloaded).

Statecharts provide a very clear yet succinct representation of orthogonal components, as shown in Figure 4-9. The dashed lines separate the orthogonal components. Each of the orthogonal components is named and operates independently of the other components. An object with this state model must be in exactly one state from *each of the orthogonal components* as long as the enclosing superstate is active. An object of class orthoClass might be in state (eRed, eDemo and TRUE) or in state (eBlue, eNormal, and FALSE).

Orthogonal components do not necessarily imply concurrent threads of execution, but they do support concurrency. Threads of control often split and proceed in parallel only to resynchronize at some later time. The state model in Figure 4-10 shows an object that begins life in state X. When the object takes transition t0, it enters the state Y, which has concurrent orthogonal components. This typically would be implemented with the temporary creation of a thread that lasts as long

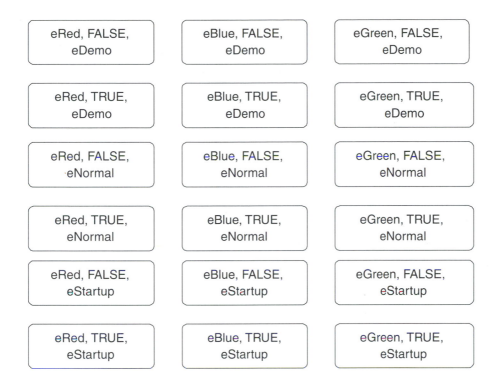

Figure 4-8: *Object with Orthogonal Components*

as the object is in state Y. When the object in state Y then takes transition t1, the concurrent threads are stopped (one is killed) and the object enters state Z.

The object's behavior is divided into two orthogonal components, S and T. As long as state Y is in effect, the S component must be in state A or B and the T component must be in state C, D, or E. When transition t1 is taken, components S and T both perform their exit actions (including the exit actions specific to the substate within the component) before the transition actions associated with t1 are taken.

When necessary or desirable, the branching or recombining of control can be shown explicitly, as in Figure 4-11. This is useful when the default substates of the orthogonal components are not entered.

Of course, most threads are only approximately independent, or life would not be nearly so interesting. Statecharts provide a total of three

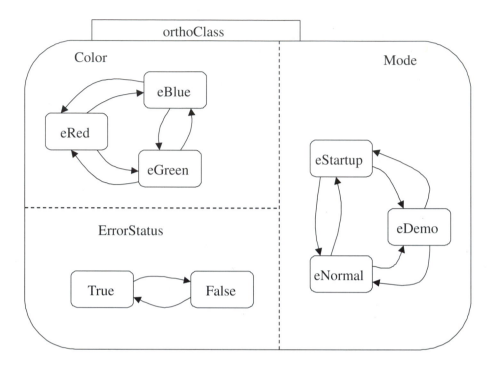

Figure 4-9: *Statechart of Object with Orthogonal Components*

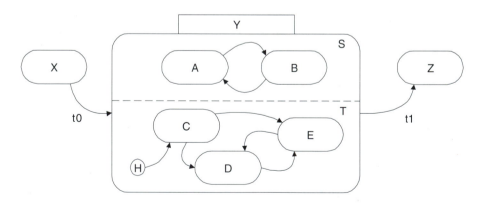

Figure 4-10: *Simple Concurrent State Model*

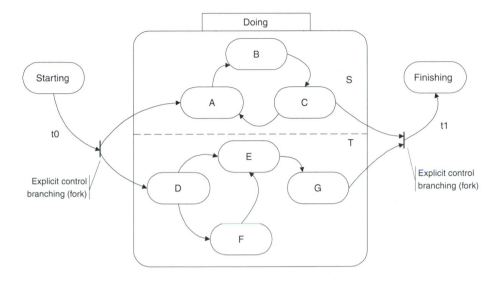

Figure 4-11: *Explicit Fork and Join*

predefined ways for orthogonal components to communicate, whether they are orthogonal components of the same object or the state machines of different objects:

- Broadcast events
- Propagated events
- The IN( ) operator

Broadcast events are simply events that more than one orthogonal component accepts. Propagated events are events that are signalled as the result of a transition being taken in one component. Finally, statecharts provide a predefined operator IN( ) that returns TRUE if another component is currently in the specified state.

Figure 4-12 shows examples of both broadcast and propagated events among the three orthogonal components, S1, S2, and S3. Transition T1 appears in both S1 and S2, just as the transition T3 appears in both S2 and S3. If the object receives a T1 event, it is logically sent to all currently active orthogonal components.[6] It need not be acted on in all components. For example, if component S1 is in state A, S2 is in state E, and S3 is in state G when the object receives the T1 event, what happens? S1 transitions to state B; S2 discards the event because T1 can cause no transition while state E is active; S3 discards it because it never acts on T1. If S1 is in state A and S2 is in state D when event T1 occurs, then both components would take a transition.

Propagated events are indicated with the caret following the event name (and optional parameters and guard). In component S1, the transition from A to C is caused by accepting event T2. When this occurs, event T3 is generated and can be acted on by other components executing concurrently.

The IN operator is used as a guard on transition T4. This allows the S3 component to take transition T4 only if S2 is currently in state D.

The last interesting thing about Figure 4-12 is the terminating connector, shown with a filled circle inside an unfilled one (an alternative syntax for this connector is to use a T circumscribed within a circle). This has the effect of killing the component thread so that it is no longer executing. Other components may continue to be active.

4.3.3 Inherited State Models

Two approaches may be taken to support inheritance of class state behavioral models. The simplest is to just ignore the parent class' state model and reconstruct the child's state model from scratch. Although this has the advantage of flexibility, it hardly seems in the spirit of object-orientation in general and reuse in particular. The second approach is to inherit the parent's state model, but to specialize and extend it where necessary.

To maximize compliance with the Liskov Substitution Principle (see Chapter 3), some rules must govern the modifications that can be made to an inherited state model:

• New states and transitions may be added freely in the child class

---

[6] In terms of implementation, it may be possible to optimize the object acceptor methods to send the event to only the components that have declared that they use it. That is a detail best left to the detailed class design.

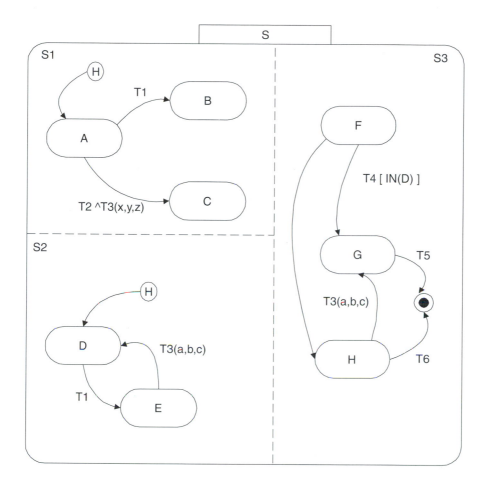

Figure 4-12: *Broadcast and Propagated Events*

- States and transitions defined by the parent cannot be deleted (the subclass must accept all events and messages that can be accepted by the parent)
- Action and activity lists may be changed (actions and activities may be added or removed) for each transition and state
- Actions and activities may be specialized in the subclass
- Substates may not alter their enclosing superstate (including adding a new one)

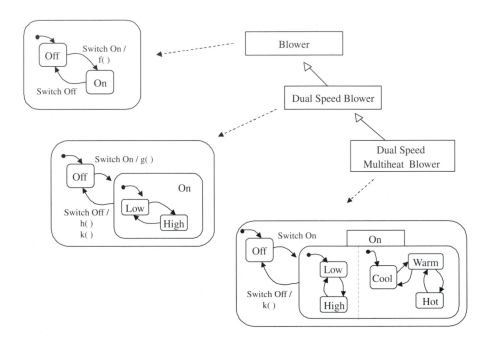

Figure 4-13: *Inherited State Models*

- Transitions may be retargeted to different states
- Orthogonal components may be added to inherited states

A simple example of inherited state models is provided in Figure 4-13. The class model is shown at the right of the figure. The class *Blower* has a simple on-off state model. The *Switch On* transition has a single action in its action list, the function f( ). The *Dual Speed Blower* class extends the *Blower* class by adding *Low* and *High* speed substates to the On state. Note that the action for the *Switch On* transition is now changed to the execution of the function g( ) and that two actions are now added to the *Switch Off* transition. The *Dual Speed Multiheat Blower* class continues the specialization by adding three heat settings as an orthogonal component to the *Low* and *High* states added by the previous subclass. Also note that the g() action for the *Switch On* transition and the h() action for the *Switch Off* transitions have been removed.

4.3.4 Cardiac Pacemaker Example

A cardiac pacemaker is an excellent example of a system in which most objects use finite state machines. The following problem statement will be developed into a class model that will allow us to see how the various statechart features can be used in a real system.

Problem Statement: A Cardiac Pacemaker

A cardiac pacemaker is an implanted device that assists cardiac function when underlying pathologies make the intrinsic heart rate too low or absent. Pacemakers operate in different behavioral modes, indicated by a three-letter acronym. The first letter is either A, V, or D depending on whether the atrium, ventricle, or both (dual) is being paced. The second letter is also A, V, or D depending on which heart chamber is being monitored for intrinsic activity. The last letter is I, T, or D, indicating inhibited, triggered, or dual pacing modes. In an inhibited mode, a sensed heart event (i.e., a detected cardiac contraction) will inhibit the delivery of a pace from the pacemaker. In triggered mode, a sensed heart event will immediately trigger a pace from the pacemaker. For example, VVI mode means that the ventricle is paced (the first V) if a ventricular sense (the second V) does not occur. If a ventricular sense does occur, then the pace is inhibited (the I). Dual modes are more complex and will not be discussed here.

Most of the time, a pacing pacemaker waits for a sense event. When it decides to pace, the pacemaker conducts an electric current of a programmable voltage (called the *pulse amplitude*) for a programmable period of time (called the *pulse width*). Following a pace, the pacemaker is put into a refractory state for a set period of time during which all cardiac activity is ignored. Following the refractory period the pacemaker resumes monitoring for the next cardiac event. The rate of pacing is determined by the programmable pacing rate. The period of time the pacemaker will wait in the waiting state is computed based on the pacing rate and the pulse width. The refractory period is fixed. This particular pacemaker operates in VVI, AAI, VVT, AAT, and AVI pacing modes as programmed by the physician.

Pacemaker parameters are programmed via a telemetric interface to an external programmer. Telemetry is sent by pulsing an electromagnetic coil a certain number of times to indicate a 0 bit, and a different number of times to indicate a 1 bit. To avoid inadvertent programming by electrical noise, a magnetically-activated reed switch must be closed before programming is enabled. The commands constructed from the bits must be checked prior to acting on them.

This short problem statement can be represented by a simple class model, as in Figure 4-14. The pacemaker itself is shown as a composite class containing the classes necessary for communicating with the external programmer and pacing the heart. The Reed Switch, Coil Driver, and Communications Gnome form the Communications subsystem, and the Chamber Model, Atrial Model, and Ventricular Model form the Pacing subsystem. These two subsystems collaborate to achieve the overall system responsibilities of communications and cardiac pacing.

A statement about the generalization relationships in the pacing subsystem is in order. The Chamber Model class defines the basic behavioral model for pacing a cardiac chamber so it seems as though the Atrial Model and Ventricular Model ought to be instances of the Chamber Model class rather than different subclasses. If, in fact, the behavior of the two chambers differed only in their context, then a single class Chamber Model would be appropriate. However, we are going to specialize the Chamber Model class in how the two cardiac chamber models behave for AVI mode. This will allow us to define the basic behavior in the superclass and specialize it for the two subclasses.

The Reed Switch has simple On-Off state behavior as shown in Figure 4-15. It propagates events into a communication subsystem to enable and disable communications.

The Coil Driver class has more elaborate behavior. The default initial state is *Disabled*. When the Reed Switch closes, it propagates an *Enable Comm* event to the Coil Driver and the Coil Driver enters the *Idle*

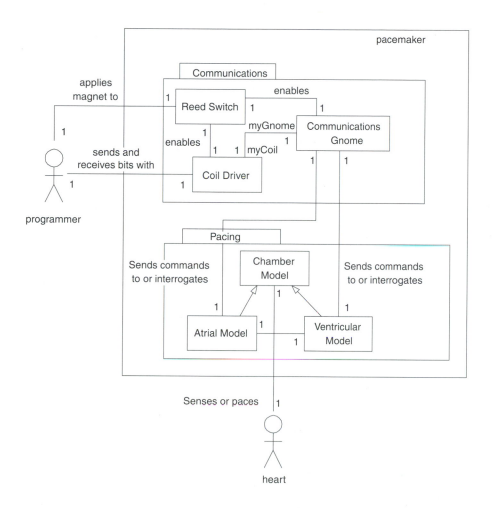

Figure 4-14: *Pacemaker Class Diagram*

substate. Once the Coil Driver is enabled, it can be idle, receiving incoming commands, or transmiting responses. The *Receiving Bit* state is entered when the Coil Driver is in its *Idle* state and detects a pulse transition in its electromagnetic coil. Once in that state, it waits for a timeout. If it receives another pulse transition before timing out, it increments a pulse count and restarts the timer. Eventually, when no more pulses arrive before the timeout, it transitions to the *Waiting for Bit* state. The actions for this transition are to decode the bit and shift the bit into the

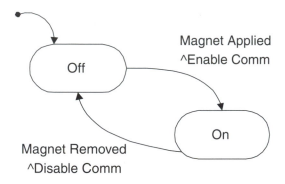

Figure 4-15: *Reed Switch State Model*

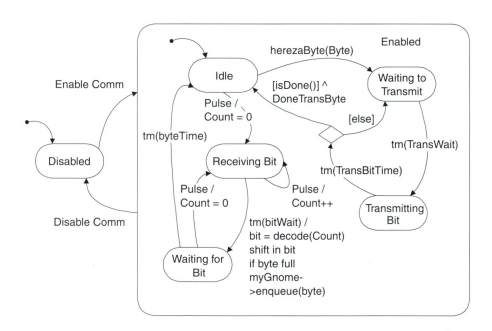

Figure 4-16: *Coil Driver State Model*

byte being constructed. If the byte is full, it is sent to the Communication Gnome (a cousin of the Elevator Gnome we met earlier) for processing.

Transmission is enabled by the receipt of a byte to transmit from the Communications Gnome while the Coil Driver is in the *Idle* state (Figure 4-16). The Coil Driver waits for a period of time (to separate transmitted bytes) and then begins transmitting the byte, one bit at a time. It pulses the electromagnetic coil for a specific period of time (depending on the value of the bit) and then transitions to the conditional connector. If the guarding function isDone() evaluates to TRUE, the Gnome is signaled via a propagated *DoneTransByte* event, and the Coil Driver reenters its Idle state. Otherwise it waits again to separate the bits in time and then sends out the next bit.

The Communications Gnome (Figure 4-17) oversees the communi-

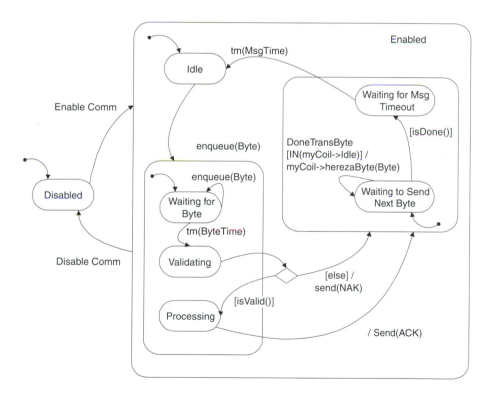

Figure 4-17: *Communication Gnome State Model*

cation process for the pacemaker. It is enabled and disabled by the *Enable Comm* and *Disable Comm* events propagated from the Reed Switch. When enabled, but in the absence of incoming or outgoing messages, the Communication Gnome spends its time in its *Idle* state.

The class diagram (Figure 4-14) names roles at both ends of the association between the Coil Driver and the Communication Gnome. These roles are used on the state machines to indicate the instance of the classes receiving the events. Specifically, the Coil Driver is sent the herezaByte(Byte) event from the Communication Gnome by using this role name, as in myCoil→herezaByte(Byte). Similarly, the Coil Driver sends the event enqueue(byte) using its role name for the Communication Gnome: myGnome→enqueue(byte). Note also the use of the IN( ) operator to synchronize the two object's state machines.

The Chamber Model is where the modal pacing behavior occurs (see Figure 4-18). It changes mode only when commanded by the external programmer. When the Communication Gnome receives a command to set the pacing mode, it validates the command and, if valid, processes it. This processing is not quite as simple as just passing it along to the Atrial Model or Ventricular Model objects because the two objects must coordinate their actions. When the Communication Gnome receives a command to put the pacemaker in VVI mode, for example, it sends a *To Inhibited* event to the Ventricular Model object and a *To Idle* event to the Atrial Model. The large-scale coordination in this model is accomplished by this reasonably smart Communication Gnome controller.

Figure 4-18 shows a big empty state for the AVI mode. It is this state that will be specialized differently in the Atrial Model and Ventricular Model subclasses. Figures 4-19 and 4-20 specialize the AVI state using the inherited state model rules given previously. By comparing the two specialized versions of the AVI state, you can see how the two objects communicate to coordinate their state machines. The pacing is controlled by the Atrial Model. When it gets a timeout, it propagates an *A Pace Start* event to the Ventricular Model. Similarly, when it completes pacing, it sends an *A Pace Done* event. The Ventricular Model controls the refractory period and the sensing. When the Ventricular Model is done with its Refractory state, it sends a *V Refract Done* event to the Atrial Model. When the Ventricular Model sees a *V Sense* event, it sends a *Got V Sense* event to the Atrial Model. By sending events back

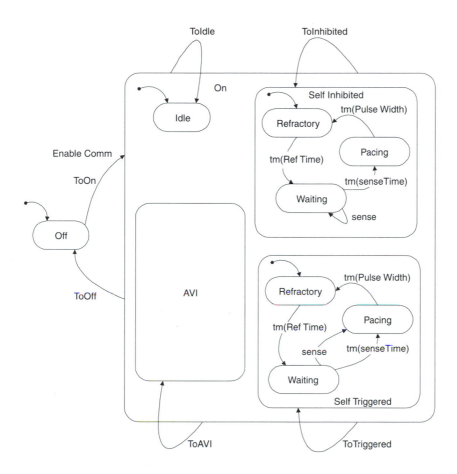

Figure 4-18: *Chamber Model State Model*

and forth between the two collaborating objects, their state machines remain synchronized.

4.4 The Role of Scenarios in the Definition of Behavior

A state diagram provides a static view of the entire state space of a system. Because the complete behavior of a state-driven object can be

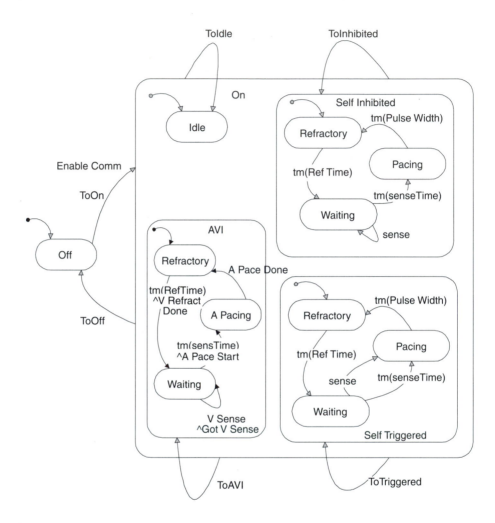

Figure 4-19: *Atrial Model State Model*

represented by a sufficiently detailed state model, state models are said to be *constructive*. This means that they can be used to generate complete executable code for the object.

What state diagrams do not show are typical paths through the state space as the system is used. These typical paths are called *scenarios*. Scenarios may not visit all states in the system nor activate all tran-

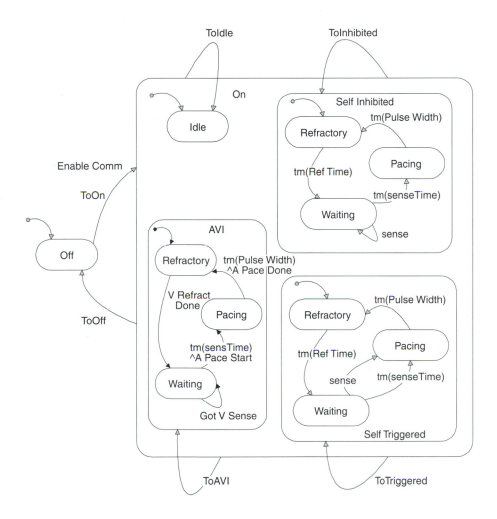

Figure 4-20: *Ventricular Model State Model*

sitions, but they provide an order-dependent view of how the system is expected to behave when actually used. Because a scenario does not have enough information to fully define the complete behavioral model of an object, scenarios are said to be *semiconstructive*. They can add operations and event handling to a state model, but they do not fully define the model.

4.4.1 Showing Scenarios

There are two methods for showing scenarios that are particularly useful in real-time systems. The first is the timing diagram, which is best used when strict timing must be shown. The other is the sequence diagram, which shows order but not strict timing.

Timing Diagrams[7]

Electrical engineers have used timing diagrams for a long time in the design of electronic state machines. A timing diagram is a simple representation with time along the horizontal axis and object state along the vertical axis. Of course, electrical engineers usually concern themselves with only two states: On and Off. Software engineers can use timing diagrams just as easily on more elaborate state machines to show the changes of state over time.

Timing diagrams depict state as a horizontal band across the diagram. When the system is in that state, a line is drawn in that band for the duration of time the system is in the state. The time axis is linear, although special notations are sometimes used to indicate long uninteresting periods of time. The simple form of a timing diagram is shown in Figure 4-21.

This timing diagram shows a particular path through the Ventricular Model state machine. It begins in the Idle state and remains there until it receives a command to enter begin pacing (*To Inhibited*). At this point, it jumps to the Waiting state. The vertical lines connecting states show that the time used for the transition is zero relative to the scale of the timing diagram. Later, a ventricular sense is detected (as shown by the transition annotation on the diagram) and the Ventricular Model returns to the Waiting state. Sometime later, the sense timeout and the Ventricular Model enters the Pacing state. In this state, the engine is actively putting an electrical charge through the heart muscle. When the pacing pulse width is complete, the object transitions to the Refractory state. Once this times out, the system reenters the Waiting state.

In this simple form, only a single object (or system) is represented. It is possible to show multiple objects on the same diagram. By separating these with dashed lines, the different (and possibly concurrent)

---

[7] Timing diagrams are not explicitly supported by the UML. If you wish to stick to only explicitly defined UML features, this section may be omitted.

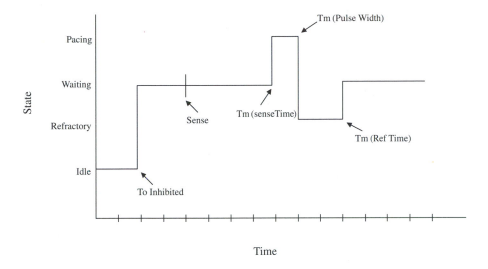

Figure 4-21: *Simple Timing Diagram*

objects can be clearly delineated. Propagated transitions can be clearly marked with directed lines showing event dependency. Figure 4-22 shows just such a diagram depicting a scenario of object collaboration of a pacemaker in AVI mode.

Timing diagrams are very good at showing precise timing behavior and are often used to analyze closely the timing of periodic and aperiodic tasks. When used in this way, some common elements shown are:

Period   The time between initiations for the same state.

Deadline   The time by which the state must be exited and a new state entered.

Initiation time The time required to enter the state completely (i.e., execute state entry actions).

Execute time   The time required to execute the entry and exit actions and the required activities of the state.

Dwell time   The time the object remains in the state after the execute time before the state is exited, including time for exit actions.

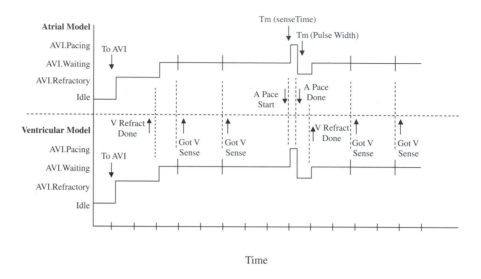

Figure 4-22: *Concurrent Timing Diagram*

Slack time   The time between the end of actions and activities
                      and the deadline.

Rise and fall time   The time required for the transition into the state
                      to complete. This includes the time necessary to
                      execute the transition actions.

Jitter   Variations in the start time for a periodic transi-
                      tion or event.

When many tasks are to be shown on a single diagram, task state can be shown using pattern shading, as in and Figure 4-23 and Figure 4-24. Although timing diagrams show no information beyond that available in annotated sequence diagrams, the absolute timing of events and state changes and the relative timing among objects is much clearer and more obvious than on sequence diagrams, even when explicit timing constraints are added.

Sequence Diagrams

Sequence Diagrams are a more common way to show scenarios as discussed earlier in this book. Sequence diagrams use vertical lines to rep-

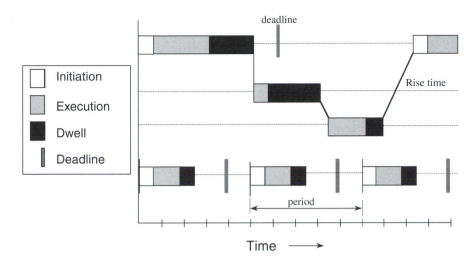

Figure 4-23: *Task Timing Diagram with Shading*

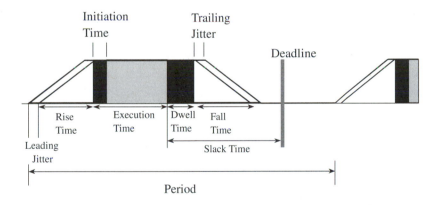

Figure 4-24: *Complex Timing Diagram*

resent the objects participating in the scenario and horizontal directed lines to represent the messages sent from one object to another. Time flows from top to bottom: that is, messages shown lower on the page take place later than ones above it.

Sequence diagrams can be related more closely with associated state

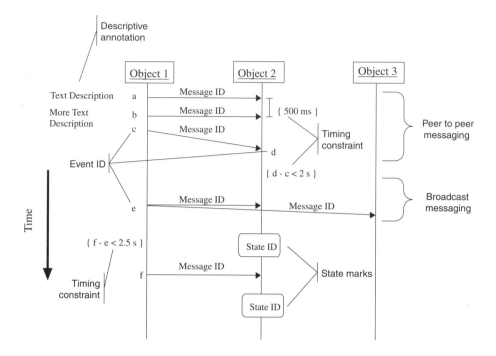

Figure 4-25: *Sequence Diagram*

models when state marks are added to the instance lines, as shown in Figure 4-25.

Sequence diagrams are discussed in more detail in Chapter 2.

4.4.2 Event Hierarchies

Events instances themselves are objects because they can have a rich structure. Because some events are specialized versions of others, it is possible to build event class generalization hierarchies. Event hierarchies are useful because they allow polymorphic acceptance of events. This means that different objects can accept events at different levels in the hierarchy.

Figure 4-26 shows a simple hierarchy for user input events. A user input active object accepting *Input Event* objects would also accept any subclass of *Input Event*, such as *Left Mouse Click* or *Keyboard Event*. The

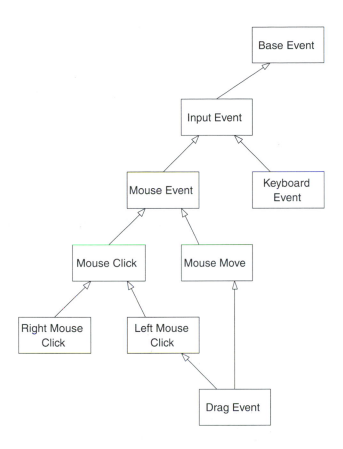

Figure 4-26: *Event Hierarchy*

active object can then dispatch all mouse events to a mouse handler class. This mouse handler class would accept *Mouse Event* objects and any of its subclasses. The mouse handler can then delegate the handling of the different mouse event subclasses and act on them appropriately.

Exception event hierarchies are normally used in just this way. Typically, general handlers accept more general exception instances and then dispatch them to more specific handlers. Alternatively, specific exception handlers may be tried first and if they cannot accept the exception then the more general handlers can be executed. Either way, event hierarchies are an important structuring tool for the handling of events.

4.4.3 Implementing State Machines

There are a number of ways to implement a state machine in software. The most common is to provide a single enumerated scalar variable called a *state variable,* and to use this as the discriminator in a switch statement. Each case clause in the switch statement can implement the various actions and activities. For example, consider the simple retriggerable one-shot timer state machine presented earlier. It might result in source code something like this:

```
void FSM(int &timer_state, message msg) {
    switch (timer_state) {
        case IDLE_STATE:
            switch (msg.msg_type) {
                case START_CMD:
                    timer.countValue = msg.cmd
                    timer.start();
                    timer_state = COUNTING_STATE;
                    break;
                default:
                    // do nothing
                    break;
            }; // end switch msg
        break;
    case COUNTING_STATE:
        switch (msg.msg_type) {
                case TIMEOUT:
                    sw_interrupt(xx);
                    timer.start();
                    break;
                case STOP_CMD:
                    timer.stop();
                    timer_state = IDLE_STATE;
                    break;
                default:
                     // do nothing
                    break;
            }; // end switch msg
            break;
        default:
                cout << "Illegal state value " << endl;
                break;
    }; // end switch
}; // end FSM function
```

This approach works well for simple state machines, but doesn't scale up well to complex FSMs, as you might imagine. Additionally, C and C++ run-time code may search switch statements for matching conditions so that the performance of this naive approach may increase linearly with the number of states and transitions. Chapter 6 provides some altenative patterns for state machine implementations that are more effective for large or complex FSMs.

4.5 Defining Operations

All class operations either handle messages or assist in their handling. This means that once a class' state machine is defined and important scenarios elucidated, the messages and events shown on those diagrams become class operations.

An operation (in this context, the terms *operation, method,* and *function* are interchangable) is the fundamental quantum of object behavior. The overall behavior of the object is decomposed into a set of operations, some of which are within the interface of the class and some of which are internal and hidden. Naturally, all objects of the same class provide the same set of operations to their clients. An object's operations must directly support its behavior and ultimately its responsibilities. In the simplest case, a 1-1 mapping exists between a class's behaviors and its operations, but this is not true in general. Often behaviors are decomposed into multiple primitive operations to produce the overall class behavior. This is similar to the functional decomposition in structured system design.

Operations have a protocol for correct usage consisting of the following:

- Preconditional invariants, that is, assumptions about the environment that must be satisfied before the operation is invoked

- A signature containing an ordered formal list of parameters and their types and the return type of the operation

- Postconditional invariants that are guaranteed to be satisfied when the operations complete

- Rules for thread-reliable interaction, including synchronization behavior

The responsibility for ensuring that preconditional invariants are met falls primarily in the client's realm. That is, the user of the operation is required to guarantee that the preconditional invariants are satisfied. However, the server operation should check as many of these as possible. Interfaces are hotbeds for common errors, and the inclusion of preconditional invariant checking in acceptor operations makes objects much more robust and reliable.

In strongly typed languages, the compiler itself will check the number and types of parameters for synchronous operation calls. However, some language type checking is stronger than others. For example, enumerated values are freely and automatically converted to integer types in C++. A caller can pass an out-of-range integer value when an enumerated type is expected and the compiler typing system will not detect it. Ada's stronger type checking[8] flags this as an error and will not allow it unless an explicit *unchecked_conversion* type cast is performed. Even in Ada, however, not all range violations can be caught at compile time. In such cases, the operation itself must check for violations of its preconditional invariants.

For example, consider an array class. Because C++ is backwardly compatible with C, array indices are not checked.[9] Thus, it is possible (even *likely*) that an array will be accessed with an out-of-range index, returning garbage or overwriting some unknown portion of memory. In C++, however, it is possible to construct a reliable array class:

```
#include <iostream.h>

template<class T, int size>
class ReliableArray {
T arr[size];
public:
    ReliableArray(void) { };
    T &operator[](int j) {
        if (j<0 || j >=size)
            throw "Index range Error";
            return arr[j];
    };
```

---

[8] It has been said "C treats you like a consenting adult. Pascal treats you like a naughty child. Ada treats you like a criminal."

[9] It is well documented that "the major problem with C++ is C."

```
    const T *operator&() { return arr; };
    T operator*() { return arr[0]; };
};

int main(void) {
    ReliableArray<int, 10> iArray;
    iArray[1] = 16;
    cout << iArray[ 1] << endl;
    iArray[ 19] = 0; // INDEX OUT OF RANGE!
    return 0;
};
```

Classes instantiated from the ReliableArray template overload the bracket ([]) operator and prevent inappropriate access to the array. This kind of assertion of the preconditional invariant ("Don't access beyond the array boundaries") should be checked by the client,[10] but nevertheless is guaranteed by the server (array class).

4.5.1 Types of Operations

Operations are the manifestations of behavior. This behavior is normally specified on state diagrams (for state-driven classes) and/or scenario diagrams. These operations may be divided into several types. Booch [2] identifies five types of operations:

- Constructor
- Destructor
- Modifier
- Selector
- Iterator

Constructors and *destructors* create and destroy objects of a class, respectively. Well-written constructors ensure the consistent creation of valid objects. This normally means that an object begins in the correct initial state, its variables are initialized to known, reasonable values,

---

[10] If known—clearly a negative index into an array is probably nonsensical, but the client may not know the upper bounds of the array. If you always put range checking in the server array class, you can be assured that even if the client forgets, the array integrity will be maintained.

and required links to other objects are properly initialized. Object creation involves the allocation of memory, either implicitly on the stack, or dynamically on the heap. The constructor must allocate memory for any internal objects or values that use heap storage. The constructor must guarantee its postconditional invariants; specifically, a client using the object once it is created must be assured that the object is properly created and in a valid state.

Sometimes the construction of an object is done in a two-step process. The constructor does the initial job of building the object infrastructure, and a subsequent call to an initialization operation completes the process. This is done when concerns for creation and initialization of the object are clearly distinct and not all the information is known at creation time.

Destructors reverse the construction process. They must deallocate memory when appropriate and perform other cleanup activities. In real-time systems, this often means commanding hardware components to known, reasonable states. Valves may be closed, hard disks parked, lasers deenergized, etc.

Modifiers change values within the object, and *selectors* read values or request services from an object without modifying them. *Iterators* provide orderly access to the components of an object. Iterators are most common with objects maintaining collections of other objects. Such objects are called *collections* or *containers*. It is important that these three types of operations hide the internal object structure and reveal instead the externally visible semantics. Consider a simple collection class:

```
class Bunch_O_Objects {
   node* p;
   node* current_node;
   public:
   void insert(node n);
   node* go_left(void);
   node* go_right(void);
};
```

The interface forces clients of this class to be aware of its internal structure (a binary tree). The current position in the tree is maintained by the current_node pointer. The implementation structure is made visible by the iterator methods go_left() and go_right(). What if the design changes to an n-way tree? A linked list? A hash table? The externally visible interface ensures that any such internal change to the class will force a change to the interface, and therefore changes to all the clients of the class. Clearly, a better approach would be to provide the fundamental semantics (the concept of a next and a previous node), as in:

```
class Bunch_O_Objects {
    node* p;
    node* current_node;
public:
    void insert(node n);
    node* next(void);
    node* previous(void);
};
```

However, even this approach has problems. This interface works fine provided that marching through the objects in the collection will always be in a sequential manner and only a single reader is active.

The first problem can be resolved by adding some additional operations to meet the needs of the clients. Perhaps some clients must be able to restart the search, or easily retrieve the last object. Perhaps having the ability to locate a specific object in the list quickly is important. Considering the client needs produces a more elaborate interface:

```
class Bunch_O_Objects {
    node* p;
    node* current_node;
public:
    void insert(node n);
    node* next(void);
    node* previous(void);
    node* first(void);
    node* last(void);
    node* find(node &n);
};
```

This interface isn't primitive or orthogonal, but does provide common-usage access methods to the clients.

Providing support for multiple readers is slightly more problematic. If two readers march through the list using next() at the same time, neither will get the entire list; some items will go to the first reader, and others will go to the second. The most common solution is to create separate iterator objects, one for each of the various readers. Each iterator maintains its own current_node pointer to track its position within the collection:

```
class Bunch_O_Objects {
    node* p;
public:
    void insert(node n);
    node *next(node *p);
    node *previous(node *p);
    friend class BOO_Iterator;
};

class BOO_Iterator {
    node* current_node;
    Bunch_O_Objects& BOO;
public:
    BOO_Iterator(Bunch_O_Objects& B) : BOO(B) {
        current_node = BOO.p; };
    node* next(void);
    node* previous(void);
    node* first(void);
    node* last(void);
    node* find(node &n);
};
```

This strategy is reified into the Container Pattern identified in Chapter 6.

4.5.2 Strategies for Defining Operations

Defining a good set of operations for a class interface can be difficult. A number of rules can help determine the operations:

- Provide a set of orthogonal primitive interface operations
- Hide the internal class structure with interface operations that show only essential class semantics
- Provide a set of nonprimitive operations to

  ▼ Enforce protocol rules

  ▼ Capture frequently used combinations of operations

- Operations within a class and class hierarchy should use a consistent set of parameter types where possible
- A common parent class should provide operations shared by sibling classes
- Each responsibility to be met by a class or object must be represented by some combination of the operations, attributes, and associations
- All messages directed towards an object must be accepted and result in a defined action

  ▼ Events handled by a class state model must have corresponding acceptor operations

  ▼ Messages shown in scenarios must have corresponding acceptor operations

  ▼ Get and set operations provide access to object attributes when appropriate

- Actions and activities identified on statecharts must result in operations defined on the classes providing those actions
- Operations should check their preconditional invariants

Just as with strategies for identifying objects, classes, and relationships, these strategies may be mixed freely to meet the specific requirements of a system.

By providing the complete elemental operations on the class, clients can combine these to provide all nonprimitive complex behaviors of which the class is capable. Consider a Set class, which provides set operations. The following class maintains a set of integers. In actual implementation, a template would most likely be used, but the use of the template syntax obscures the purpose of the class so it won't be used here.

```
class Set {
    int size;
    SetElement *bag;

    class SetElement {
    public:
        int Element;
        SetElement *NextPtr;
        SetElement(): NextPtr(NULL); {};
```

```
          SetElement(int initial): Element(initial),
          NextPtr(NULL) { };
     };
  public:
     Set(): size(0), bag(NULL) { };
     Set union(set a);
     Set intersection(set a);
     void clear(void);
     void operator +(int x); // insert into set
     void operator -(int x); // remove from set
     int numElements(void);
     bool operator ==(set a);
     bool operator !=(set a);
     bool inSet(int x); // test for membership
     bool inSet(Set a); // test for subsethood
  };
```

This simple class provides a set type and all the common set operations. Elements can be inserted or removed. Sets can be compared for equality, inequality, and whether they are subsets of other sets. Set unions and intersections can be computed.

Often, a series of operations must be performed in a specific order to get the correct result. Such a required sequence is part of the protocol for the correct use of that object. Whenever possible, the operations should be structured to reduce the amount of information the clients of an object must have in order to use the object properly. These protocol-enforcing operations are clearly not primitive, but they help ensure the correct use of an object.

A sensor that must first be zeroed before being used is a simple example. The sensor class can simply provide the primitive operations doZero() and get(), or it can provide an acquire() operation that combines them:

```
class sensor {
   void doZero();
   int get();
public:
   int acquire(void) {
      doZero();
      return get();
   };
};
```

The acquire() operation enforces the protocol of zeroing the sensor before reading the value. Not only does this enforce the preconditions of the get() operation, but also simplifies the use of the class. Since the doZero() and get() operations are always invoked in succession, combining them together into an operation provides a common-use non-primitive.

Polymorphic operations are operations of the same name that perform different actions. Depending on the implementation language, polymorphism may be either static or dynamic. Static polymorphism is resolved at compile time and requires that the compiler has enough context to unambiguously determine which operation is intended. Dynamic polymorphism occurs when the binding of the executable code to the operator invocation is done as the program executes. Both static and dynamic polymorphism are resolved on the basis of the type and number of parameters passed to the operation.[11] Ada 83 operator overloading is purely static. C++ polymorphism may be either static or dynamic. Smalltalk polymorphism is always dynamic.

4.6 Summary

We have now seen both parts of analysis. The previous chapter covered means to identify the object structure of a system, find the classes of those objects, and link them together with relationships and associations. This chapter covered the dynamic aspects of objects—the definition of behavior, with special attention given to state-driven objects, and the operations necessary to implement those behaviors.

The task of analysis is to find the object structure required of all acceptable solutions to the problem. Put another way, analysis finds the essential objects, classes, and relationships inherent in the system under study. Analysis defines the *what* of the system. The next process

---

[11] C++ class operations have an invisible *this* pointer in their parameter lists. Thus, even an operation with an otherwise identical parameter list can be polymorphic if a subclass redefines the operation, since the *this* pointer is a pointer to a different type.

step, design, will add the *how*. We have deferred many questions about implementation strategies and structures, such as the number of tasks running, how messages will be implemented, and the internal design of the objects themselves. Let's continue with the large-scale architectural design in the next chapter.

4.7 References

[1] Harel, David "Statecharts: a Visual Formalism for Complex Systems," *Science of Computer Programming* 8 (1987): 231–274.
[2] Booch, Grady, *Object-Oriented Analysis and Design with Applications*. 2nd ed. Redwood City, CA: Benjamin/Cummings, 1994.

Chapter 5

Architectural Design

The last three chapters have dealt with analysis of the system. Chapter 2 looked at ways of capturing requirements using the context diagram and use cases. Chapters 3 and 4 presented approaches for identifying and characterizing classes and objects inherent in the problem. Analysis looks at key concepts and structures in the system that are independent of how the solution is implemented.

Now we're ready for design. Design specifies a particular solution that is based on the analysis model. Design can be broken into three parts according to the scope of decisions made: architectural, mechanistic, and detailed. This chapter discusses the first: architectural design.

Architectural design identifies the key strategies for the large-scale organization of the system under development. These strategies include the mapping of software packages to processors, bus, and protocol selection, and the concurrency model and task threads. UML provides notation and semantics for the specification of large-scale architecture. This chapter presents the features available in the UML for architectural design and shows how they can be applied to real-time systems.

Large-scale design strategies can be based on architectural patterns found useful in a variety of similar systems. A number of patterns are presented in this chapter that exemplify how pattern-based architectures can simplify architectural design.

5.1 Overview of Design

If you've been following this book along, you should have a good grasp by now of the process and products of analysis. Analysis identifies the criteria of acceptance of any solution. The first part of analysis studies system-environment interaction and explores and captures this interaction with context and use case diagrams. The second part of analysis drills down inside the system to identify the fundamental concepts within the system that must be represented both in terms of structure and dynamics. These concepts are captured as classes and objects.

Design is the process of specifying an implementation that is consistent with the analysis model. It is useful to divide design into three primary categories based on the scope and breadth of decisions within that category: architectural, mechanistic, and detailed design (see Figure 5-1). Architectural design details the largest scale software structures, such as subsystems, packages, and tasks. The middle layer of design is called mechanistic design because it includes the design of mechanisms composed of classes working together to achieve common goals. Detailed design specifies the internal primitive data structures and algorithms within individual classes.

For simple systems, most of the design effort may be spent in the mechanistic and detailed levels. For larger systems, including avionics and other distributed real-time systems, the architectural level is crucial to project success. This chapter will focus on the process of architectural design.

The design process can be either translative or elaborative. Translative design takes the analysis model and, using a translator, produces an executable system more or less autonomously. Great care must be put into the design of the translator and this is often highly customized for a particular problem domain and business environment. The other approach elaborates the analysis model by adding increasing amounts of design detail until the system is fully specified. The UML is process-independent and applies equally to both design approaches. Since the elaborative approach is much more common and generally applicable, we will continue in an elaborative spirit in this book.

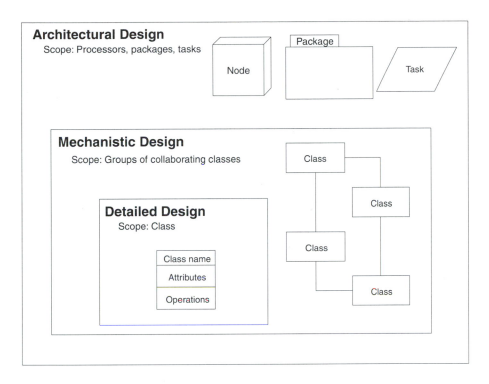

Figure 5-1: *Three Levels of Design*

5.2 What Is Architectural Design?

The analysis model identifies objects, classes, and relationships but does not specify how they are organized together into large-scale structures. As shown in Table 5-1, architectural design is concerned with large-scale design decisions involving collaborations of packages, tasks, or processors.

System architectural design is broader in scope than just software and involves the physical architecture as well including electronic and mechanical design. Naturally, physical architecture has a great impact on the software architecture. Together, physical and software architectures combine to form the *system architecture*. In most embedded systems, the system architecture is by necessity a collaborative effort

Table 5-1: *Phases of Design*

Design Phase	Scope	What is Specified
Architectural	System-wide	Number and type of processors
	Processor-wide	Packages of objects running on each processor Inter-processor communication media and protocols Concurrency model and inter-thread communication strategies Software layering and vertical slices Global error handling policies
Mechanistic	Inter-object	Instances of design patterns of multiple objects collaborating together Containers and design-level classes and objects Medium-level error handling policies
Detailed	Intra-object	Algorithmic detail within an object Details of data members (types, ranges) Details of function members (arguments, internal structure)

including engineers from a wide variety of disciplines, including software, electronics, mechanics, safety, and reliability. The system design must ensure that all the pieces will ultimately fit together and achieve the system objectives in terms of functionality, performance, safety, reliability, and cost.

The software must ultimately map to the physical structure. This mapping occurs primarily at the architectural and detailed levels of design. The detailed design level deals with the physical characteristics of the individual hardware components and ensures that low-level interface protocols are followed. The architectural level maps the large-scale software components such as subsystems, packages, and tasks onto the various processors and devices. Mechanistic design is insulated away from most aspects of physical architecture.

5.2.1 Physical Architecture Issues

The electronic design decisions that are particularly relevant to the software architecture are the number and type of devices in the system (particularly the processors) and the physical communications media linking them together.

It is crucial to the success of the system that the electrical and software engineers collaborate on these decisions. If the electrical engineers don't understand the software needs, they are less able to adequately accommodate them. Similarly, if the software engineers don't have a sufficient understanding of the electronic design, their architectural decisions will be at best suboptimal, and at worst unworkable. For this reason, both disciplines must be involved in device selection, particularly processors, memory maps, and communication buses. It is an unfortunate truth that many systems do not meet their functional or performance requirements when this collaboration is missing in the development process.

The software concerns for each processor are:

- Envisioned purpose and scope of the software executing on the processor
- The computational horsepower of the processor
- Availability of development tools such as compilers for the selected language, debuggers, in-circuit emulators
- Availability of third-party components including operating systems, container libraries, communication protocols, and user interfaces
- Previous experience and internal knowledge with the processor

How the processors are linked together is another far-reaching set of electronic design decisions. Should the communication media be arranged in a bus or star topology? Should it be bus-mastered or master-slave? Should it arbitrate on the basis of priority or fairness? Point-to-point or multidrop? How fast must the transmission rate be? These are the requirements of just the physical communications media. The software must layer appropriate communications protocols on top of that to ensure timely and reliable message exchange.

Naturally, these electronic design decisions can have a tremendous impact on the software architecture. Smaller processors can be used if there are more of them and they are linked together appropriately, or a smaller number of larger processors can do the same work. If the bus mastering is not arbitrated in hardware, it becomes more difficult to implement the peer-to-peer communications protocol required for distributed processing. Only by working together can the electronic and software engineers find an optimal solution given the system constraints. The optimal solution itself is specific to both the application domain and the business goals and approaches.

5.2.2 Software Architecture Issues

Within the confines of the physical architecture, the software itself has large-scale structures. The UML defines a subsystem as a subordinate system within a larger system [1]. In the embedded world, it is useful to further constrain our use of the term to mean *an integrated set of software components residing on a single physical processor.* These components will typically be packages that in turn contain other packages, tasks, objects, and classes. Software architecture then becomes the process of designing subsystems, packages, tasks, and their interconnections.

The building blocks of subsystems are packages and tasks. Packages may contain subpackages but their primary components are objects and classes. Packages model a single area of concern or *domain*.[1] Specifically, they contain objects and classes representing important concepts within a given domain. Class generalization hierarchies are always within a single package. The icons used to represent these features, shown in Figure 5-1, will be elaborated in this chapter.

Subsystems are often organized as a set of layered packages. Many complex systems have several layers ordered hierarchically from the most abstract (closest to the system problem domain) down to the most concrete (closest to the underlying hardware). For example,

- Application
- User interface
- Communication

---

[1] We will use the term *domain* to refer to an independent subject matter that has its own set of concepts that can be modeled as classes and objects.

- OS

- Hardware abstraction

Layering packages and subsystems in this way is an example of the Microkernel Architecture Pattern discussed in Section 5.4.

Just because the subsystems and packages are logically layered in terms of abstraction does not in any way imply that systems should be implemented layer by layer. In fact, the opposite is true. It is most efficacious to design a layered architecture and actually implement the system as a series of vertical slices of functionality that cut through all layers.

The OSI's seven-layer reference model is a common layered architecture for communications protocols, as shown in Figure 5-2 (the physical layer is not shown in the figures since it usually does not involve software). The lollipop at the left of each package represents its *interface*, a set of classes and objects that may be externally accessed (these are Service Access Points [SAPs] in OSI's nomenclature). The dashed arrow is the dependency relationship, and indicates that each package depends on the packages below it. This is an example of the Microkernel Architectural Pattern described on page 221.

The Microkernel Architectural Pattern is fundamentally a set of client-server relationships among the layers. The more abstract layers are the clients that invoke the services of the more concrete layers. This one-way dependency makes it possible to use the same lower-level server layers in different contexts because they know nothing of their clients. Similarly, since the lower layers offer a well-defined set of interfaces, they can be replaced with different lower layers making the entire subsystem easily portable to other physical environments.

A layered implementation strategy would build each layer independently and link them together as they are completed. However, this approach has been proven to be risky and expensive in practice because fundamental flaws that affect the overall subsystem functionality are not caught until integration. A better implementation strategy is to implement vertical slices, as shown in Figure 5-3.

Each vertical slice implements only the portion of each layer relevant to the purpose of the slice. This approach to implementation is called *iterative prototyping* and each slice is called a *prototype*. The prototypes are implemented so that each prototype builds upon the features implemented in its predecessors. The sequence of prototypes is de-

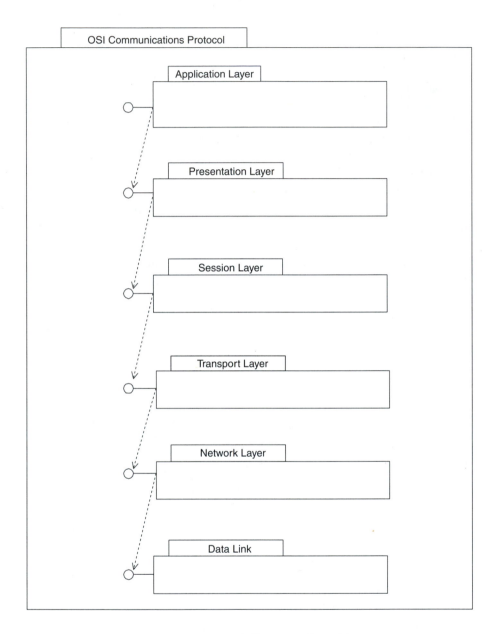

Figure 5-2: *OSI Model's Layered Architecture*

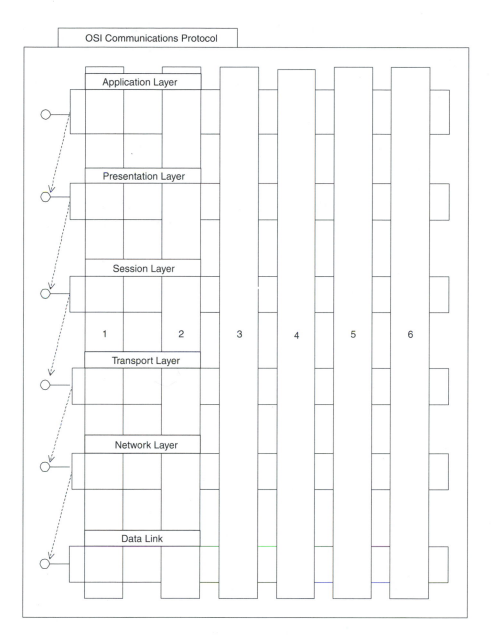

Figure 5-3: *Vertical Slices*

cided based on which features logically come first as well as which represent the highest risk. By doing risk-based development, higher risk items are explored and resolved as early as possible. This typically results in less rework and a more integrated, reliable system.

A typical set of prototypes for Figure 5-3 might be those shown in Table 5-2.

Note how the later prototypes build upon the services implemented in their predecessors. This is the essence of the iterative prototyping development philosophy—gradually adding capability until the entire system is complete. Naturally, iterative prototyping applies to more than just communication protocol design. Any sufficiently complex piece of software can be broken down into a set of hierarchical layers in a client-server topology. (We leave you the formal inductive proof of this statement as an exercise.)

It is common for these vertical slices to contain one or more threads. The concurrency model is another piece of architectural design that can greatly impact system performance. In a soft real-time environment,

Table 5-2: *Typical Protocol Implementation Strategy*

#	Prototype Name	Description
1	Hello World	Implement enough of each layer (and stub the remainder) to send a message from one node to another.
2	Data Format	Mostly presentation layer—implement data encode, decode, and network data format conversions. Also include timed ACK/NAK transport layer protocol.
3	Routing	Mostly network and data link layers to control routing of messages.
4	Flow Control	Data-link Xon/Xoff flow control, and message CRCs to implement data integrity checks with automatic retry on message failure.
5	Connections	Connections and sessions (transport, data-link, session layers).
6	Performance	Performance tuning of all layers to optimize throughput.

average throughput must be ensured, but individual deadlines are not crucial to system correctness. In hard real-time environments, however, each deadline must be met and the concurrency model must ensure the ability of the system to meet all deadlines. For most multitasking systems, this is a nontrival problem because the exact arrival patterns are not periodic and synchronous. Commonly, the system must respond to periodic events with vastly different periods as well as aperiodic events that may be bursty.[2] Concurrency design is the subject of the latter half of this chapter.

The last primary architectural goal is to design the global error handling policies to ensure correct system performance in the presence of faults. Many different strategies are possible, ranging from each object assuming full responsibility for all errors to a single global error handler that decides the correct action to take in all error conditions. Most systems are a hybrid of such approaches. One popular strategy is to have multiple levels of error handling with the general rule that each error will be handled at the point at which enough context is available to make the correct decision. An object with enough redundancy of its data members (such as triple storage for important data) might process an invalid data value by reconstructing the appropriate data value or assigning a default value in the event of an error. A subsystem might reboot itself and let the remainder of the system function when it discovers some particular error. Some errors may require a global handler to intervene and coordinate a correct system shutdown, such as in the event of a failure in a nuclear power plant.

Error handling policies are usually at least as complex as the primary software functionality and may result in systems three times as large and an order of magnitude more complex. Complicating error handling is the fact that it is highly system dependent, yet only through clear error handling policies can safety-critical systems be deployed safely (something for you to think about the next time you fly off to visit grandma). This is an important aspect of the software architecture.

---

[2] A bursty event arrival pattern is one in which the events often arrive in great numbers separated by relatively long quiet intervals. To make a system deterministic, this bursty behavior must be bounded in both the maximum number of events and the minimum arrival time between events within a burst.

5.3 Representing Physical Architecture in UML

The UML represents physical architectures with deployment diagrams. The are two primary diagrammatic elements, as shown in Figure 5-4. The icon of primary importance on deployment diagrams is the *node*. Nodes represent processors, sensors, actuators, routers, displays, input devices, memory, custom PLAs, or any physical object of importance to the software. Typically, nodes are stereotyped to indicate the type of

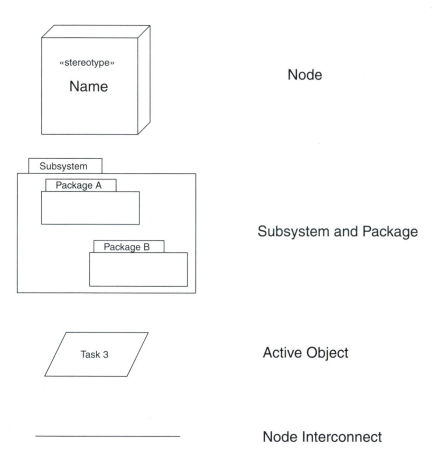

Figure 5-4: *Deployment Diagram Notation*

node. Interconnects represent physical interconnections among nodes. They are most commonly electronic, but can as easily be optical or telemetric.

Processor nodes are occasionally shown containing classes or objects, but usually processor nodes contain packages that may be broken down into subpackages and tasks. To show tasks, include only the active objects in the package. Of course, these packages ultimately contain objects and classes, but they usually appear only on class and object, not deployment, diagrams.

Figure 5-5 shows a simple example for a telescope position control

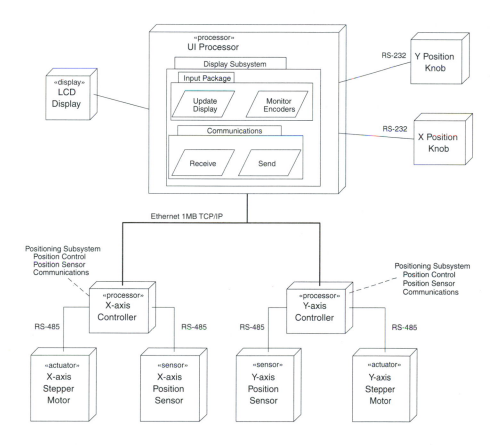

Figure 5-5: *Telescope Position Controller Deployment Diagram*

system. The user interface consists of an LCD display and two rotary encoder knobs, which are tied to the same processor. The positioning subsystem consists of two independent subsystems each containing a stepper motor and an independent sensor. The processors are linked together across an Ethernet network, and both use Ethernet controller boards to access the network.

This figure shows two methods for specifying the software running on the processors. The first is shown in the *User Interface (UI) Processor* node. The software components are shown as nested packages. The other notation is to list the packages in a textual annotation, as is done for the position controllers.

The description for the user interface processor in the figure shows that it contains two primary threads—one for monitoring the encoders and one for updating the display. The positioning subsystem also has two threads—one for controlling the stepper motor and one for monitoring the position of the telescope. Both processors have additional task threads for communicating across the network. Since this is a large-scale view, it typically does not include individual classes and objects.

You should also note that the same package can reside on multiple processors. The *User Interface* package usually resides on a single processor, but packages such as *Communications, Device I/O*, and *Containers* may very well reside on every processor node in the system.

5.3.1 Multiprocessor Systems

Multiprocessor embedded systems use more than one processor linked together to achieve a common system goal. Simple applications may use a single processor, but a great many interesting problems require multiple processors working together. In addition, dual channel architectures for safety-critical systems use different processors to ensure safety in the presence of errors and failures.

Distribution of Control in Systems

The primary complexity in multiprocessor systems arises in the coordination of the separate subsystems. The two primary strategies are centralized and decentralized control. There are advantages and disadvantages of each.

Centralized control means that one processor is in charge and all others do its bidding. Also known as *master-slave architecture*,[3] the primary advantage is the simplicity of the code running on the peripheral processors. By centralizing the control, a single point of complexity (the *master*) allows for easy modification and maintenance—up to a point. When the system gets too complex, it becomes simpler to distribute the processing load more evenly among the processors.

Distributing the intelligence and control is an alternative approach. In a fully decentralized system, all processors share the computational load more-or-less evenly. Peripheral processors become a little smarter, simplifying their coordination. The usefulness of decentralized systems lies in the fact that it is usually far easier to build a lot of half-smart systems than a single really smart one. Additionally, the computational requirements for a large system may overwhelm a single master. When the system complexity gets too high, decentralizing control may be your only option.

Naturally, this is not a black-and-white choice. There is an entire spectrum from master-slave to peer-to-peer. You can think of slaves as servers in a client-server architecture. The range of control distribution varies from very thin clients (very little centralized client control with smart servers) to very fat clients (all control is centralized within the clients).

The decision of thin versus fat clients should be based on several factors. Fat clients (i.e., smart masters) are most effective when there is an excess of processor horsepower in one node and the system itself is either relatively simple, very deterministic, or fundamentally single-threaded. Then the structure of the master is very simple and can often be implemented as a cyclic executive or some equally primitive control structure. Thin clients are more appropriate when available computation horsepower is distributed among several nodes, and the system environment is complex enough to make it difficult to predict when different events will occur.

One of the control issues is the arbitration of shared resources. This problem is usually very simple in fat clients, because the master is the

---

[3] The master-slave pattern defined in [3] assumes identical slaves, since it uses this pattern to achieve fault tolerance via redundancy. In this book, we call that the *Homogeneous Redundancy Pattern*. *Master-slave* as used here refers to the dispatching and coordination of control by a master controller to subordinate slave processes.

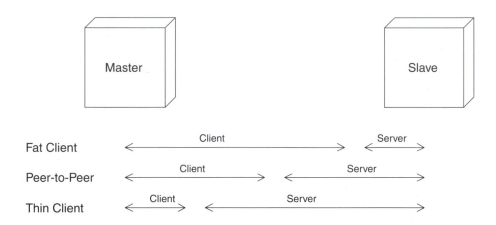

Figure 5-6: *Distribution of Control*

one making all the decisions. In thin clients, the servers may all act as masters at different points in time, and so a scheme for arbitration of shared resources must be designed. For example, when multiple processors must share a bus, should a master poll the slaves or should the different nodes talk when they have something interesting to say?

Arbitration schemes run the gamut from cyclic executives to priority-arbitration scheduling. These algorithms can be complex, but for systems with sufficiently rich behavior, it is the simplest approach to take.

5.4 Architectural Patterns

So far, we've discussed some of the issues that must be addressed by a system architecture and we've even given a simple example of it. Rather than give dozens of specific examples of architectures in real-time systems, let's present some abstractions of architectures and weigh their pros and cons.

Architectural design may be approached in many different ways.

Each different approach to solving a problem can be generalized into a pattern of organizing and marshalling these large-scale structures to achieve system goals. A *pattern* is the formalization of an approach to a common problem within a context [4].

Many useful software patterns have been identified in the literature, and the next chapter will present several patterns that appear at the mechanistic level of design. In following sections, we'll present some architectural patterns that have been particularly useful in the design of real-time systems.

The UML notation for a design pattern is an oval with a dashed border. It connects to a participating entity with a dash line. The label on these associations is the role of the entity within the pattern. Patterns can be applied to nodes and packages as well as objects, and that will be how they are used in this chapter. This book will show both the structure and a scenario illustrating the use of each pattern.

The patterns presented in this section include those shown in Table 5-3.

5.4.1 Distribution of Control Patterns

The patterns in this section show common ways to assign control in multitasking and multiprocessor systems.

Master-Slave Pattern

The Master-Slave Pattern is a control pattern in which an intelligent controller issues commands and receives inputs from slave devices. The slaves typically don't initiate communication but must be actively polled by the master.

This pattern applies to both symmetric and asymmetric multiprocessing. In *symmetric multiprocessing,* the slaves are more or less identical, and the master distributes tasks to the slaves dynamically. This is particularly useful when the master must dynamically balance the processing load among a set of processors. An advantage of symmetric processing is that the addition of processors to an existing system can result in improved performance with no modifications to the software, because the symmetric RTOS dynamically loads tasks to lightly-loaded processors.

Table 5-3: *Architectural Patterns*

Category	Pattern Name	Purpose
Control	Master-Slave	Coordinate the activities of several processors.
	Microkernel	Decompose complex components into sets of hierarchical abstraction layers to facilitate portability and reuse.
	Proxy	Handle the distribution of data from a central server to multiple remote clients.
	Broker	Handle the distribution of data from a central server to multiple remote clients when the location of the servers and clients is not known at compile time.
Safety and Reliability	Homogeneous Redundancy	Increase reliability and safety in the presence of single point failures.
	Diverse Redundancy	Increase reliability and safety in the presence of single point failures and systematic errors.
	Monitor-Actuator	Low-cost improvement in safety with a specific type of diverse redundancy.
	Watchdog	Mechanism to detect failures and faults during execution.
	Safety Executive	Manage potentially complex safety processes in the presence of faults.

Asymmetric multiprocessing is defined to be when the processors are dedicated to specific tasks at compile-time. This approach makes smaller demands on the RTOS scheduling software and is more efficient for a specific configuration, but is less flexible. Most real-time systems are asymmetric because each processor usually has different interfaces to specific hardware devices.

A third approach that I've found useful for larger hard real-time systems is what I call *semisymmetric multiprocessing (SSM)*. In this compromise approach, the allocation of tasks is not determined at compile-time, but rather during system boot. A task broker queries the set of processors available and allocates tasks that are not tightly coupled to the hardware, to the available processors. The advantage of SSM is that it remains highly flexible and has minimal software run-time impact.

The advantages of the Master-Slave Pattern lie in its simplicity (see Figure 5-7). It can be used to implement distributed concurrent processing algorithms or to simplify arbitration of shared resources. Master-slave control normally is performed as a cycling executive where the master cycles through actions that invoke services of the slaves in a predefined sequence. When the action sequence is known at design time, the Master-Slave Pattern is an obvious choice. The cyclic scheduling of actions makes the system extremely deterministic. It is literally possible to stop the CPU clock at any (known) point in time and tell from the design what CPU instruction it is executing. Aperiodic events are handled with polling, but because the scheduling is so deterministic it is a simple matter to compute the worst-case latency for event handling.

The simplicity of the Master-Slave Pattern is also its primary disadvantage. Many systems must respond to episodic events that are impossible to predict. Depending on the complexity of the control algorithms and the computational horsepower available on the master, it may be difficult to meet all deadlines in a master-slave arrangement. Cyclic schedulers are simple, but they tend to be inefficient in their use of CPU resource. It is possible to meet all deadlines using a preemptive scheduling policy yet be unable to do so with a cyclic scheduler.[4]

Microkernel Architectural Pattern

This pattern is also known as the Layered Pattern. The basic concept of this pattern is to layer the structure of the subsystem into distinct sets of classes or packages that can be arranged in a set of hierarchical client-server associations. Commonly, the lowest level in the hierarchy directly interfaces with the underlying hardware or operating system, and the highest layer contains high-level application domain objects.

The layer interfaces are transparent from above but opaque from

---

[4] Although most current avionics flight-control systems for both planes and spacecraft, such as the Galileo Jupiter probe, use cyclic schedulers, the Mars Pathfinder mission used priority-based scheduling with great success.

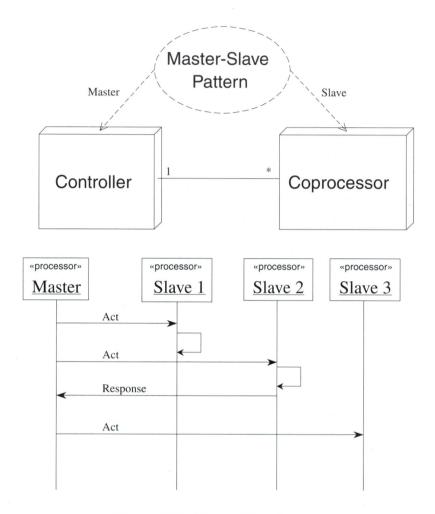

Figure 5-7: *Master-Slave Pattern*

below. The classes defined in the package interface are visible only to classes in packages at or above the package in the hierarchy. A *closed-layered architecture* is one in which each layer knows only about the layer immediately below it in the hierarchy. In an *open-layered architecture*, a layer can request services of any layer lower in the hierarchy. Closed-layered architectures tend to sacrifice some performance for increased encapsulation and reusability. See Figure 5-8.

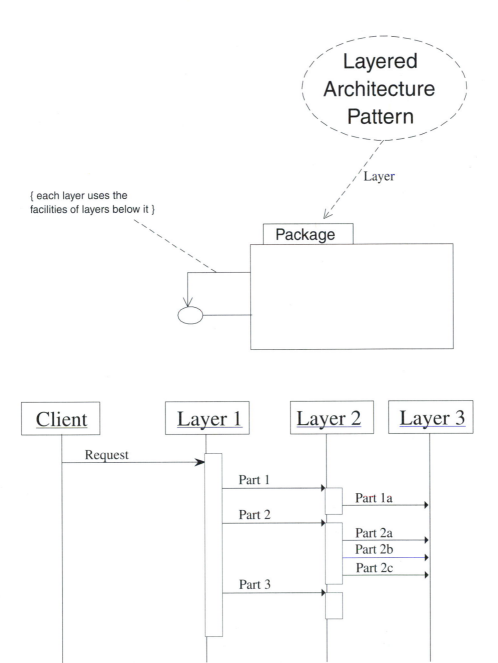

Figure 5-8: *Layered Architecture Pattern*

There is much to recommend layered designs, as they provide good portability at both the top and bottom layers. The bottom layers can be reused with different upper layers because the latter are more concrete and more primitive. For example, a device I/O layer can be used in a wide set of applications on the same hardware platform. The upper layers can be reused on different hardware platforms by replacing only the device-specific lower layers. This is a great aid in porting a system to new physical architectures.

The primary disadvantage of the microkernel architecture is a potential loss in performance. A layered strategy often means that an execution path must pass through several layers in order to invoke the required service, when it would be more efficient to call the service directly. Also, because the lower layers know nothing of the higher layers, they must of necessity be general and not apply any optimization that would require knowledge of their clients. This inefficiency can be mitigated by identifying the high bandwidth among the objects and optimizing the propagation of the data along those paths.

Proxy Pattern

The Proxy Pattern is only marginally an architectural pattern, but it is included here because it serves as the basis for the Broker Pattern, which is clearly architectural. The Proxy Pattern is applicable when a normal reference or pointer to an object is inappropriate or impossible, such as when the object resides in another thread or processor. This pattern decouples clients from their servers by creating a local proxy, or stand-in, for the less accessible server. When the client needs to request a service from the server, such as retrieving a value, it asks its local proxy. The proxy can then marshal a request to the original server or it can use an asynchronous policy that periodically or episodically receives updated values from the server.

The decoupling of client and server means that the server can reside in a different address space than the client and is useful in distributed systems for this reason. Different proxy objects can provide different access rights to data, such as when your system must interface to third-party systems over which you have little or no control. Finally, the Proxy Pattern can provide reference counting for load-on-demand objects and assist in the creation and destruction of servers when memory is extremely tight.

Figure 5-9 shows the Proxy Pattern and an example. In this scenario, the server contains the heart rate as measured from its ECG leads. The client resides on a separate display processor and displays the current heart rate. Since the objects reside on different processors, the display processor uses a proxy object to hold a local copy of the heart rate. This proxy can have many clients, such as an alarm manager (to check for arrhythmia), a trending client, and several display clients. The proxy maintains its own link over the communications bus to the heart rate server. The proxy subscribes to the server (which might have several proxy clients distributed throughout the system) and every so often the server sends an update to its proxies. The proxy insulates the clients from knowing anything about the location of the server and how to marshal bus messages to get the data. Further, the proxy is more efficient when multiple clients reside on the same processor because bus bandwidth is usually at a premium and this way only the proxy must communicate with the server directly.

The primary disadvantage of the Proxy Pattern is again a possible loss of performance when only a single client resides on the processor. Another weakness is the coupling between the proxy objects and the server. The proxy must know how to find the server, so it must know not only the operational syntax for requesting the data, but also the location of the server and how to marshal requests using the communication protocol. The Proxy Pattern can be elaborated to decouple the proxy from the server using the Broker Pattern, described next.

Broker Pattern

The Broker Pattern is an elaborated Proxy Pattern that goes another step towards decoupling the clients from the servers. An object broker is an object that knows the location of other objects. The broker can have the knowledge *a priori* (at compile-time) or can gather the information dynamically as objects register themselves, or a combination of both. The primary advantage of the Broker Pattern is that it is possible to construct a Proxy Pattern when the location of the server isn't known when the system is compiled. This makes it particularly useful for systems using symmetric or semisymmetric multiprocessing.

The architectural components of the Broker Pattern are the Object Broker, Client, and Server Subsystems. It is rare to have a broker with an isolated client and server, and when it is used the Broker Pattern is

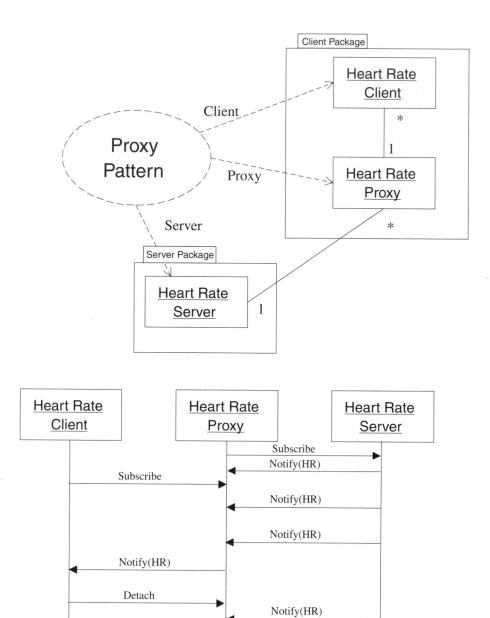

Figure 5-9: *Proxy Pattern*

normally a key strategic design decision. Although many real-time systems may be able to use commercial object brokers, it is not uncommon to implement a custom broker to optimize system resource usage.

In fault-tolerant and safety-critical systems, the object broker may play a key role in the maintenance of system integrity. For example, the broker can contain a watchdog (see the Watchdog Pattern on page 233) that maintains connections with all safety-relevant subsystems.[5] When a subsystem becomes unstable or shuts down, the object broker can initiate safety actions, such as de-energizing lasers, inserting control rods into the nuclear reactor core, and so on.

The scenario in Figure 5-10 shows how the participant objects collaborate with two levels of indirection. The first level is that provided by the proxies, insulating the clients and servers from each other. The second level is provided by the object broker, which insulates the proxies from the servers. Note that the server object first registers with the broker so that it can handle incoming requests for the server. When the client subscribes to its local proxy, the proxy in turn subscribes to the server proxy. The object broker handles this request since only it knows the location of the server.

5.4.2 Safety and Reliability Patterns

By *safe*, we mean that the system does not create accidents leading to injury, the loss of life, or damage to property. By *reliable*, we mean a system that continues to function for long periods of time. It is possible to have reliable but unsafe systems as well as safe but unreliable systems. A safe system can fail, as long as it does so without creating an accident. For example, an accounting program can fail requiring a system reboot, but this can occur without the loss of life. Such an unreliable accounting system continues to be safe. On the other hand, a reliable system can function correctly but can still lead to accidents. A handgun is a very reliable piece of equipment but it is not particularly safe.

In many real-time systems, safety and reliability go hand-in-hand. This is especially true when there is no predetermined fail-safe condi-

---

[5] This connection is often implemented with special "life tick" messages that indicate that the client subsystem is alive and well.

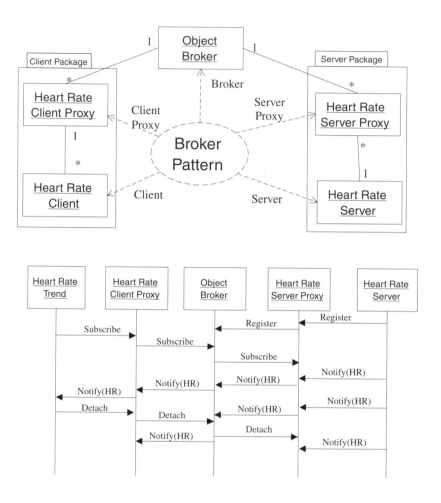

Figure 5-10: *Broker Pattern*

tion. When flying at 35,000 feet, what is the fail-safe condition in the event of an engine malfunction? It may not be to shut down the engine! In such systems, safety is enhanced when the reliability is increased. But this is not always the case. Many systems are fault-tolerant by having redundancy, but if a redundant channel fails, the system may no longer be safe.

In safety-critical environments, applications must not only do the right thing when everything is OK—they must continue to do the right thing in the presence of single point failures.[6] It is possible to improve both safety and reliability through an appropriate architecture, although not always at the same time. This section will explore some of the architectural patterns relevant to safety and reliability.

Homogeneous Redundancy Pattern

The Homogeneous Redundancy Pattern (Figure 5-11) uses identical channels[7] to increase reliability. All redundant channels are run in parallel and the output of the channels is compared. If an odd number of channels is used, then a majority-wins policy can be implemented that can detect and correct failures in the minority channels.

The advantages of this pattern are improved robustness in the presence of failures in the channels without a large development overhead. Since all the channels are identical, they need only be cloned rather than redeveloped. Care should be taken that the channels are not only identical but also fully redundant so that single point failures do not take out all channels simultaneously.[8]

A *failure* is an event that happens at a particular point in time. This is distinct from an *error,* which is a systematic fault. An error is a flawed system condition—a system with an error has always had the error. The big disadvantage of homogeneous redundancy is that it only detects failures but not errors. Homogeneous redundancy cannot detect errors because by definition all channels are identical. If one channel contains an error then all redundant channels contain the same error. This implies that homogeneous redundancy only protects against hardware failures, but does not protect against software faults because *software cannot fail.* Software can be wrong and full of errors, but it cannot suddenly break.

There are other disadvantages of redundancy. There is an increase in recurring cost due to the duplicated hardware devices. The redun-

---

[6] In highly safety-critical systems where the lives of thousands or millions may be put at risk (such as nuclear power plants), double-point failure safety may be required.

[7] A *channel,* in this context, means a set of devices (including processors and software running on processors) that handle a related cohesive set of data or control flows from incoming event to ultimate system response.

[8] A Bell-Boeing V22 Osprey crashed because two roll-rate sensors were cross-wired, allowing the two faulty units to outvote the correct one. Similar faults were found in other flying V22 Ospreys as well [6].

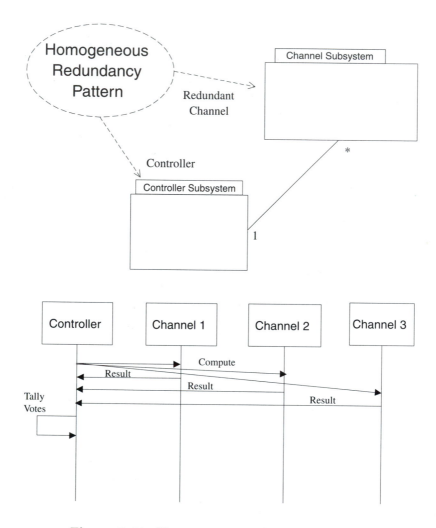

Figure 5-11: *Homogeneous Redundancy Pattern*

dant hardware also requires more space and power and generates more heat. In some real-time systems, this can be an important limitation.

Diverse Redundancy Pattern

The Diverse Redundancy Pattern mitigates the primary disadvantage of homogeneous redundancy by providing redundant channels that are implemented using different means. This can be accomplished in many ways:

- Different but equal
- Light-weight redundancy
- Separation of monitoring and actuation

The first option is similar to the Homogeneous Redundancy Pattern in that the channels are all approximately equal in terms of accuracy, throughput, and reliability. Each channel is implemented differently, using different software and hardware components and so will provide additional protection against errors as well as failures. This is the most expensive of the three but can not only detect failures and errors, but can also continue to execute correctly in the presence of such faults.

The second option is to use a light-weight secondary channel to ensure the correctness of the primary. This light-weight channel provides a reasonableness check on the results from the primary channel, but does not have the same accuracy and/or range. It costs less to implement and manufacture, but is much better at fault detection than fault tolerance. The secondary channel can identify when the primary channel is broken but typically cannot take over all its duties when this occurs. Other fault tolerance means must be present if the system must remain operational in the presence of errors.

The last of these, the separation of monitoring and actuation, is discussed as a separate pattern, next.

You will note in Figure 5-12 that the diverse channels share a common interface but have different implementations. It is not strictly required that the interfaces be identical but it simplifies the software development. The requirement is that the channels do not have any common mode faults; that is, that they do not have the same systematic errors nor can a single point failure bring down multiple channels.

Monitor-Actuator Pattern

The Monitor-Actuator Pattern is a special type of diverse redundancy. In this case, however, the channels are separated into monitoring and actuator channels. The actuator channel performs the actions, such as controlling the wing flaps, moving the control rods, or pacing the heart. The monitor channel keeps track of what the actuation is supposed to

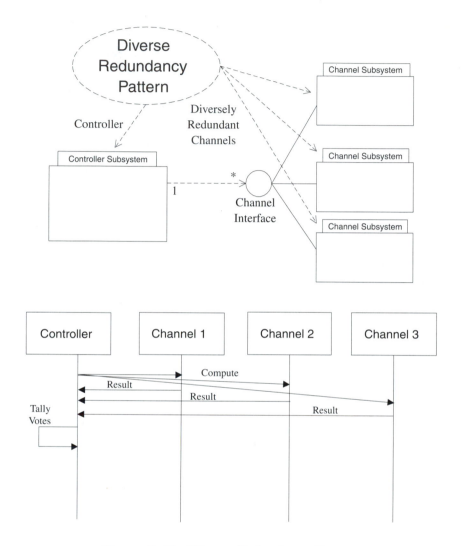

Figure 5-12: *Diverse Redundancy Pattern*

be doing and monitors the physical environment to ensure that the results of the actuator are appropriate. Note that the actuator itself cannot
rely on this monitor—closed loop actuators must use separate sensors
that are independent of the sensor used in the monitoring channel.

The basic concept behind the Monitor-Actuator Pattern is that the
monitor channel identifies actuation channel failures so that appropri-

ate fault-handling mechanisms can be executed. If the monitor channel fails, then it means that the actuator didn't fail, so it continues to be correct. As with all forms of redundancy, common mode failures must be eliminated to achieve the safety and fault-tolerance goals of the redundancy. The monitor and actuator channels often exchange messages periodically to ensure both are operating properly as well. The messages can also be sent to the controller, which decides the appropriate actuation.

The primary downside to this pattern is the (small) increased recurring cost due to the additional monitoring channel. Nevertheless, in safety-critical or fault-sensitive situations it can be a very cost-effective means for improving safety and reliability when compared to full homogeneous or diverse redundancy.

The scenario in Figure 5-13 shows how the desired result is sent to both the actuator and the monitor channels. The actuator uses this result to decide the exact action it should take. The monitor uses this to check up on the result of the action to see if the goal is achieved. In the first case, the actuation was correct but in the second case the monitor detected a large discrepancy between the commanded result and the actual environment. The Controller can then take whatever corrective action seems appropriate.

Notice also the exchange of life tick messages in the middle of the scenario. In this way, the actuator can detect when the monitor fails and vice versa.

Watchdog Pattern

A watchdog is a very common concept in real-time embedded systems (Figure 5-14). A watchdog is a subsystem that receives messages from other subsystems on a periodic or sequence-keyed basis. If a service of the watchdog occurs too late or out of sequence, the watchdog takes some corrective action, such as reset, shutdown, alarming, or initiating a more elaborate error recovery mechanism. Watchdogs themselves tend to be very simple and are often implemented in hardware to protect them from software faults. Although watchdogs are rather more mechanistic in their level, they are usually used within a global scope of safety and redundancy and so are included here.

Sometimes software watchdogs are more active. Such watchdogs are woken up periodically and perform some Built-In Test (BIT) suite,

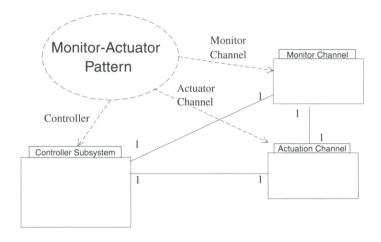

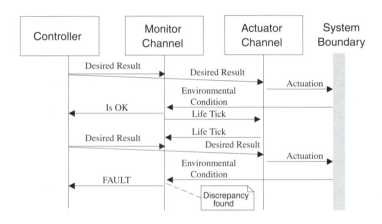

Figure 5-13: *Monitor-Actuator Pattern*

such as performing CRC checks over the executable code, checking RAM, looking for evidence of stack overflow, etc. Although these are not watchdogs in the classic sense, they are simple to implement and are required in many safety-critical environments.

The advantage of using watchdogs is that they are cheap and easy to implement. They don't require a lot of hardware or software support. However, many systems do not have a simple response to the detection of a system fault. Simply resetting an unattended ICU patient

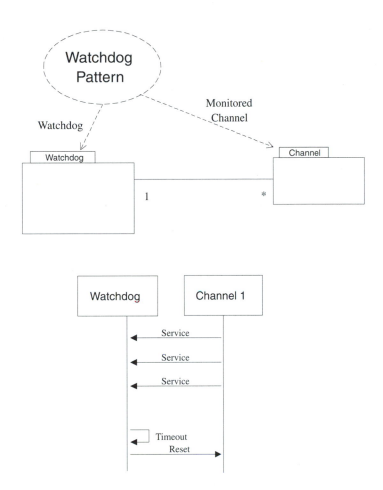

Figure 5-14: *Watchdog Pattern*

ventilator may not be the most appropriate action. This is their primary disadvantage—they may be too simple to support complex error handling and fault recovery.

Safety Executive Pattern

The Safety Executive Pattern (Figure 5-15) uses a centralized coordinator for safety monitoring and control of system recovery from faults. It also goes by the name of the Safety Kernel Pattern. The safety executive

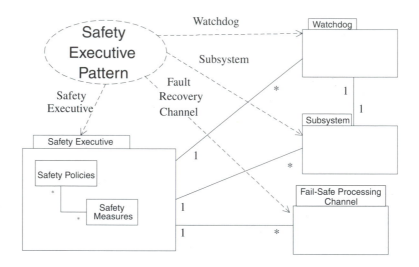

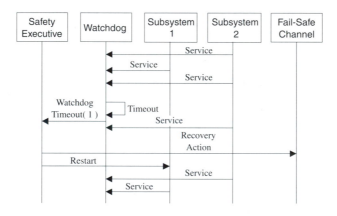

Figure 5-15: *Safety Executive Pattern*

acts like a really smart watchdog that tracks and coordinates all safety
monitoring. Typically it captures the following inputs:

- Watchdogs timeouts
- Software error assertions
- Continuous or periodic BITs
- Faults identified by monitors in the Monitor-Actuation Pattern

For larger and more complex systems, a safety executive provides a consistent, centralized point for safety processing. This simplifies the application software that might otherwise be riddled with extra checks and resulting actions that obscure the primary application purpose. Because the safety control is centralized, it becomes a simpler process to verify and validate the safety measures.

5.5 Communication Infrastructure

Another aspect of architectural design is the structure and control of communication among devices. Multiprocessor systems require a communications path linking the processors together.[9] Two separate, but related issues are the communications bus topology and the protocol operating over the bus. The overall structure of the protocol represents a set of important architectural decisions.

A *protocol* is defined to be the rules, formats, and procedures agreed upon by objects wanting to communicate. By this definition, a protocol includes not only the physical characteristics of the medium but also the additional rules of behavior governing the use of the medium.

Protocols are constructed of five distinct parts:

1. Services to be performed

2. Assumptions the protocol makes about its environment

3. Vocabulary of messages defined within the protocol and their implied semantics[10]

4. Encoding format of information within the messages

5. Procedural rules that govern high-order use of the protocol (the *meta-protocol*)

The only conditions for a usable protocol are:

- All communicating parties understand how communication is started and ended

---

[9] We will call this a *bus* in this discussion regardless of the specific topology of the communications link.

[10] Grammars with similar vocabularies but different semantics can lead to all sorts of havoc. For compelling examples, see [5, 6].

- Synchronization between communicating parties is achieved
- Errors in communication are detected and corrected
- Information is formatted and stored in the messages

The embedded system developer frequently ends up designing protocols for custom hardware devices, which communicate over novel physical media. Even when the physical media is standard, such as the ubiquitous RS-232, there is no corresponding standard for logical messaging that meets all the needs of the various embedded environments (or rather, there are many incompatible standards, none of which may actually meet your specific needs). The requirements levied against a protocol vary widely. Many embedded systems are highly safety relevant and have strict reliability requirements. In others, occasional message dropouts may be an annoyance, but otherwise harmless. The protocol may need only support a single point-to-point pair or a large distributed communications network containing dozens or hundreds of nodes. Feedback may be immediate or it may be transmitted to a space probe light-hours away. How are changes to your communications channel likely to manifest themselves—need for greater speed? More nodes? New application information?

In the field of embedded real-time systems, protocol designers generally use one of two approaches in the definition of their own custom protocols. The first are *data-driven* protocols. In a data-driven protocol, the specific application vocabulary drives all else in the protocol. The structure of the protocol is fundamentally based on the information that must be communicated. This makes for a highly specialized protocol. Data-driven protocols are simple and can be made very efficient. On the downside, they are not very reusable, flexible, or extensible. They tend to be less robust, because error detection and correction concerns are not fully addressed.

The other kind of protocol is *grammar-driven.* In such a protocol, the *type* of things that need to be said are the primary focus, not the *specific things* themselves. These protocols are more general and can be used in a variety of settings. Because they are more general, they are much more flexible and extensible. Error detection and correction can be dealt with in much greater detail. On the downside, this generality increases the protocol overhead and makes them less efficient than is possible with data-driven protocols. The SCSI bus protocol, for example, can have an average 75% of its bandwidth associated with arbitration of control rather than data transmission. Because of the benefit of generality, in this book, we will consider only grammar-driven protocols.

A good protocol should be:

Stable	Protocol state reachability graph is known
	Protocol is deadlock free
Bounded	Cannot overflow system limits and queues
Reliable	Meets needs for error detection and correction
Timely	Hard deadlines can be guaranteed to be met
	Soft deadlines are met on the average
Adaptive	Can dynamically adjust to meet current system demands

The relative importance of each of these aspects must correspond with your target environment. Are the applications safety related (e.g., nuclear power plant control system)? Are there hard real-time requirements (e.g., control surfaces of aircraft)? Is the environment likely to cause message corruption (as in electrically noisy environments)? Are the reliability requirements abnormally high (such as in a distributed automated factory)?

5.6 Concurrency Design

Real-time systems typically have multiple threads of control executing simultaneously. A *thread* can be defined as a set of executable *actions* that execute sequentially. Actions are statements executing at the same priority in a particular sequence or performing some cohesive function. These statements can belong to many different objects. The entirety of a thread is also known as a *task*. Multiple objects typically participate within a single task. In some systems, a distinction is made between *heavyweight* and *lightweight* threads. Heavyweight threads use different data spaces and must resort to expensive messaging to communicate data among themselves. Such threads have relatively strong encapsulation and protection from other threads. Lightweight threads coexist within an enclosing data space. Lightweight threads provide faster inter-task communication via this shared "global" space, but offer weaker encapsulation. Some authors use the terms *thread* to refer to lightweight threads and *task* or *process* to refer to heavyweight threads. We shall use thread and task as synonyms in this book.

5.7 Representing Tasks

The UML can show concurrency models in a couple of ways. Class and object diagrams can show the tasks (represented as active objects) directly and state diagrams can show the orthogonal components participating in multiple threads. Collaboration and sequence diagrams show specific scenarios of these active objects and their components with other tasks.

Class and object diagrams can use the stereotype «active» or the active object stereotype icon to represent tasks. By showing only classes and objects with this stereotype, the task structure is clear. A task diagram is nothing more than a class diagram with only active objects and their associations.[11]

State diagrams show the state space for classes and objects. Since active objects are just a special kind of object, their behavior can be captured on state diagrams as well. Using the complex transition notation (e.g., join and fork), it is possible to show multiple threads rooted within a single active object. Broadcast and propagated events allow communication between active objects. These concepts were dealt with in some detail in the previous chapter.

Scenarios can be single or multithreaded. In multithreaded scenarios, threads are included in the message label by preceding the sequence number with the thread name.

---

[11] The system specification must be kept distinct from the diagrams. The specification resides in the repository, and diagrams provide a view into that repository. Many different and redundant views are possible, so it is perfectly all right to create new diagrams that contain only partial information, such as the System Task Diagram.

5.7.1 System Task Diagram

Class and object models are fundamentally concurrent. Objects are themselves inherently concurrent and it is conceivable that each object could execute in its own thread (this is, after all, how biological neural systems work; see [7]). During the course of architectural design, the objects must be aligned into a smaller set of concurrent threads solely for efficiency reasons. For this reason, the partitioning of a system into threads is always a design decision.

In UML, tasks are rooted in a single active object. The active object is a composite, aggregating the objects participating within the thread. It has the general responsibility to coordinate internal execution by dispatching messages to its constituent parts and providing information to the underlying operating system so that the latter can schedule the task. By applying a filter on the active stereotype, only the threads are shown. This is the System Task Diagram.

The packaging of objects appropriately into nodes and threads is vital for system performance. The relationships among the tasks are fundamental architectural decisions that have great impact on the performance and hardware requirements of the system. Besides just identifying the tasks and their relationships to other tasks, the characteristics of the messages must themselves be defined. These characteristics include the:

- Message arrival patterns and frequencies
- Event response deadlines
- Synchronization protocols for inter-task communication
- "Hardness" of deadlines

Defining these characteristics is at the very heart of multithreaded systems design.

The greatest advantage of the System Task Diagram is that the entire set of tasks for the system can be shown on a single diagram, albeit at a high conceptual level. It is easy to trace back from the diagram into the requirements specification and vice versa. By elaborating each task symbol on the task diagram into either a lightweight task diagram or an object diagram, the tasks can be efficiently decomposed and related to the class, object, and behavioral models.

The Elevator class diagram provided in Chapter 3 identified the pri-

mary classes from the original problem statement, along with their relationships and multiplicity. Figure 5-16 shows the task diagram for the
same set of classes. The diagram shows a number of useful things. First,
notice that the processors have been identified. The *Elevator Gnome* resides on a singleton processor since it acts as a controller/event dis-
patcher. The *Central Station* is likewise a singleton. The elevator and
floor processors are not—there is an instance of the elevator processor
for every elevator, and an instance of a floor processor in every floor.
Note the instance multiplicity defined in the upper left-hand corner of
each processor icon.

Within each processor, objects are busy collaborating to achieve the
goals of that processor. However, on the system task diagram, only the
tasks are shown. Remember that each task is rooted in a single active
composite object that receives the events for that task and dispatches
them to the appropriate object within the task.

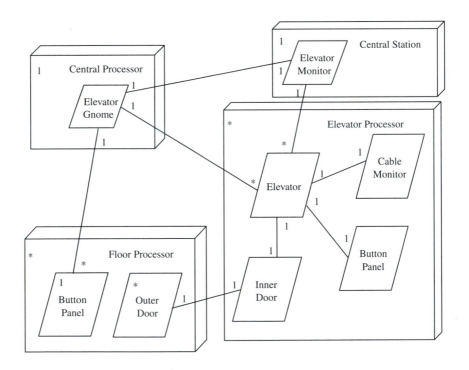

Figure 5-16: *Elevator Task Diagram*

The associations among the tasks are shown using conventional association notation. These associations indicate that the tasks must communicate in some fashion to pass messages.

Compare Figure 5-16 with Figure 3-10 in Chapter 3. Can you identify in which threads the various objects and classes reside?

5.7.2 Concurrent State Diagrams

Rumbaugh [2] has suggested a means by which concurrent tasks can be diagrammed using the statecharts. He notes that concurrency with objects generally arises by aggregation; that is, a composite object is composed of component objects, some of which may execute in separate threads. In this case, a single state of the composite object may be composed of multiple states of these components.

Active objects respond to events and dispatch them to their aggregate parts. This process can be modeled as a finite state machine. The other orthogonal component is due to the task thread itself having a number of states. Since the active object represents the task characteristics to the system, it is very natural to make this an orthogonal component of the active object.

Figure 5-17 shows the two orthogonal components of a typical Active object class. The dashed line separates the orthogonal components of the Running superstate. Each transition in the event processing component can take place only while the active object is in one of the substates of the Running superstate of the thread component. After all, that is the only time it actually consumes CPU cycles. On the other hand, if the running thread becomes preempted or suspended, the event processing component will resume where it left off, as indicated by the history connector.

Table 5-4 provides a brief description of the states.

5.8 Defining Task Threads

During analysis, classes and objects were identified and characterized and their associations defined. In a multitasking system, the objects must be placed into task threads for actual execution. This process of task thread definition is two-fold:

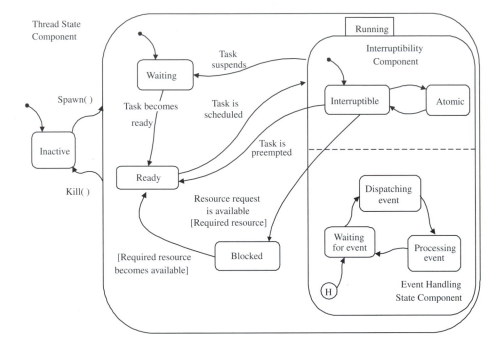

Figure 5-17: *Concurrency in Active Objects*

1. Identify the task threads
2. Populate the task threads with classes and objects from the analysis and design process

A number of strategies can help you define the threads based on the external events and the system context. They fall into the general approach of grouping events in the system so that a thread handles one or more events, and each event is handled by a single thread.

There are conditions under which an event may be handled by more than one thread. One event may generate other *propagated* events, which may be handled by other threads. For example, the appearance of waveform data may itself generate an event to signal another thread to scale the incoming data asynchronously. Occasionally, events may be broadcast to more than one thread. This may happen when a number of threads are waiting on a shared resource or are waiting for a common event that permits them all to move forward independently.

Table 5-4: *States of the Active Object Thread Component*

State	Description
Inactive	Task is not yet created.
Waiting	Task is not ready to run, but is waiting for some event to put it in the *Ready* state.
Ready	Task is ready to run and is waiting to be executed. It is normally stored in a priority FIFO queue.
Running	Task is running and chewing up CPU cycles. This superstate contains two orthogonal, concurrent components.
Interruptible	Task is running and may be preempted. This is a substate of the *Interruptibility Component* of the *Running* state.
Atomic	Task is running but may not be preempted. Specifically, task switching has been disabled. This is a substate of the *Interruptability Component* of the *Running* state.
Blocked	Task is waiting for a required resource to become available so that it may continue its processing.
Waiting for event	Task is waiting for an event to handle. This is a substate of the *Event Handling State Component* of the *Running* state.
Dispatching event	Object is handling an incoming event and deciding which aggregates should process it. This is substate of the *Event Handling State Component* of the *Running* state.
Processing event	Designated aggregate of the active object composite is responding to the event. This is a substate of the *Event Handling State Component* of the *Running* state.

5.8.1 Identifying Task Threads

Internal and external events can be grouped together in a variety of ways into threads. Some common event grouping strategies are:

- Single Event Groups
  In a simple system, it may be possible to create a separate task for each external and internal event. This usually is not feasible in complex systems with dozens or even hundreds of possible events, or

when task switch time is significant relative to the event response timing.

- Sequential Processing
  When it is clear that a series of steps must be performed in a sequential fashion, this may be grouped within a single thread.

- Event Source
  This strategy groups events from a common source together. For example, group all the events related to ECG numerics into one thread (such as HR Available, ECG Alarms, etc), all the NIBP (Non-Invasive Blood Pressure) data in another, the ventilator data in another, the anesthetic agent in another, and the gas mixing data in yet another. In an automobile, sources of events might be the ignition, braking, and engine control systems. In systems with clearly defined subsystems producing events that have roughly the same period, this may be the simplest approach.

- Interface Device (a.k.a. *port*)
  This grouping strategy encapsulates control of a specific interface within a single thread. For example, the (periodic) SDLC data can be handled in one thread, the (episodic) RS-232 data to the external models by another, and the (episodic) user buttons and knobs by another. This strategy is a specialization of the Event Source grouping strategy.

- Related Information
  Consider grouping all waveforms to be handled by a single task, and all measured numeric parameters within another task. Or, all information related to airfoil control surfaces in each wing and tail section might be manipulated by separate threads. This grouping may be appropriate when related data is used together in the user problem domain. Another name used for this grouping is *functional cohesion*.

- Event characteristics
  If data arrives at a given rate, a single periodic task thread could handle receiving all the relevant data and dispatching it to different objects as necessary. Aperiodic events might be handled by a single interrupt handler and similarly dispatch control to appropriate objects. Generally, this grouping may be most useful with internal events, such as timer interrupts, or when the periods of events naturally cluster around a small set of periods.

- Target Object/Computationally Intense Processing
  One of the purposes of rendezvous objects is to encapsulate and provide access to data. As such, they are targets for events, both to insert and remove data. A waveform queue object server might have its own thread for background scaling and manipulation, while participating in threads depositing data within the queue object and removing data for display.

- Purpose
  Alarms serve one purpose—notifying the user of the system of anomalies, so that he or she can take corrective action or vacate the premises, whichever seems more appropriate. This might form one event group. Grouping safety checks within a watchdog task, such as checking for stack overflow or code corruption, might form another.

- Safety Concerns
  The system hazard analysis may suggest threads. One common rule of thumb in safety-critical systems is to separate monitoring from actuation (see the Monitor-Actuator Pattern discussed earlier in this chapter). In terms of task identification, this means that a task that controls a safety-relevant process should be checked by an independent task. From a safety perspective, it is preferable to run safety checks on a separate processor, so that common-mode hardware and software faults do not affect both the primary and the safety processing simultaneously.

During concurrency design, you must add events to groups where it appears appropriate so that each event is represented in at least one group. Any events remaining after the initial grouping can each be considered independently. Create a task diagram in which the processing of each group is represented by a separate thread. Most events will only occur within a single task, but sometimes events must be dispatched to multiple tasks.

Frequently, one or more of these groupings will emerge as the primary decomposition strategy of the event space, but it is also common to mix grouping strategies. When the grouping seems complete and stable, you have identified an initial set of tasks that handle all events in your system. As the product development evolves, events may be added to or removed from groups, new groups may suggest themselves, or alternative grouping strategies may present themselves. This will lead the astute designer to alternative designs worth consideration.

5.9 Assigning Objects to Tasks

Once a good set of tasks is identified, you may start populating the groups with objects. Note that the previous sentence referred to objects and not classes. Objects are specific instances of classes that may appear in different tasks or as an interface between tasks. Some classes create only a single instance in an application (singletons), and some classes instantiate to multiple objects that all reside within a single thread, but in the general case, classes instantiate a number of objects that may appear in any number of threads. For example, there may be queues of tasks, queues of waveform data, queues of numeric data, queues of network messages, command queues, error queues, alarm queues, etc. These might appear in a great many tasks, even though they are instances of the same class (queue).

5.10 Defining Task Rendezvous

So far in this chapter, we have looked at what a task is, strategies to select a set of tasks, and how to populate tasks with objects. The remaining piece is to define how the tasks communicate with each other.

There are a number of strategies for intertask communication. The simplest by far is to use the OS to send messages from one task to another. Although this approach maintains encapsulation and limits coupling among threads, it is expensive in terms of compute cycles and is relatively slow. Light-weight expeditious communication is required in many real-time systems in order for the tasks to meet their performance requirements. In this chapter, we will consider some methods for intertask communication that are both light-weight and robust.

The two main reasons for task communication are to share information and to synchronize control. The acquisition, manipulation, and display of information may all occur in different task threads with different periods and may not even take place on the same processor, necessitating some means to share the information among these tasks. Synchronization of control is also very common in real-time systems. In asynchronous tasks that control physical processes, one task's completion (such as emptying a chemical vat) may form a precondition for another process (such as adding a new volatile chemical to the vat). The task synchronization strategy must ensure that such preconditions are satisfied.

When tasks communicate, the rendezvous itself has attributes and behavior, which make it reasonable to model it as an associative class. The important questions to ask about task synchronization are as follows:

- Are there any preconditions for the tasks to communicate? A precondition is generally a data value that must be set, or an object that must be in a particular state. If a precondition for task synchronization exists, it should be checked by a guarding condition before the rendezvous is allowed to continue.
- What should happen if the preconditions are not met, as when the collaborating task is not available? The rendezvous can:
  - ▼ Wait indefinitely until the other task is ready (a *waiting rendezvous*)
  - ▼ Wait until either the required task is ready or a specified period has elapsed (*timed rendezvous*)
  - ▼ Return immediately and ignore the attempt at task communication (*balking rendezvous*)
  - ▼ Raise an exception and handle the task communication failure as an error (*protected rendezvous*).
- If data is to be shared via the rendezvous class, what is the relationship of the rendezvous object with the object containing the required information? Options include:
  - ▼ The rendezvous object contains the information directly
  - ▼ The rendezvous object holds a reference to the object containing the information, or a reference to an object serving as an interface for the information
  - ▼ The rendezvous object can temporarily hold the information until it is passed to the target thread.

Remember that objects must ensure the integrity of their internal data. If the possibility exists that shared data can be simultaneously *write* or *write-read* accessed by more than a single task, then it must be protected by some mechanism, such as a mutual-exclusion semaphore. In general, synchronization objects must handle:

- Preconditions
- Access control
- Data access

One approach is typified using a specialization of the Abstraction Strategy Pattern (see Chapter 6) called the Rendezvous Pattern.

5.10.1 Sharing Resources

Rendezvous objects control access to resources and classical methods exist to handle resource usage in a multitasking environment. In the simplest case, resources can be simultaneously accessed—that is, access is nonatomic. Many devices use predetermined configuration tables burned into FLASH or EPROM. Since processes can only read the configuration table, many tasks can access the resource simultaneously without bad effects.

When data access involves writing, it requires some form of access control to ensure data integrity. Clearly, if multiple internal attributes must be simultaneously updated, another reader task cannot be permitted to read these values while only some of them are updated.

With large collections of objects, it may be necessary to allow read accesses in one or more portions of the data base even while other sections are being updated. Large airline reservation databases must function in this fashion, for example. Algorithms to control these processes are well defined and available in texts on relational and object data bases.

5.10.2 Assigning Priorities

Task *priority* is distinct from the importance of the actions executed by the task. Priority in a preemptive priority scheme determines the *required timeliness* of the response to the event or precondition. For example, in an ECG monitor, in order to have smoothly drawn waveforms, waveform tasks must have a high priority to ensure that they run often enough to avoid a jerky appearance. ECG waveforms have tight timeliness requirements. On the other hand, a jerky waveform is not as important to patient outcome as is alarming when the patient is at risk. An asystole alarm is activated when the monitor detects that the heart is no longer beating. Clearly, bringing this to the attention of the physician is very important, but if the alarm took an extra second to be annunciated, it would not affect patient outcome. Such an alarm is very important, but does not have a very high priority.

In *Rate Monotonic Scheduling (RMS)*, the assignment of priorities is simple: the priority of all tasks is inversely proportional to their periods. The shorter the period, the higher the priority. The original RMS scheme assumed that the deadline is equal to the period. When this is not true, the priority should be assigned based on the deadline, rather than the period. In general, the RMS scheduling makes intuitive sense—those tasks with short deadlines must be dealt with more promptly than those with longer deadlines. It is not uncommon to find a few exceptions to the rule, however. RMS scheduling and the associated mathematics of proving schedulability are beyond the scope of this book. For a more detailed look, see [8, 9].

5.11 Summary

Architectural design consists of specification of the kind and quantity of devices, the media and rules they use to communicate, and the large-scale software components mapping to the physical architecture. The units of software architecture are subsystems and tasks. Subsystems are typically layered sets of packages arranged in a hierarchical fashion. Tasks cut through all layers, although they are rooted in a single active object.

The software architecture must map to the set of physical devices. The UML shows this mapping with the deployment diagram. This diagram shows not only nodes and communication paths, but can also show the large-scale software components.

The iterative refinement implementation strategy builds these layered subsystems using vertical slices passing through all layers as well. Each vertical slice constitutes an iterative prototype. Prototypes build upon the services defined in the previous prototypes. The order of prototypes is determined by both required services as well as the level of risk. By elaborating high-risk prototypes early, overall project risk is lowered as early as possible with a minimum of rework.

The specification of the concurrency model is very important to performance in real-time systems. This concurrency model identifies a relatively small number of threads and populates these threads with the objects identified in the analysis model. Intertask communication allows tasks to share information and to synchronize control. This is often accomplished using a Rendezvous Pattern to ensure robust exchange of information.

The next step is to specify the middle layer of design, known as mechanistic design. This level of design focuses on the collaboration of small groups of classes and objects. In the process of mechanistic design we will add classes to improve information flow and to specify details that so far have been ignored.

5.12 References

[1] *UML Semantics Appendix M1-UML Glossary Version 1.0.* Santa Clara, CA.: Rational Corporation, 1997.

[2] Rumbaugh, James, Michael Blaha, William Premerlani, Frederick Eddy, and William Lorensen, *Object-Oriented Modeling and Design.* Englewood Cliffs, NJ: Prentice Hall, 1991.

[3] Buschmann, Frank, Regine Meunier, Hans Rohnert, Peter Sommerlad, Michael Stal, *A System of Patterns: Pattern-Oriented Software Architecture.* Chichester: John Wiley & Sons, 1996.

[4] Alexander, C., S. Ishikawa, and M. Silverstain, *A Pattern Language.* New York: Oxford University Press, 1977.

[5] Gray, John, *Men are From Mars, Women are From Venus.* New York: Harper-Collins Books, 1992.

[6] Barry, Dave, *Dave Barry's Complete Guide to Guys.* New York: Fawcett Columbine Books, 1995.

[7] Douglass, Bruce Powel, *Statistical Analysis of Simulated Multinerve Networks: Use of Factor Analytical Methods.* Ph.D. Dissertation. Vermillion, SD: USD Medical School, 1984.

[8] Douglass, Bruce Powel, *Doing Hard Time: Using Object Oriented Programming and Software Patterns in Real Time Applications.* Reading, MA: Addison Wesley Longman, 1998.

[9] Klein, Mark, Thomas Ralya, Bill Pollak, Ray Obenza, and Michael Gonzalez Harbour, *A Practitioner's Handbook for Real-Time Analysis: Guide to Rate Monotonic Analysis for Real-Time Systems.* Boston: Kluwer Academic Publishers, 1993.

[10] Neumann, Peter G., *Computer Related Risks.* Reading, MA: Addison Wesley Longman, 1995.

Chapter 6

Mechanistic Design

This chapter explains the middle level of design, called mechanistic design. Mechanistic design deals with how small sets of classes and objects collaborate to achieve common goals. Mechanistic design is organized primarily around the discovery and use of patterns of object collaboration. These design patterns are reified solutions to structurally similar problems. Some architectural patterns are given in the previous chapter, but this chapter will identify several smaller scale patterns useful in real-time embedded systems.

6.1 What Is Mechanistic Design?

Mechanistic design is concerned with adding and organizing classes to support a particular implementation strategy. The mechanistic design process elaborates the analysis model and iterates it by adding objects to facilitate a particular design. A set of classes and objects collaborating together is called a *mechanism*.[1] A typical real-time system may have dozens or even hundreds of mechanisms operating concurrently.

---

[1] One of my favorite mechanisms is *Crazy Ed's Original Cave Creek Chili Beer,* in which beer is tightly coupled with a jalapeño chili (Black Mountain Brewing Company, Cold Spring, MN and Cave Creek, AZ). I find it a keen programming-skill enhancer.

Whereas the analysis model identifies the classes and objects fundamental to the problem domain, mechanistic design reorganizes these entities and adds objects to facilitate their collaboration. A common example is the addition of container classes to handle *multivalued* roles (one with a nonunity multiplicity, such as 0,1 or *) in associations.

In the analysis model, many associations will have multivalued roles. For example:

- A customer can have many bank accounts
- An autopilot can use many sensors and actuators
- A physiological parameter can be shown in many different views simultaneously

The most common implementation of a 1-to-1 association is a pointer or reference in the client allowing the client to send messages to the server (e.g., call one of the server's member functions), such as:

```
class Actuator {
    int value;
public:
    int gimme(void) { return value; };
    void set(int v) { value = v; };
};

class Autopilot {
    Actuator *s;
public:
    void AutoPilot(Server *YourActuator):s(YourActuator)
    { };
    // send msg to Server object s
    void setIt(int a) { s->set(a); }
    void IncIt(void) {
        int a = s->gimme();
        s->set(++a);
    };
};
```

The class *Autopilot* uses pointer *s* to locate its *Actuator* object. It can then send the object messages like *s→set(a)* and *s→gimme()*. The use of a simple pointer is appropriate because the multiplicity of the association is 1-to-1. But what if the association is 1-to-*?

It is entirely possible to build the ability to manage collections of *Ac-*

tuator objects directly into the *Autopilot* class. A strategy could be used, such as using a vector, linked-list, or binary tree to manage the collection by adding operations into the class *Autopilot* for adding, finding, sorting, and deleting these objects in the collection.

This simple approach has a number of drawbacks. First of all, the machinery to manage the collection is entirely unrelated to the primary purpose of the class *Autopilot*. Inserting such methods would obscure this purpose. Secondly, depending on the nature of the collection itself, the management of the collection may be quite complex, such as balancing AVL or Red-Black trees. Adding this behavior would make the class large and complex as well. Further, managing collections is a subject domain of its own and such collection class packages may be purchased. Building the behavior directly into the *Autopilot* class makes reuse of these libraries impossible. If the system has 20 classes with multivalued roles, this behavior must be rewritten for each such class. Building the behavior directly into each class that uses it makes changing to a different kind of collection much more difficult.

The more common approach is to introduce a new class during mechanistic design, one to handle the vagaries of managing the contained objects. Such a class is called a *collection* or *container* class. This allows third-party libraries to be used, separates out unrelated concerns of container management, and allows the type of collection to be changed fairly easily. The analysis model identified the association and its multiplicity, but the use of a container class is a design decision because it is a specific way to implement the analysis model. The use of collection classes is so common that it can be reified into a design pattern:

> *When a class must manage a number of objects of the same class, a useful design approach is to add a container class between the primary class and the set of multiple objects.*

So it is with all of mechanistic design. Classes are added to facilitate the implementation of the analysis model. This is the classic elaborative or iterative development method—repeated refinement of the model via reorganization and addition.

In the following section, we'll present a number of design patterns that can be profitably applied in the design of real-time systems. The use of these patterns simplifies the system's design and allows reuse on a grander scale than the reuse of individual objects and classes.

6.2 Mechanistic Design Patterns

As discussed in the previous chapter, design patterns consist of

- A common problem, including common problem context
- A generalization approach to a solution
- Consequences of the pattern

The problem statement describes the general characteristics of the problem at hand. This description may include context and preconditions. For example,

> *Problem: When exception handling is used, raw pointers can lead to memory leaks when exceptions are thrown. The use of temporary pointers within normal C++ functions or class member functions may not be cleaned up properly if an exception is thrown because the inline delete operator may be bypassed. This does not apply to objects because when objects go out of scope, their destructors are called. Raw pointers do not have destructors.*

This problem statement identifies a problem common to many designs within many domains. The context is broad—programs using C++ with exception handling. Since a generally applicable solution to this problem is available, it can be reified into a design pattern, as follows:

> *Solution: A smart pointer object can be used instead of a raw pointer when a temporary pointer must be used. The smart pointer is responsible for identifying if it must deallocate memory when the pointer is destroyed. This requires an internal mechanism, such as reference counting, to determine whether other smart pointers are referring to the same object in memory.*

Naturally, design patterns have pros and cons. Following are the consequences of the design pattern.

Consequences: The smart pointer makes the design more ro-bust in the presence of thrown exceptions, but it increases the code complexity somewhat and requires an additional level of indirection for each pointer reference. Although this can be made syntactically invisible to the user, it involves a small run-time overhead. Enforcement of the smart pointer policy cannot be automated, but must be ensured by consensus and review. Further, if smart and raw pointers are both applied against the same object, reference counting should be disabled.

Mechanistic design patterns are medium scale, involving as few as two or as many as a dozen classes. Several patterns are provided in this chapter, but this is a rich area of active research [1–4]. The interested reader is referred to the references for more patterns.[2]

As specified, you may find these patterns too specific or too general. Feel free to adapt these patterns to the particular needs of your system.

This chapter presents the patterns outlined in Table 6-1.

6.2.1 Simple Patterns

A number of useful patterns are small, involving few objects. This section identifies a number of these.

Observer Pattern[3]

It is common that a single source of information acts as a server for multiple clients who must be updated autonomously when the data value changes. This is particularly true with real-time data acquired through sensors. The problem is how to design an efficient means for all clients to be notified.

The Observer Pattern (a.k.a. *Publish-Subscribe*) is one design solution, shown in Figure 6-1. A single object, called the *server,* provides the data automatically to its clients, called *observers.* These are abstract classes that may be subclassed (into *Concrete Server* and *Concrete Observer*) to add the specialized behavior to deal with the specific information being served up.

---

[2] Another good source of patterns is the Patterns Home Page at http://stwww.cs.uiuc.edu/users/patterns/patterns.html.

[3] This rendition of the Observer Pattern is somewhat different than that found in most pattern references, but I've found it particularly useful in hard real-time environments.

Table 6-1: *Mechanistic Patterns*

Category	Pattern Name	Purpose
Simple Patterns	Observer	Allow multiple clients to share a server effectively and be updated autonomously.
	Model-View-Controller	Separate concerns of user input, data maintenance and manipulation, and display.
	Transaction	Control communication between objects with various levels of reliability.
	Smart Pointer	Avoid problems associated with dumb pointers.
Reuse	Container	Abstract away data structuring concepts from application domain classes simply to model and facilitate reuse.
	Interface	Abstract away the type of an object from its implementation to support multiple implementations of a given type and to support multiple types with a common internal structure.
	Policy	Provide the ability to easily change algorithms and procedures dynamically.
	Rendezvous	Provide a flexible mechanism for light-weight intertask communication.
State Behavior	State	Provide an optimal state machine implementation when some state changes are infrequent.
	State Table	Provide an efficient means to maintain and execute large complex state machines.

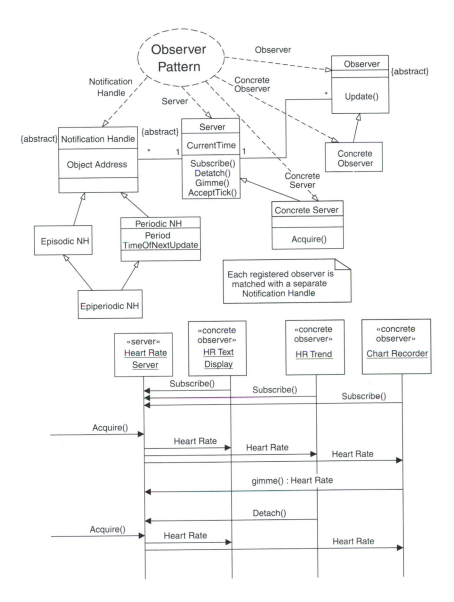

Figure 6-1: *Observer Pattern*

The observers register with the server by calling the server's *Subscribe()* method and deregister by calling the *Detach()* method. When the server receives a subscribe message, it creates a Notification Handle object that includes the address of the object. This address may be either a pointer, if the object is in the same data address space, or a logical address or identifier to be resolved by a separate communications subsystem or object broker if the target object is in a remote address space.

The Notification Handle class is subclassed to distinguish its update policy. The update policy defines the criteria for when data is sent to the observer. Typically, this is periodic, episodic, or epiperiodic (both). In some cases, it may be sufficient to use the same policy universally, but using a policy makes the design pattern more general. It is very common for an episodic policy to be used exclusively, but this is insufficient for many applications. In safety critical systems, for example, a lost message could result in an unsafe system. By periodically sending the data to the observers, the system is hardened against random message loss.

Notification of the observers is straightforward. When the server acquires data via the *Acquire()* method, it scans its notification list looking for Notification Handles that refer to objects with an episodic update policy. The *AcceptTick()* method is called on a timer event. When this method is called, the notification list is scanned for Notification Handles that are due for an update. When data is sent, the time of the next update for that target object is computed and stored in the *TimeOfNextUpdate* attribute.

To manage the notification list, this pattern is usually combined with the Container Pattern. For distributed or multiprocessor systems, this pattern is often elaborated into the Proxy or Broker Patterns, described in the previous chapter.

This pattern is useful when many clients need to access a single server object. This pattern simplifies the creation of these clients because once they register, they will be automatically notified of the data based on their selected policy. This continues until they detach from the server.

The following entities participate in the pattern:

- Server
  The Server is an abstract class defining the interface to which the abstract observer class adheres. It uses the Update() method of the

Observer to pass the value to the Observer. The methods of interest are:

▼ Subscribe(target address, policy)
This method adds the object indicated by target address to the notification list by creating a Notification Handle object. The particular subclass created depends on the policy parameter. The policy parameter is of an enumerated type updatePolicy consisting of values [episodic, periodic, epiperiodic]. Address may be a pointer value if the object is within the local address space, or an object identifier that a broker or communications system can resolve into a pointer in its target address space.

▼ Detach(target address)
This method undoes the action of the Subscribe() method by deleting the Notification Handle object corresponding to the target address.

▼ Gimme()
This method allows a direct query of the data value. It is not uncommon to have the return value for this method be a parameterized value requiring template instantiation of the Server class.

▼ AcceptTick()
This method is called by a timing object (such as OS-provided timers) to indicate either the passage of time or the counting of an event sequence. This increments the CurrentTime attribute. When this method is called, the server scans its notification list for Periodic Notification Handle objects that are due for an update.

• Concrete Server
This is a subclass of the Server. This class extends the Server class with the data attributes of interest and the Acquire() method. This may either be a passive class with an active object calling the Acquire() method, or it may itself be active. It has the method:

▼ Acquire()
This method gets the data for the server. When this method is called, data messages are sent to all objects with Episodic Notification Handles.

- Observer
  The abstract Observer class calls the Subscribe() method of the Server so that it will be updated automatically and Detach() when it no longer wishes to be updated. It has the method:

  ▼ Update(value)
   This method is called by the Server to pass the value. It is logically a callback function.

- Concrete Observer
  This class subclasses the Observer and adds local storage for the attribute needed, and methods required to perform its client function.

- Notification Handle
  This is a local reference to a registered Observer owned and managed by the Server. It is created when an Observer calls *Subscribe()* and destroyed when it calls *Detach()*. It contains the attribute Object Address, which is the reference to the *Update()* function of the Observer. The set of all Notification Handles is referred to here as the notification list. The notification list is maintained by the Server so that it can call the Update() method of registered Observers when appropriate.

- Episodic Notification Handle
  This is a subclass of Notification Handle. It adds no attributes or methods, but helps define the Notification Handle class hierarchy. Observers registered with this update policy are updated only when the data changes.

- Periodic Notification Handle
  This is a subclass of Notification Handle that is used to notify Observers on a periodic basis. This hardens the Observer in the event of message loss or corruption. This subclass adds the attributes of Period and TimeOfNextUpdate. The Server scans the Periodic Notification Handles periodically. When the notification time has elapsed, the referenced Observer is updated and the TimeOfNextUpdate is recomputed.

Model-View-Controller (MVC) Pattern

Many objects have orthogonal components that accept and respond to user-generated events, maintain the model data, and display this data to the user. If these components are combined into a single monolithic object, they are artificially tightly coupled. This results in more work to maintain these objects and limits the reusability of the components. A very common set of orthogonal components of objects is:

- Model—the data component of the object
- View—how the data values are displayed
- Controller— receives and processes events from the view

This is captured in the classic design pattern Model-View-Controller, popularized by Smalltalk many years ago. For example, an ECG monitor senses and determines heart rate. Heart rate can be viewed in many different ways:

- As an icon—perhaps using different symbols to represent normal rates, bradycardia, and tachycardia, varying the size or color if desired
- As a number—it can be shown as a single string of numeric characters, or a textual array of the last n values, or as a computed average
- As a graphic—pie charts, histograms, rulers can all be used
- As an alarm—used to indicate potential life-threatening conditions
- As sound—a computer-generated voice can announce the heart rate periodically

How it is displayed has little consequence on how the data is acquired or manipulated. By separating these concerns, a small set of collaborating objects work together. Each of these objects is concerned with a different subject matter as it applies to the model. This pattern is applicable in real-time systems that have displays, particularly when data must be both controlled and displayed.

The MVC Pattern, as shown in Figure 6-2, is a simplified and specialized form of the Observer Pattern. This pattern can be implemented using pointers or the publish-subscribe method, as in the more general Observer Pattern. If the objects participating in the pattern are relatively static, then using pointers is the easier implementation. If the objects will change dynamically or the Controller or View objects may not be known to the Model at compile-time, then the subscription approach is preferable.

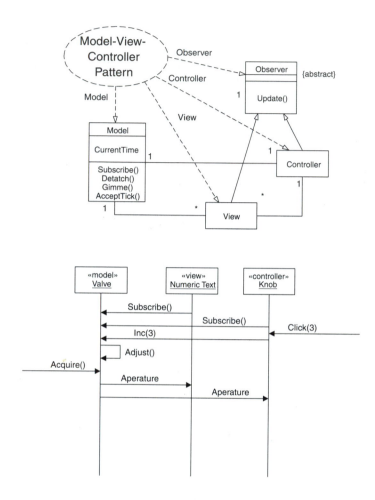

Figure 6-2: *Model-View-Controller Pattern*

The following objects participate in this pattern:

- Model
  The Model object holds the data of interest. It is also known as the *application object*. It updates the view and the controller as necessary, usually using an episodic update policy.

- View
The View object represents a view of the data to the user. The View registers with the Model so that it can be updated automatically when the data changes, or periodically, or both. The View also creates the Controller object because the controller must handle events specific to the kind of view that is currently active.

- Controller
This object receives and responds to events related to the view of the model. It may receive knob turns, mouse moves, key presses, or button clicks. It responds to these events appropriate to the semantics of the model.

The scenario in Figure 6-2 shows a valve that is controlled by a knob with a numeric view of the aperture size on the screen. In this case, the knob sends the events to the model, which changes the position. As a result of the position being changed, the view is updated. This allows the display to track the actual position of the knob in the event that knob messages are lost or corrupted. The knob, receiving the updated aperture value, knows that its message has been received so it need not be resent.

Transaction Pattern

Real-time systems use communication protocols to send and receive critical information, both among internal processors, and with external actors in the environment. Within the same system, different messages may have different levels of criticality, and so may have different requirements for the reliability of message transfer. Further, different media have different reliability as do different environments.

The *transaction* is used when reliable communications is required over unreliable media or when extraordinary reliability is required. For example, suppose the system needs three distinct levels of communications reliability:

1. At Most Once (AMO)—a message is transmitted only once. If the message is lost or corrupted, it is lost. This is used when light-weight transfer is required and the reliability of message transfer is high compared to the probability of message loss.

2. At Least Once (ALO)—a message is transmitted repeatedly until either an explicit acknowledgement is received by the sender or a maximum retry count is exceeded. This is used when the reliability of message transfer is relatively low compared to the probability of message loss, but receipt of the same message multiple times is OK.

3. Exactly Once (EO)—a message is treated as an ALO transaction except that should a message be received more than once due to retries, only the first message instance will be acted upon. This is used when message transfer reliability is relatively low but it is important that a message is acted on only once. *Increment* or *toggle* messages, for example, must only be acted on once.

The Transaction Pattern (Figure 6-3) is particularly suited to real-time systems that use a general communication protocol with a rich grammar. It allows the application designers flexibility in their choice of communications method so that they may optimize for speed or reliability.

The following objects participate in this pattern:

- Source
  The source is the originator of the message.

- Sender
  The sender is the communication protocol engine that marshals and transmits the message. It parses enough of the message to know if it must create a Sender Transaction (Transaction Type is ALO or EO). The Sender also accepts Acknowledgments and searches its list of Send Transactions for matching transactions. If one is found, the Send Transaction is destroyed. Sometimes, an explicit receipt is requested by the Source, in which case the Source is notified. If the acknowledgement does not match any existing Send Transactions, it is quietly discarded.

- Sender Transaction
  This is the transaction created (and destroyed) by the Sender. Each transaction corresponds to a single ALO or EO message. It tracks the number of times the message has been transmitted as well as its retry period. If an acknowledgement specifiying the original MsgID is not received within the retry period, the message is retransmitted and the transmit count is incremented. If the count exceeds Max Retries, the Source is notified.

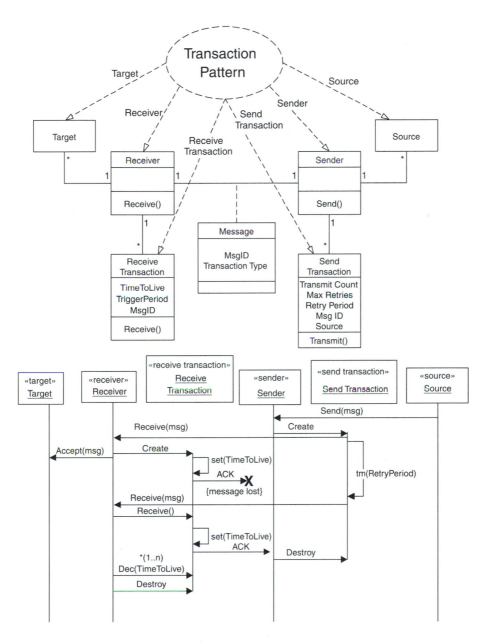

Figure 6-3: *Transaction Pattern*

- Message
  The Message contains the data of interest to the Source and Target, but also metadata as well, such as a MsgID and Transaction Type. The MsgID must be unique within the lifespan of the transaction object so that it uniquely identifies the message. The Transaction Type tells the Sender and Receiver whether or not transaction objects are required for this message.

- Receiver
  This is the communication protocol engine on the receiving side that accepts messages over the communications media, demarshals them, and passes them off to the target objects. If necessary (Transmission Type for the incoming message is EO), the Receiver creates a Receive Transaction. Before creating a new Receive Transaction, the current transaction list is searched for a match. If one is found, it means that the message is a duplicate, and so may be discarded after resetting the transaction's TimeToLive attribute. Periodically, the TimeToLive attribute is decremented. Once it decrements to zero, the Receive Transaction is discarded.

- Receiver Transaction
  This object tracks the receipt of messages using EO semantics. It is created when the Receiver gets a message with the EO transaction type. It has a TimeToLive attribute that is periodically decremented. If another message is received with a matching MsgID, the TimeToLive is reset to its original value, and the duplicate message is quietly discarded. Finally, when the TimeToLive attribute decrements to 0, the Receiver destroys the Receiver Transaction object.

- Target
  This is the ultimate destination of the message sent from the Source.

The AMO semantics are the simplest to implement. To implement AMO semantics, no transaction objects are required. The reliability of the communication medium and protocol are sufficiently high, and the consequences of a lost message are sufficiently low, so that no extra measures are required. Transferring messages using AMO semantics is fast and requires the least computation resources.

ALO semantics require that the Sender object maintain a transaction object until an explicit acknowledgement is received from the receiver. If an acknowledgement is received, the transaction object is destroyed. If no acknowledgement is received within the retry period, then the Sender automatically retransmits the message to the Receiver. If the Sender fails to get the message to the receiver successfully (i.e., the Max Retries count is exceeded), the Source originator is notified so that corrective measures can be initiated.

The Sender cannot distinguish between a loss of the message and a loss of the acknowledgement, so it can happen that the Receiver object receives the message more than once. This is normally not a problem for operations like Set() when setting an absolute value, but becomes problematic when the operation is something like increment(). ALO semantics are incompatible with incremental operations.

EO semantics require transaction objects on both sides. The Sender and Send Transaction objects function exactly as they do to support ALO semantics. What is different it that the Receiver object must now manage Receive Transactions. When the Receiver receives a message with an EO transaction type, it creates a Receive Transaction object and sets its TimeToLive, TriggerPeriod, and MsgID. Once the TimeToLive attribute decrements to zero, the Receive Transaction object is destroyed. If a duplicate message is received before that occurs, the TimeToLive is reset back to its TriggerPeriod. The scenario in Figure 6-3 shows an EO transaction.

Smart Pointer Pattern

The problems with pointers are well known to C and C++ programmers. They fall into several distinct categories:

- Pointers may be used before they are initialized
- Pointers may be used after the memory they point to has been released (dangling pointer)
- Memory may not be released (memory leak)
- Pointer arithmetic may result in erroneous addresses being used
- Target objects may be in different memory addresses

Every experienced C and C++ programmer has not only seen these problems—they have also committed these offenses against Truth, Justice, and the Object Way. These languages make it easy to misuse pointers and hard to find these errors. Even programs that appear to be robust can lead to subtle pointer problems. Just to prove how easy it is, we'll provide some simple examples of memory leaks.

The first example is a procedure that accepts and uses a pointer.

```
void test(int* p) {
    int* a = p;  // line 1
    *p = 17;     // line 2
    delete a;    // line 3
    *p = 99;     // line 4
};
```

What if the parameter p is not initialized? Then lines 2 and 4 will wreak havoc. This is a very common problem in C and C++ programs. What about when line 3 is executed? Then line 4 is in error because p now points to memory that is released. Further, does the caller of *test* know that the memory to which p points has been released? What further use of this pointer is made in the remainder of the program?

Many pointer problems are more subtle. For example, can you identify the problem in the following code?

```
class myClass {
    int a;
public:
    int get(void) { return a; }
    void put(int temp) { a = temp; }
};

class usesMC {
public:
    void test(void) {
       myClass *pMC = new myClass;
       pMC->put(75);
       //
       // function defined outside class
       myTestFunction();
       //
       delete pMC;
    };
};
```

The problem is that if myTestFunction() throws an exception, the myClass object pointed to by pMC will not be deleted. Using raw pointers in C++ for local function objects is always an error whenever the compiler puts in exception handling code. By default, all ANSI compliant C++ compilers must put in exception handling code because 1) they're required to, and 2) the standard C++ libraries throw exceptions. Thus, this ostensibly correct code can lead to memory leaks.

The smart pointer is a common pattern meant to eliminate, or at least mitigate, the myriad problems that stem from the manual use of raw pointers:

- Though raw pointers have no constructor to leave them in a valid initial state, smart pointers can use their constructors to initialize them to NULL or force the precondition that they are constructed pointing to a valid target object.

- Raw pointers have no destructor and so may not deallocate memory if they suddenly go out of scope, but smart pointers determine whether or not it is appropriate to deallocate memory when they go out of scope and call the delete operator.

- A raw pointer to a deleted object still holds the address of the memory where the object used to be (and hence can be used to reference that memory illegally), but smart pointers can detect that condition automatically and refuse access.

The simplicity of the smart pointer pattern shown in Figure 6-4 belies its usefulness. Although the mechanism is so simple, significant functionality is hidden within the detailed design of the smart pointer class.

6.2.2 Reuse Patterns

The patterns in this section use encapsulation and abstraction to improve reuse of classes. They may also provide other advantages as well, but their primary purpose is to separate and encapsulate different areas of concern within an object into separate objects.

Container Pattern

Analysis models the "what" of a system—what is it, what are the fundamental concepts involved, and what are the important relations and associations among them. Design specifies the "how" of all the unspec-

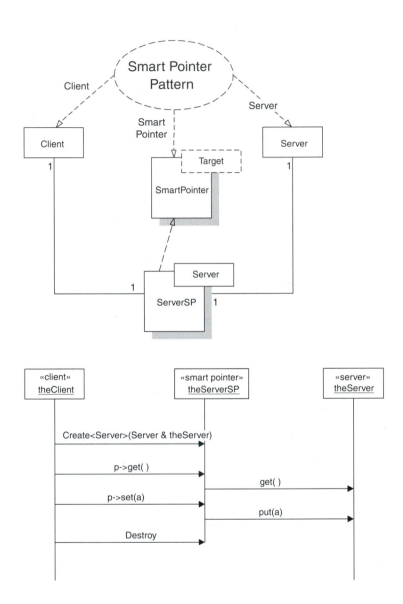

Figure 6-4: *Smart Pointer Pattern*

ified portions of the system. One of the important "hows" of design is how each and every object-object message will be implemented; is it a function call, an OS mail message, a bus message, or something even more exotic? Another important "how" is the resolution of associations with multivalued roles.

When one object has a 1-to-many association, the question arises as to the exact mechanism the 1 class will use to access the many objects. One solution is to build features into the 1 class to manage the set of contained objects. These facilities typically manifest themselves as operations such as add(), remove(), first(), next(), last(), and find(). Often the semantics of the association dictate elaborate operations, such as maintaining the set of objects in a specific order or balancing the tree. Building these features into each and every class that must maintain a 1-to-many association is repugnant for several reasons, outlined in Section 6.1. The common solution to these problems is to insert a container object (a.k.a. *collection object*) between the 1 and the many.

Adding a container object to manage the aggregated objects doesn't solve the entire problem because often the container must be accessed from several different clients. If the container itself keeps track of the client position, then it will become confused in a multiclient environment. To get around this, *iterators* are used in conjunction with the containers. An iterator keeps track of where the client is in the container. Different clients use different iterators so that the separate concerns of managing the collection and tracking position within the container are abstracted away from each other. A single client may use several different iterators. The Standard Template Library (STL), a part of the ANSI C++ standard, provides many different containers with a variety of iterators, such as *first, last,* and so on.

Like the previous pattern, the Container Pattern is very simple, although the container itself may be quite complex internally (see Figure 6-5). This pattern will be elaborated more in the next pattern.

The following objects participate in the Container Pattern:

- Container
  The container manages the collection and provides accessor operations.

- Iterator
  The iterator acts like a smart pointer and mediates access to the parts for the client. An iterator query access, such as first() or next(),

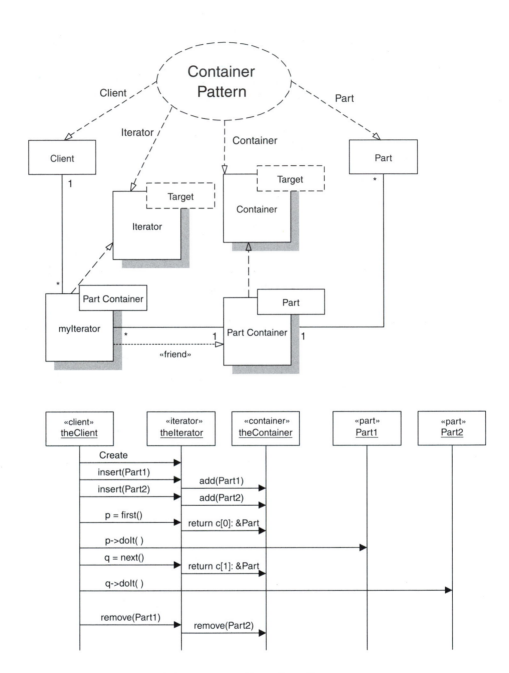

Figure 6-5: *Container Pattern*

typically returns a pointer to a Part object. Insertion and deletion parts may also be mediated through the iterator.

- Client
  The Client is the object needing access to the Part objects managed by the Container.

- Part
  The Part objects are the objects managed by the container. In a system managing bank accounts, this might be individual accounts or transactions within those accounts.

Interface Pattern

In languages like C++, the interface provided by a class is bound tightly to its implementation. As discussed previously, strictly speaking the interface of an object is its *type* and the implementation specification is its *class.* C++ mixes these metaphors so that most of the time the difference is unnoticeable. Unfortunately, binding the type and class together limits the reusability of a class. There are a number of cases in which explicit separation of interface and implementation is useful.

First, a common implementation may be appropriate for a variety of uses. If a class could provide different interfaces, a single underlying implementation could meet several needs. For example, many common computer science structures, such as trees, queues, and stacks, can actually use a single underlying implementation, such as a linked list. The relatively complex innards of the common implementation can be used in different ways to implement the desired behavior, even though the ultimate clients are clueless as to what happens behind the scenes.

Second, by separating an interface, it becomes easier to change an implementation or add a new and different interface. As in our container example in the previous paragraph, it becomes a simple matter to add a new container (for example, an extensible vector) by creating an interface that provides the correct services to the client but implements those services in terms of primitive operations of existing containers.

Last, it happens sometimes that you want different levels of access into the internals of an object. Different interfaces can be constructed to provided different levels of access for different client objects and environments. For example, you might want classes providing services to users to be able to use only a subset of all operations, a different set provided in service mode, and a much different set in remote debugging mode.

The Interface Pattern (a.k.a., the Adapter Pattern) solves all of these problems. It is a very simple pattern but is so common that UML actually provides the stereotype «type» in the language specification.

The scenario shown in Figure 6-6 illustrates how the Interface Pattern separates the interface from its implementation. The client object needs a stack-like container and so associates to the myStack object. The myStack object itself does not directly manage the collection. Instead, myStack associates to a linked list object that actually manages the collection. The myStack provides the proper interface to the client (such as push() and pop()) but implements this interface by using the operations provided by the linked list class (such as insertAtEnd(), getLast(), and deleteLast()). Thus, given a linked list, it is a simple matter to provide a stack or queue.

Policy Pattern

Many times classes are structurally similar or even identical, but differ in terms of how they operate internally. For example, it is possible that a class looks the same but makes different time/space/complexity/safety/reliability optimization choices. The selection of different algorithms to implement the same black box behavior is called a *policy*. Policies can be abstracted away from the main class to simplify the interface, improve reuse, and even allow dynamic choices of policies based on operating condition or state.

The objects participating in the Policy Pattern are:

- Client—Uses the services and operations of the Context object.
- Context—Provides services to the Client and a context for the Policy object. It will invoke the services of the Policy object necessary to implement the policy within its context.
- Abstract Policy—Provides a virtual interface to the Concrete Policy object for the Context Object.
- Concrete Policy—Implements the algorithm and services for the selected policy.

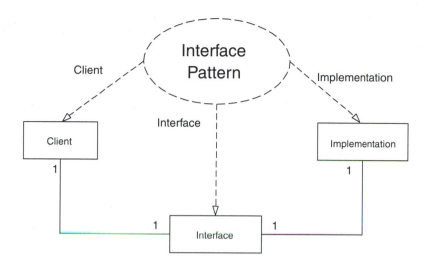

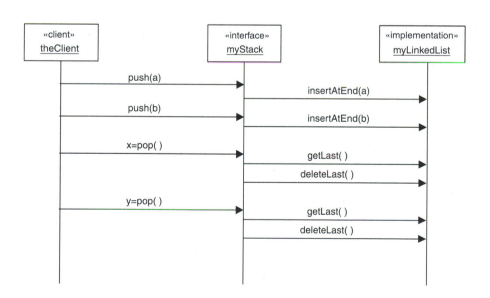

Figure 6-6: *Interface Pattern*

The scenario in Figure 6-7 shows a typical use of a Policy Pattern in safety-critical applications. A client associates with the Heart Rate Server to get patient information. If this information is corrupted (and EMI in an operating room can be extremely high), then patient safety may be compromised. To improve safety, the Heart Rate Server uses a safety policy to detect corruption. Such policy may use feedback error detection schemes, such as checksums, cyclic redundancy checks, and one's complement storage or feedforward error correction, such as triple redundancy or Hamming codes. A CRC error detection policy is used in the scenario in Figure 6-7.

This particular scenario shows a Heart Rate Source object updating the Heart Rate Proxy. When new data is received from the Heart Rate Source, the Heart Rate Proxy requests that the CRC Policy object compute a CRC on the data. theClient object gets the heart rate from the Heart Rate Proxy via its get() operation. The Heart Rate Proxy's get() operation checks the data against the CRC stored in the CRC Policy object via the latter's check() member function. If it returns OK, then the heart rate is returned to the client. If it returns BAD, then the Heart Rate Proxy requests a new value from the Heart Rate Source, recomputes the CRC and then checks the CRC. If this now works, then the heart rate is returned. If it still fails (not shown in the scenario), the Heart Rate Proxy could retry or throw an exception to theClient.

Rendezvous Pattern

A rendezvous refers to the synchronization of concurrent tasks. In fact, the use of a mutual exclusion semaphore is also called a *unilateral rendezvous*. The more common use of the term rendezvous refers to the synchronization of more than one task. For example, the rendezvous of more than two tasks is referred to as a bilateral rendezvous.

The problem of task synchronization occurs in many real-time systems. Formally speaking, a rendezvous is a means for enforcing the preconditional invariants of both participant tasks. Consider the state model in Figure 6-8.

Figure 6-8 shows a trilateral rendezvous in which three threads (shown as orthogonal state components) must synchronize. One thread is involved in the preparation of the vat to be used to mix the reagents for the desired reaction. The other two threads prepare the reagents— one that must be heated and one that must be cooled. Only when all

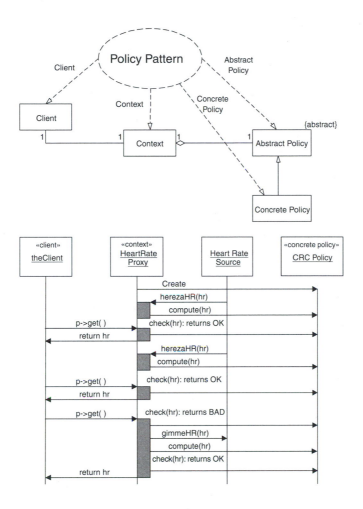

Figure 6-7: *Policy Pattern*

three orthogonal state components have completed their preparatory activities are the components allowed to be mixed together (mixing details are not shown).

Synchronization of threads can be solved with the Rendezvous Pattern, as shown in Figure 6-9.

This pattern consists of a coordinating passive object (called the rendezvous object), clients that must synchronize, and mutex blocking

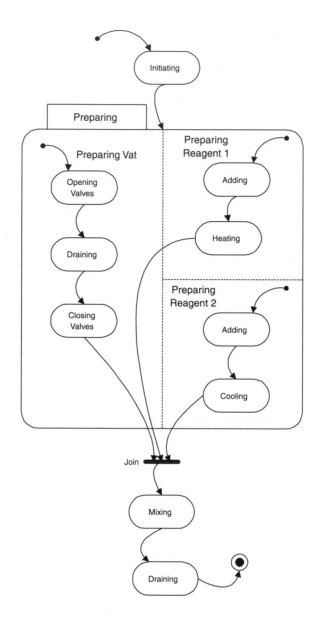

Figure 6-8: *Trilateral Rendezvous Problem*

semaphores. Blocking semaphores are used to force the threads to wait until all preconditions are met. More elaborate behavior can be implemented using timed or balking semaphores, if desired.

The following objects participate in this pattern:

- Rendezvous Object

  The Rendezvous object coordinates the synchronization process and glues the mutex semaphores to client thread objects. Each Rendezvous object typically handles a single synchronization point. Each participant client thread has an association with the Rendezvous so that it can call its wait() operation. The Rendezvous handles the coordination of the Lock objects and identifies when all Locks are in their locked state. When this is true, all locks are signaled that they may release their captured threads and enter their unlocked state.

- Lock

  The Lock objects have two states—locked and unlocked (the default initial state). When a client thread calls the wait() operation on the Rendezvous, it uses the ObjectID to select the appropriate lock and change its state. Each client has its own lock, created when the Rendezvous is initially created. Locks may be implemented in several ways. The most common are the busy-wait and the sleep-wait. In the busy-wait approach, the lock() operation loops until the synchronizing condition (all required threads are waiting) is met. Care must be taken with this approach that the OS will allow the other threads to run while the current client thread loops. The sleep-wait solution puts the client thread to sleep, pending on an OS event. This OS event is issued by the Rendezvous object when the preconditions are satisfied.

- Thread

  The Thread object in the pattern is a normal object that operates within an asynchronous thread. It calls the Rendezvous object's wait() method and remains blocked until the Lock allows its lock() call to complete and returns control back to the Thread object.

The scenario shows a typical bilateral rendezvous. The rendezvous object is created knowing the number of objects required to meet the precondition and their Object IDs. The thread objects are some objects

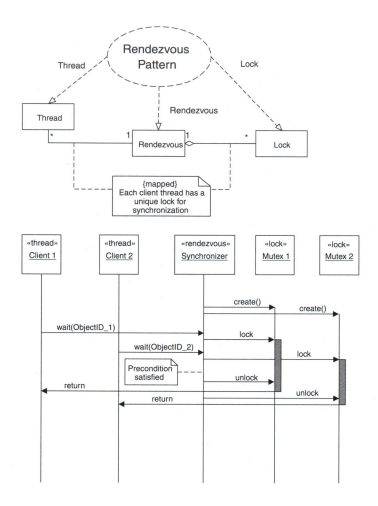

Figure 6-9: *Rendezvous Pattern*

executing within separate OS threads that associate with the (passive) rendezvous object. As each client thread becomes ready to synchronize, it sends a wait() message to the rendezvous object, identifying itself with its Object ID. The Rendezvous object registers each pending client in a separate Lock created for this purpose. Once all clients have registered with the Rendezvous object, the precondition is satisfied and the threads may now continue.

6.2.3 State Behavior Patterns

There are many different ways to implement state machines using programming language constructs. The simplest is to use nested conditional statements something like this:

```
switch(state) {
case state1:    // we're in state 1, so process events
   switch(event) {
      case ev1:    action1( );
                   action2( );
                   state = state2;
                   break;
      case ev2:    action3( );
                   state = state3;
                   break;
   }; // switch event

   case state2:
      switch(event) {
      case ev3:    action4( );
                   action5( );
                   state = state1;
   };
}; // switch(state)
```

This approach has the advantage that it is conceptually simple, but can become unmanageably complex when applied to large state machines. Additionally, switch-case statements may be searched so that handling transitions can be an O(n) process, where n is the product of the number of states and the number of events handled in each state.

State patterns are design approaches meant to simplify or optimize performance of large state machines. In many real-time systems, performance is a critical issue even though the state machines are complex. For example, a cardiac pacemaker may be thought of as a battery with some hardware attached. When the battery is exhausted, the pacemaker must be surgically removed and discarded. If the software requires only a few additional CPU instructions on each event to handle dispatching that event, the pacemaker may require replacement months or years earlier (bringing a whole new meaning to the term "End of Life"). A more optimal design strategy is required in such cases.

The last two patterns in this chapter deal with patterns for the efficient implementation of state machines. The State Pattern simplifies the implementation by identifying long-term persistent states and making those transitions heavier weight in order to make the transitions within those long-term persistent states lighter weight. The State Table Pattern uses a table-driven approach with good performance characteristics for large machines with many states and transitions.

State Pattern

Many systems spend most of their time in only a few states. For such systems, it is more efficient to have a heavy-weight process for transitioning to the less-used state if it can make the more-used state transitions lighter weight. The state model shown in Figure 6-10 illustrates this problem.

A cardiac pacemaker is programmed by the physician into a pacing mode after it is implanted in the patient's chest. In a VVI pacing mode, the ventricle is paced (the first V), the ventricle is sensed (the second V) and when an intrinsic beat is sensed, pacing is inhibited (the I). The patient leaves the office with a pacemaker in this mode and may return on a yearly or biyearly basis. Since only the doctor can reprogram the pacemaker[4], the transitions between available pacing modes are very infrequent. However, it is very important that within a pacing mode, the state transitions be very lightweight to reduce battery drain.

The participants in the State Pattern (see Figure 6-11) are as follows.

- Context
  The Context is a composite object that manages the state behavior. It accepts the transitions and either processes the transition directly (for heavy-weight transitions) or dispatches it to the currently active State object.

- Abstract State
  The Abstract State class defines the structure for a state class. This includes the events accepted and the actions executed. As you might guess, this class is never directly instantiated.

---

[4] Now *there's* an after-market niche for the Home Shopping Network—*"Hot date tonight? Not sure if you're up to it? Now you can be! Reprogram your pacemaker in the privacy of your own home!"*

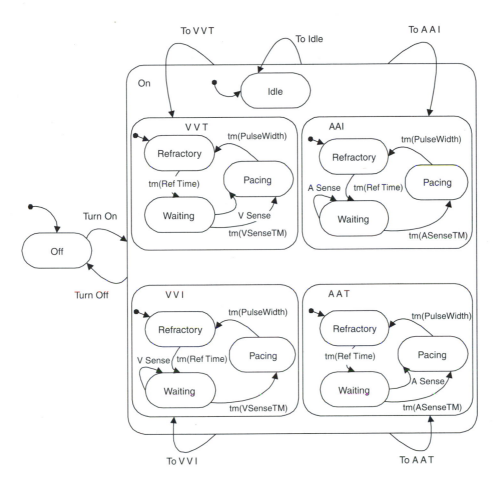

Figure 6-10: *Pacemaker State Machine Example*

- Concrete State
  The Concrete State objects implement a state—each corresponds to a single heavy-weight state. Frequently, Concrete States themselves have substates, and so directly and clearly map to the nested hierarchical states found in statecharts. Concrete States implement superstates and the substates within the Concrete States are implemented using a lighter-weight mechanism, such as nested switch-case statements or state tables (see the State Table Pattern, on page 287).

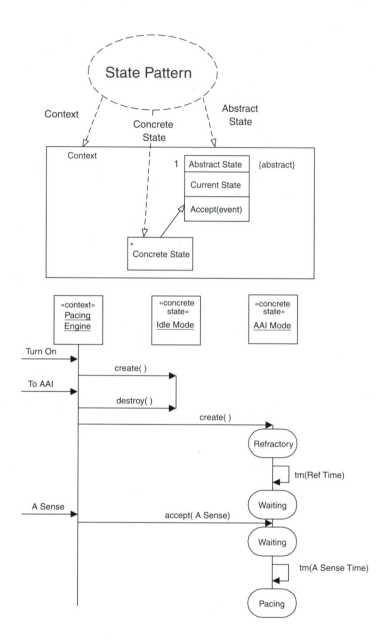

Figure 6-11: *State Pattern*

The scenario shows how the Context handles events in two distinct fashions. Some events cause the currently active Concrete State to change. If the event is not one of those, then it is dispatched to the Concrete State for processing. If the event is handled by the Concrete State, then it may be quietly discarded or cause an exception to be thrown, whichever is semantically appropriate in your system. Self-caused events, such as the timeouts shown in the scenario, are usually handled directly by the active state object.

The scenario uses a modified sequence chart syntax, which permits the states of an object to be shown in the object line in sequence with the events. This expanded syntax isn't strict UML notation, but is useful because it clearly shows the relationship between the scenario and the state model, and is supported by some UML-compliant CASE tools.

State Table Pattern

The State Table Pattern provides a simple mechanism for managing state machines with an efficiency of $O(c)$, where c is a constant. This is a preferred mechanism for very large state spaces because the time to handle a transition is a constant (not including the time to execute actions associated with state entry or exit, or the transition itself). Another advantage is that this pattern maps directly to tabular state specifications, such as those used to develop many safety-critical systems.

The State Table pattern hinges upon the state table. This structure typically is implemented as an n x m array, where n is the number of states and m is the number of transitions. Each cell contains a single pointer to a Transition object that handles the event with an *accept* operation. The operation returns the resulting state. Both events and states are represented as an enumerated type. These enumerated types are used as indices into the table to optimize performance. Because this pattern is specifically designed to execute fast, it has a relatively high initialization cost, but execution cost is low.

The State Table Pattern in Figure 6-12 is relatively complex (in this case, due to the tight coupling of the classes involved), although it contains only the following elements:

- Context
  This is the class for which the state table is managing the state machine. It also contains all the actions to be executed, including the

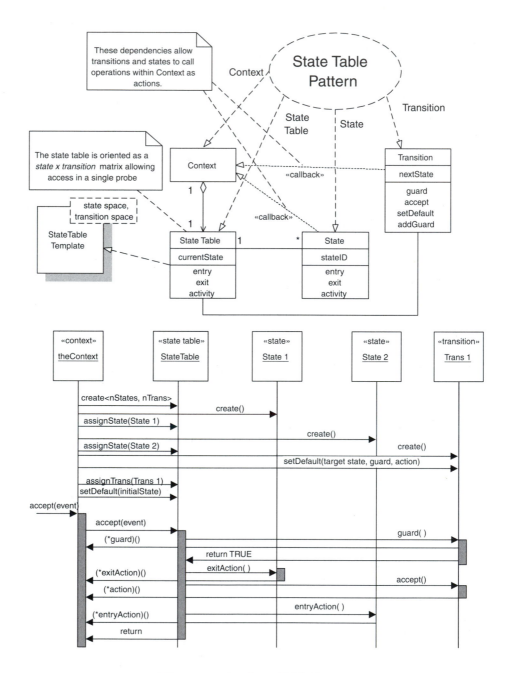

Figure 6-12: *State Table Pattern*

transition actions and the state entry, exit, and activity actions. Context creates the state and transition objects and then passes responsibility for their management over to the State Table.

- State Table Template
  A template or generic that is refined based on the number of states and transitions.

- State Table
  The State Table is basically a nState x nTransition matrix of pointers to state transitions, and a vector of nStates, with some supporting methods, such as

  ▾ accept—accepts an incoming event and processes it based on the current state by indexing into the array. If the matrix cell is empty, the event is discarded, otherwise the guard (if any) is evaluated. If the guard evaluates to TRUE, then the current state's exit action is executed, followed by the transition's action and the new state's entry action.

  ▾ setDefault—sets the default initial state.

  ▾ assignState—accepts state objects created by the Context.

  ▾ assignTrans—accepts transition objects created by the Context.

  ▾ destructor—destroys state and transition objects originally created by the Context.

- State
  State objects contain a state ID (so it can be queried if necessary) and action statements. These action statements are all implemented using function pointers pointing back to operations defined within the Context. This is done because, almost always, actions to be executed must be defined within the Context and must manipulate its member variables. The following behaviors are defined for State Objects:

  ▾ idState—identifies the state using an integer or enumeration value.

  ▾ entryAction—action to be executed when the state is entered.

  ▾ exitAction—action to be executed when the state is executed.

  ▾ doActivitiy—action to be executed as long as state is active.

- Transition

  In the simplest case, a transition has a single guard (implemented as a function pointer to an operation defined within the Context that returns a Boolean), a single action (similar to State object actions), and a single target state to be entered when the transition is taken. However, to handle conditional connectors, Transitions must handle multiple guards, each with a separate associated action and target state. Thus, this class contains the following elements:

  ▼ nGuard—identifies the number of conditions to be handled. If this is 0, then there are no branching conditions.

  ▼ lastTrueGuard—for efficiency reasons, this attribute identifies the index of the last guard that evaluated to TRUE. It is normally maintained to a testable sentinel value indicating NOT TESTED.

  ▼ setDefault—when there are no branches, this operation sets the guard and action operations to point to the specified operations defined within the Context.

  ▼ addGuard—when there are conditional branches, this operation sets a {guard, action, target state} triad, so that if the guard evaluates to TRUE, its corresponding action will be executed, and its corresponding target state will be entered.

  ▼ guard—executes the guards in order until one evaluates to TRUE or it runs out of guards. The attribute lastTrueGuard is set to the first guard evaluating to TRUE.

  ▼ accept—assumes that the guard has been passed. It uses the lastTrueGuard attribute to identify the guard that evaluated to TRUE and then executes its associated action. It returns the new target state and resets lastTrueGuard back to its sentinel value.

The scenario in Figure 6-12 illustrates how the pattern works showing details that are not immediately apparent from the pattern's class diagram. This scenario shows the creation of a state machine with only two states and a single transition.

The code to implement this pattern in C++ is straightforward, if somewhat lengthy:

```
//
// State Table pattern
//

typedef void (*fPtr)();
#define FNULL (fPtr)0
typedef int (*fIntPtr)();
#define FINULL (fIntPtr)0
class stObject {
protected:
   const int theState;
   fPtr pEntry, pExit, pActivity;
public:
   stObject(int stateName, fPtr ptEntry=FNULL, fPtr
      ptExit=FNULL,
      fPtr ptAct=FNULL):theState(stateName),
      pEntry(ptEntry),
      pExit(ptExit), pActivity(ptAct){ };
   int idState(void) { return theState; }; // query
   void entryAction(void) { if (pEntry) (*pEntry)();
   };
   void exitAction(void) { if (pExit) (*pExit)(); };
   void doActivity(void) { if (pActivity)
   (*pActivity)(); };
}; // stObject

typedef stObject* pStObject;

#define MAXGUARDS 5
class trObject {
protected:
   int nGuards;
   // guard that passed. Set to -1 when fails.
   int lastTrueGuard;
   // next state when transition taken
   int targetState[MAXGUARDS];
   // pGuard[0] is intentionally blank
   fIntPtr pGuard[MAXGUARDS];
   // pAction[0] is "default" (no guards)
   fPtr pAction[MAXGUARDS];
public:
   trObject(void):nGuards(0), lastTrueGuard(-1){
      for (int j=0; j=0; j<MAXGUARDS; j++) {
      pGuard[j]=FINULL;
      pAction[j]=FNULL;
```

```
      targetState[j] = 0;
      };
   };

   // the default targetstate and action are only
   // valid
   // when there are no guards
   void setDefault(int tState, fPtr ptAction) {
      targetState[0] = tState;
      pAction[0] = ptAction;
   };

   int addGuard(int tState, fIntPtr ptGuard,
      fPtr ptAction) {
      if (nGuards >= MAXGUARDS-1)
         throw "Max Guards Exceeded";
      nGuards++;
      targetState[nGuards] = tState;
      pGuard[nGuards] = ptGuard;
      pAction[nGuards] = ptAction;
      return nGuards;
   };

   int guard(void) {
      // if there are no guards, return TRUE
      if (nGuards == 0) {
         lastTrueGuard = 0;
         return 1; // return TRUE if there is no guard
         }
      else {
         for (int j=1; j<nGuards; j++)
         if (pGuard[j]) {
            lastTrueGuard = j;
            return 1;
         };
      };
      lastTrueGuard = -1;
      // return FALSE if no guard conditions met
      return 0;
   };

   // accept(...)
   // takes event, assumes the guard is already
   // checked and has set
   // lastTrueGuard as a result
   // returns new state
```

```cpp
   int accept(void) {
   // last time it evaluated to TRUE
   if (lastTrueGuard >= 0) {
      int temp = lastTrueGuard;
      lastTrueGuard = -1; // reset to not passed
      // execute the transition action
       (*pAction[temp])();
      return targetState[temp]; // new state entry
      // actions are performed by caller
      }

   else
      return 0; // no target state
   }; // accept(...)
}; // trObject


typedef trObject* pTrObject;


template <int nS, int nE> class stateTable {
protected:
   pTrObject trTable [nS][nE];
   pStObject stTable[nS];
   int currentState;

   int inEventRange(int checkEvent) {
      return (checkEvent>0 && checkEvent< nE);
   };

   int inStateRange(int checkState) {
      return (checkState>=0 && checkState<nS);
   };

   int validState(int checkState) {
      return (inStateRange(checkState) &&
            (stTable[checkState] != (pStObject)0));
   };

   int handledEvent(int eventNum) {
      return (inEventRange(eventNum) &&
            trTable[currentState][eventNum] !=
            (pTrObject)0);
   };
```

```
public:
   // constructor
   stateTable(void) {
      for (int j=0; j<nS; j++)
            for (int k=0; k<nE; k++)
               trTable[j][k] = (pTrObject)0;
            stTable[j] = (pStObject)0;
      }; // for j
   }; // constructor


   // assignTrans allows the specification of a
   // transition object
   // to a table cell
   void assignTrans(int stateNum, int eventNum,
         pTrObject ptr) {
      if (inStateRange(stateNum))
         if (inEventRange(eventNum))
            trTable[stateNum][eventNum] = ptr;
            else
               throw "Invalid event";
      else
               throw "Invalid state";
   }; // assignTrans


   // assignState allows the build up of the
   stateTable
   void assignState(int stateNum, pStObject pS) {
      if (inStateRange(stateNum))
      stTable[stateNum] = pS;
else
   throw "Invalid state";
}; // assignState


// setDefault sets up the default state. This must be
// called after assign has been called repeatedly to
set up the table.
int setDefault(int initialState) {
   if (validState(initialState)) {
      currentState = initialState;
      stTable[initialState]->entryAction( );
      }
   else
      throw "Invalid State";
   return currentState;
```

```
}; // setDefault

// accept accepts and processes an event.
// returns the new current state
// handling consists of
// 1. performing current state exit actions
// 2. performing transition actions
// 3. setting current state to the new state
// 4. executing new state current entry actions
int accept(int event) {
    int newState;
    // check that we are in a valid state
    if (validState(currentState)) {
        if (handledEvent(event)) {
            if (trTable[currentState][event]
            ->guard()) {
                stTable[currentState]->exitAction();
                newState = trTable[currentState][event]
                ->accept();
                if (validState(newState)) {
                    currentState = newState;
                    stTable[currentState]->entryAction( );
                    }
                else
                    throw "Invalid target state";
            }; // end if guard passes
        } // if (handledEvent(...))
        else // unhandled event
            return currentState;
        }
    else
        throw "State not initialized";
    return currentState;
}; // accept

~stateTable(void) {
    for (int j=0; j<nS; j++) {
        for (int k=0; k<nE; k++)
            delete trTable[j][k];
        delete stTable[j];
        };
    }; // destructor
}; // class stateTable
```

The main class is stateTable (a template, actually). Internally, it contains two arrays: trTable, a two-dimensional array of pointers to trObjects (i.e., transition objects), arranged as a state x event matrix, and stTable, a one-dimensional array of pointers to stObjects (i.e., state objects). Construction of the tables is a multistep process. The constructor initializes the tables to null pointers. Subsequent calls to assignTrans and assignState populate the tables with pointers to existing trObject and stObject objects. Once the tables have been fully initialized, the default state is specified with a call to setDefault. It is now ready to process events via calls to its accept operation.

A Context class is a domain class that has state behavior. Consider the simple communications class with the state machine shown in Figure 6-13. Although relatively simple, this state machine does include transition actions, state entry actions, default states, and conditional connectors. The C++ code for this domain class follows:

```cpp
//// sample context class (see diagram)//
enum eEvent{evNone, evByteReceived1, evByteReceived2,
evEndOfMsg,
    evDoneValidating, evMsgReady, evDoneTransmittingByte,
    evDoneMarshalling, evEnd};enum eState {esNone, esIdle,
    esByteIncoming, esValidating, esMarshalling,
    esTransmitting, esEnd};

#define MAXLENGTH 255

class commGnome {
protected:
    stateTable<evEnd, esEnd> myStateSpace;

    // members variables & functions used for
    communications
    static char ACK[];
    static char NAK[];
    static int msgLength;
    static char msg[MAXLENGTH];
    // reads the next byte from the hw
    static char readByte(void);
    static int isValid(void); // validates msg
    // does something with incoming msg
    static void process(char* msg);
    // sends the msg static int bytesSent;
    static send(char* msg);
    // write a byte to the transmitter
    static writeByte(char b);
```

```
static void addCRC(void);

// define all actions (void return, no parameters);
// static is required to use the member function
// pointers as generic function pointers
static void enableTransmitter(void);
static void disableTransmitter(void);
static void fByteReceived1(void) {
   msgLength = 1;
   msg[msgLength] = readByte();
   };
```

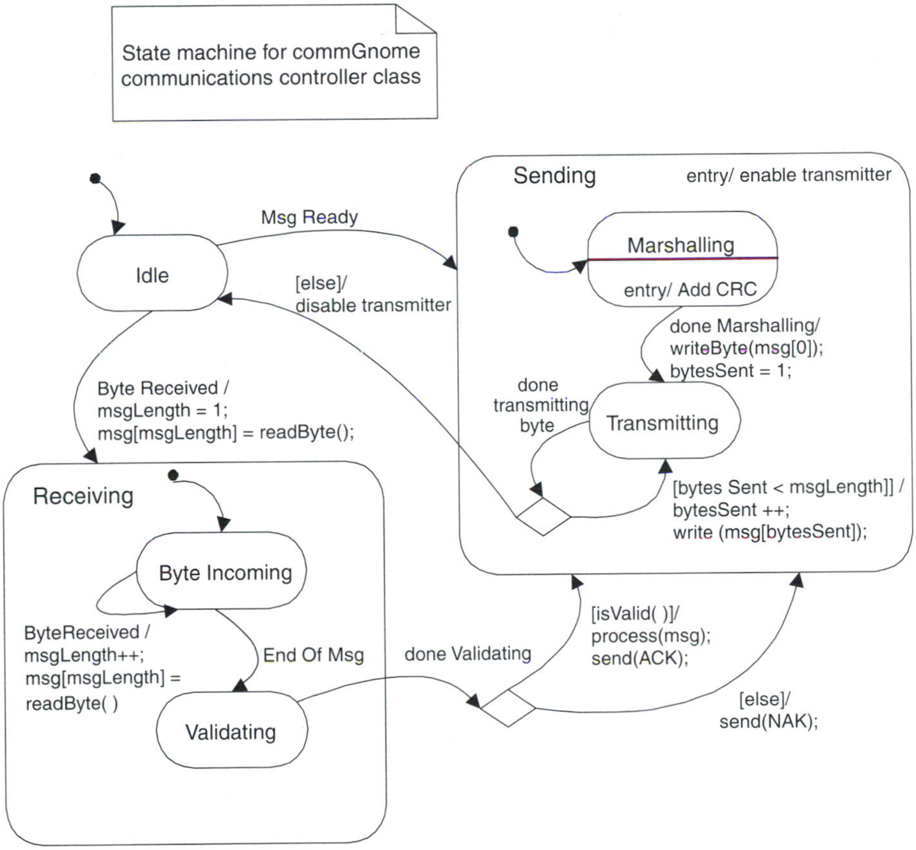

Figure 6-13: *Example for State Table Pattern*

```
static void fByteReceived2(void) {
   msgLength++;
   msg[msgLength] = readByte();
   };

static int doneV1_guard(void) {
   return isValid( );
   };

static void doneV1_action(void) {
   process(msg);
   send(ACK);
   };

static int doneV2_guard(void) {
   return 1;       // since it's an else,
                   // assume other condition checked
                   // first
   };

static void doneV2_action(void) {
   send(NAK);
   };

static void fDoneMarshalling(void) {
   writeByte(msg[0]);
   bytesSent = 1;
   };

static int doneTr1_guard(void) {
   return bytesSent < msgLength;
   };

static void doneTr1_action(void){
   writeByte(bytesSent);
   bytesSent++;
   };

// is an [else] guard
static int doneTr2_guard(void) {
   return 1;
   };

static void doneTr2_action(void) {
   disableTransmitter();
   };
```

```
public:
    //
    // create all state objects for the state machine
    //
    void createStates(void) {
        pStObject pS;
        fPtr p1;
        pS = new stObject(esIdle);
        myStateSpace.assignState(esIdle, pS);
        pS = new stObject(esByteIncoming);
        myStateSpace.assignState(esByteIncoming, pS);
        pS = new stObject(esValidating);
        myStateSpace.assignState(esValidating, pS);

        // the following states have entry actions
        p1 = enableTransmitter;
        pS = new stObject(esMarshalling, p1);
        myStateSpace.assignState(esMarshalling, pS);

        p1 = addCRC;
        pS = new stObject(esTransmitting, p1);
        myStateSpace.assignState(esTransmitting, pS);
        }; // createStates

    //
    // create all transition objects for the state
    // machine
    void createTrans(void) {
        pTrObject pT;
        fPtr pF;
        fIntPtr pFi;

        // evByteReceived1
        pF = fByteReceived1;
        pT = new trObject();
        // target state, action
        pT->setDefault(esByteIncoming, pF);
        myStateSpace.assignTrans(esIdle,
            evByteReceived1, pT);

        // evByteReceived2
        pF = fByteReceived2;
        pT = new trObject();
        pT->setDefault(esByteIncoming, pF);
        myStateSpace.assignTrans(esByteIncoming,
            evByteReceived2, pT);
```

```
// evEndOfMsg
pT = new trObject();
pT->setDefault(esValidating, FNULL);
myStateSpace.assignTrans(esByteIncoming,
    evEndOfMsg, pT);

// evDoneValidating conditional w/ 2 guards
// they will be checked in order, so the [else]
// guard is last
pT = new trObject();
pFi = doneV1_guard;
pF = doneV1_action;
pT->addGuard(esMarshalling, pFi, pF);
pFi = doneV2_guard;
pF = doneV2_action;
pT->addGuard(esMarshalling, pFi, pF);
myStateSpace.assignTrans(esValidating,
    evDoneValidating, pT);

// evMsgReady
pT = new trObject();
pF = enableTransmitter;
pT->setDefault(esMarshalling, pF);
myStateSpace.assignTrans(esByteIncoming,
    evEndOfMsg, pT);

// evDoneMarshalling
pF = fDoneMarshalling;
pT = new trObject();
pT->setDefault(esTransmitting, pF);
myStateSpace.assignTrans(esMarshalling,
    evDoneTransmittingByte, pT);

// evDoneTransmittingByte conditional with 2
// guards
pT = new trObject();
pFi = doneTr1_guard;
pF = doneTr1_action;
pT->addGuard(esTransmitting, pFi, pF);
pFi = doneTr2_guard;
pF = doneTr2_action;
pT->addGuard(esIdle, pFi, pF);
myStateSpace.assignTrans(esValidating,
    evDoneValidating, pT);
```

```
   }; // createTrans

   // construct state space table here
   commGnome(void) {
      createStates();
      createTrans();
   }; // constructor

   void accept(int eventNum) {
      myStateSpace.accept(eventNum);
      };

   }; // commGnome

   // initialize commGnome static members
   char commGnome::ACK[] = "YUP";
   char commGnome::NAK[] = "NAH";

   void main(void) {

      commGnome theGnome;

      // do stuff with commGnome
      // ...
   };
```

The action statements are implemented as C++ static member functions so that they can be called using simple function pointers (yet another C++ idiosyncrasy).

6.3 Summary

Mechanistic design is concerned with specifying the details of inter-object collaboration. Groups of objects acting together to achieve a common goal are referred to as *mechanisms*. Mechanistic design takes the collaborative groups of objects identified in analysis and adds design-level objects to facilitate and direct their implementation. For example, containers and iterators are added to manage associations consisting of multiple objects. Smart pointer objects glue associations together in such a way as to eliminate memory leaks and inappropriate pointer dereferencing. Policy objects abstract away strategies and algorithms from their context so that they can be easily modified or replaced, even while the system executes.

Many of the objects added during mechanistic design reappear in many designs because they solve problems common to many systems. These collaborations are reified into mechanistic design patterns. These patterns are templates of object interaction consisting of a problem, context, and a structural solution. The reification of the patterns allows them to be cataloged and studied systematically, allowing them to be reused in future projects. This chapter presented a number of patterns useful in mechanistic design. If interested, you are invited to explore the references for more patterns.

The final chapter in this book will discuss the detailed design of object-oriented systems in a real-time context. Detailed design is concerned with the implementation of data structures and algorithms within the scope of a single class. Space and time complexity tradeoffs are made during detailed design to achieve the performance requirements specified for your system.

6.4 References

[1] Gamma, Erich, Richard Helm, Ralph Johnson, and John Vlissides, *Design Patterns: Elements of Reusable Software*. Reading, MA: Addison Wesley Longman, 1995.

[2] Buschmann, Frank, Regine Meunier, Hans Rohnert, Peter Sommerlad, Michael Stal, *A System of Patterns: Pattern-Oriented Software Architecture*. Chichester: John Wiley & Sons, 1996.

[3] Coplien, James and Douglas Schmidt, ed., *Pattern Languages of Program Design*. Reading, MA: Addison Wesley Longman, 1995.

[4] Vlissides, John, James Coplien and Norman Kerth, ed., *Pattern Languages of Program Design 2*. Reading, MA: Addison Wesley Longman, 1996.

Chapter 7

Detailed Design

In the preceding chapters, we've seen how architectural design defines the largest scale strategic design decisions and mechanistic design specifics exactly how groups of objects collaborate together. Now it is time to peer inside the objects themselves and design their internal structure. Detailed design specifies details such as the storage format used for attributes, how associations are implemented, the set of operations the object provides, the selection of internal algorithms, and the specification of exception handling within the object.

7.1 What Is Detailed Design?

You're just about at the point where you can actually run code on that pile of wires and chips cluttering up your Geekosphere,[1] so if you're like me, you're getting pretty excited (see [4] for a detailed explanation of the phenomenon). If architectural design is deciding which planet to fly to and mechanistic design is the flight path to the selected planet, then detailed design is deciding on which rock you want to eat your

---

[1] Geekosphere (n): the area surrounding one's computer (*Jargon Watch,* Hardwired, 1997).

"tube of salami" sandwich once you arrive.[2] It is the smallest level of decomposition before you start pounding code.

The fundamental unit of decomposition in object-oriented systems is the *object*. As we have seen, it is a natural unit from which systems can be specified and implemented. We have also seen that it is necessary but insufficient for large-scale design. Mechanistic design deals with mechanisms (groups of collaborating objects) and architectural design is connected with an even larger scale—domains, tasks, and subsystems. At the root of it all remains the object itself, the atom from which the complex chemistry of systems is built.

Although most objects are structurally and behaviorally simple, this is certainly not universal. Every nontrivial system contains a significant proportion of interesting objects that require further examination and specification. The detailed design of these objects allows the objects to be implemented correctly, of course, but also permits designers to make trade-off decisions to optimize the system. One definition of an object is "data tightly bound to its operations forming a cohesive entity." Detailed design must consider both the structure of information and its manipulation. In general, the decisions made in detailed design will be:

- Data structure
- Implementation of associations
- Set of operations defined on the data
- Visiblity of data and operations
- Algorithms used to implement those operations
- Exceptions handled and thrown

7.2 Data Structure

Data format in objects is generally simple because if it were not, a separate object would be constructed to hold just the data. However, not only must the structure of the data be defined, the valid ranges of data,

---

[2] My personal choice would be the *Sagan* rock on Mars (see http://mpfwww.jpl.nasa.gov, a public mirror site for the Mars Pathfinder mission).

accuracy, preconditions, and initial values must also be specified during detailed design. This is just as true of "simple" numeric data as of user-defined data types. After all, aircraft, spacecraft, and missile systems must perform significant numeric computation without introducing round-off and accuracy errors or "bad things" are likely to happen.[3] Consider a simple complex number class. Complex numbers may be stored in polar coordinates, but let's stick to rectilinear coordinates for now. Most of the applications using complex numbers require fractional values, so that using ints for the real and imaginary parts wouldn't meet the need. What about using floats, as in:

```
class complex_1 {
public:
    float iPart, rPart;
    // operations omitted
};
```

That looks like a reasonable start. Is the range sufficient? Most floating point implementations have a range of 10^{-40} to 10^{+40} or more, so that is probably OK. What about round-off error? Because the infinite continuous set of possible values are stored and manipulated as a finite set of machine numbers, just representing a continuous value using floating point format incurs some error. Numerical analysis identifies two forms of numerical error—absolute error and relative error [1]. For example, consider adding two numbers, 123456 and 4.567891, using six-digit precision floating point arithmetic:

$$123456.000000$$
$$\underline{+000004.567891}$$
$$123460.567891 = 0.123460567891 \times 10^6$$

Because this must be stored in six-digit precision, the value will be stored as 0.123460×10^6, which is an absolute error of 0.567891. Relative error is computed as:

$$\frac{(A - B) - [m(A) - m(B)]}{A - B}$$

where m(x) is the machine number representation of the value x. This gives us a relative error of 4.59977 x 10⁻⁸ for this calculation. Although this error is tiny, errors can propagate and build during repeated calculation to the point of making your computations meaningless.

Subtraction of two values is a common source of significant error. For example,

$$
\begin{array}{r}
0.991012312 \\
-\ 0.991009987 \\
\hline
0.000002325 = 0.2325 \times 10^{-5}
\end{array}
$$

But truncating these numbers to six digits of precision yields:

$$
\begin{array}{r}
0.991012 \\
-\ 0.991010 \\
\hline
0.000002 = 0.20 \times 10^{-5}
\end{array}
$$

which is an absolute error of 0.325 x 10⁻⁶ and a relative error of 14%. This means that we may have to change our format to include more significant digits, change our format entirely to use infinite precision arithmetic,[4] or change our algorithms to equivalent forms when a loss of precision is likely. For example, when computing 1-cos(x) an angle close to zero can result in the loss of precision. You can use the trigonometric relation

$$
1 - \cos(\emptyset) = 2\sin\left(\frac{\emptyset}{2}\right)
$$

to avoid round-off error.[5]

Data is often constrained beyond its representation limit by the problem domain. Planes shouldn't pull a 7g acceleration curve, array indices shouldn't be negative, ECG patients rarely weigh 500 Kg, and

---

[4] Infinite precision arithmetic is available in some Lisp-based symbolic mathematics systems, such as Derive and MacSyma.
[5] Widely different computational results of algebraically equivalent formulations can lead to hazardous situations. See [5].

automobiles don't go 300 miles per hour.[6] Attributes have a range of valid values and when they are set unreasonably, these faults must be detected and corrective actions must be taken. Mutator operations (operations that set attribute values) should ensure that the values are within range. These constraints on the data can be specified on class diagrams using the standard UML constraint syntax, such as {range 0..15}.

Subclasses may constrain their data ranges differently than their superclasses. Many designers feel that data constraints should be monotonically decreasing with subclass depth; that is, that a subclass may constrain a data range further than its superclass. Although systems can be built this way, this violates the Liskov Substitution Principle (LSP):

> *An instance of a subclass must be freely substitutable for an instance of its superclass.*

If a superclass declares a color attribute with a range of {white, yellow, blue, green, red, black} and a subclass restricts it to {white, black} then what happens if the client has a superclass pointer and set the color to red, as in:

```
enum color {white, yellow, blue, green, red, black};
class super {
protected:
   color c;
public:
   virtual void setColor (color temp); // all colors
   valid
};

class sub: public super {
public:
   virtual void setColor (color temp); // only white
   and black now valid
};
```

---

[6] Normally, that is. The Darwin Award, given to the person who finds the most ingenious way to kill him- or herself each year, was bestowed upon the guy who strapped a JATO (Jet-Assisted Take Off) pack to his 1967 Chevy Impala and hit a rocky cliff several miles away going well over 350 miles per hour. (To his credit, he tried to stop—the brake pads melted away before he became airborne for 1.4 miles and left a blackened 3-foot deep crater in the rock wall 125 feet above the roadway).

Increasing constraints down the superclass hierarchy is a dangerous policy if the subclass will be used in a polymorphic fashion.

Aside from normal attributes identified in the analysis model, detailed design may add *derived attributes* as well. Derived attributes are
values that can in principle be reconstructed from other attributes
within the class, but are added to optimize performance. They can be
indicated on class diagrams with a «derived» stereotype, and defining
the derivation formula within an associated constraint, such as {age =
currentDate – startDate}.

For example, a sensor class may provide a 10-sample history, with a
get(index) accessor method. If the clients often want to know the average measurement value, they can compute this from the history, but it
is more convenient to add an average() operation like so:

```
class sensor
    float value [10];
    int nMeasurements, currentMeasurement;
public
    sensor(void) : nMeasurements(0),
    currentMeasurement(0) {
        for (int j = 0; j<10; j++) value [10] = 0;
};

    void accept(float tValue) {
        value[currentMeasurement] = tValue;
        currentMeasurement = (++currentMeasurement) \
        10;
        if (nMeasurements < 10) ++nMeasurements;
        };

    float get(int index=0) {
        int cIndex;
        if (nMeasurements > index) {
            cIndex = currentMeasurement-index-1; // last
            valid one
            if (cIndex < 0) cIndex += 10;
            return value[cIndex];
        else
            throw "No valid measurement at that index";
        };

    float average(void) {
        float sum = 0.0;
        if (nMeasurements > 0) {
```

```
            for (int j=0; j < nMeasurements-1; j++)
                sum += value[j];
            return sum / nMeasurements;
            }
        else
            throw "No measurements to average";
    };
};
```

The average() operation exists only to optimize the computational path. If the average value was needed more frequently than the data was monitored, the average could be computed as the data is read:

```
class sensor {
    float value[10];
    float averageValue;
    int nMeasurements, currentMeasurement;
public:
    sensor(void): averageValue(0), nMeasurements(0),
                currentMeasurement(0) {
        for (int j = 0; j<10; j++) value[10] = 0;
    };

    void accept(float tValue) {
            value[currentMeasurement] = tValue;
            currentMeasurement =
            (++currentMeasurement) \ 10;
            if (nMeasurements < 10) ++nMeasurements;
                // compute average
            averageValue = 0;
            for (int j=0; j < nMeasurements-1; j++)
                averageValue += value [j];
                averageValue /= nMeasurements;
            };

    float get(int index=0) {
            int cIndex;
            if (nMeasurements > index) {
                cIndex = currentMeasurement-index-1; //
                last valid one
                if (cIndex < 0) cIndex += 10;
                return value [cIndex];
            else
                throw "No valid measurement at that
                index":
            };
```

```
float average(void) {
        if (nMeasurements > 0)
            return averageValue;
        else
            throw "No measurements to average";
    };
};
```

In this case, the derived attribute averageValue is added to mini-mize the required computation when the average value is needed fre-quently.

7.2.1 Data Collection Structure

Collections of primitive data attributes may be structured in myriad ways, including stacks, queues, lists, vectors, and a forest of trees. The layout of data collections is the subject of hundreds of volumes of re-search and practical applications. UML provides a role constraint no-tation to indicate different kinds of collections that may be inherent in the analysis model. Common role constraints for multivalued roles in-clude:

{ordered}   Collection is maintained in a sorted manner

{bag}   Collection may have multiple copies of a single item

{set}   Collection may have at most a single copy of a given item

{hashed}   Collection is referenced via a keyed hash

Some constraints may be combined, such as {ordered set}. Another common design scheme is to use a key value to retrieve an item from a collection. This is called a *qualified association* and the key value is called a *qualifier*.

Figure 7-1 shows examples of constraints and qualified associa-tions. The association between Patron and Airline is qualified with *Fre-quent Flyer Num*. This qualifier will be ultimately implemented as an attribute within the Patron class and will be used to identify the Patron to the Airline class. Similarly, the Patron has a qualified association with Library using the qualifier *Library Card Num*. The associations be-tween Airline and Flight and between Library and Book have con-strained multivalued roles. The former set must be maintained as an

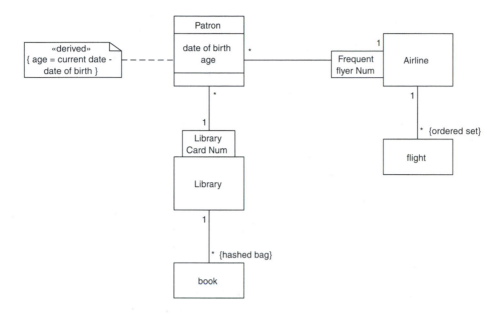

Figure 7-1: *Role Constraints and Qualified Associations*

ordered set, and the latter are a hashed bag. Note also the use of a text note to constrain the Patron's *age* attribute. The stereotype indicates that it is a derived attribute and the constraint shows how it is computed. Other constraints can be added as necessary to indicate valid ranges of data and other representational invariants.

Selection of a collection structure depends on what characteristics should be optimized. Balanced trees, for example, are very fast to search but inserting new elements is complex and costly because of the need to rotate the tree to maintain balance. Linked lists are simple to maintain, but searching takes relatively long.

7.3 Associations

Associations among objects allow client objects to invoke the operations provided by server objects. There are many ways to implement associations depending on the nature and locality of the objects and their association. Implementations appropriate for objects within the same thread will fail when used across thread or processor boundaries. Accessing objects with multivalued roles must be done differently than with a 1-to-1 association. Some implementation strategies that work for composition don't work for client-server associations. One of the purposes of detailed design is to resolve the management of associations within the objects.

The simplest cases are the 1-to-1 or 1-to-(0,1) association between objects within the same thread. The 1-to-(0,1) is best down with a pointer to the server object, since there are times when the role multiplicity will be zero (i.e., the pointer will be null). A 1-to-1 association may also be implemented with a reference (in the C++ sense) because the association link is always valid (C++ requires that references always be valid; that is, a null reference is semantically illegal). A 1-to-1 composition association may also use an inline class declaration which would be inappropriate for the more loosely-coupled client-server association. Normal aggregation is implemented in exactly the same way as an association. The following class shows these simple approaches:

```
class testAssoc {
    T myT;    // appropriate only for 1-to-1 composition
    T* myT2; // ok for 1-to-1 or 1-to-(0,1) association
             // or composition
    T& myT3; // ok for 1-1 association or composition
};
```

As discussed in the previous chapter, multivalued roles are most often resolved using the Container Pattern. This involves inserting a container class between the two classes with the multivalued role, and possibly iterators as well, as shown in Figure 7-2. Refer to the previous chapter for more details on the Container Pattern.

Crossing thread boundaries complicates the resolution of associations somewhat. Simply calling an operation across a thread boundary is not normally a good idea because of mutual exclusion and re-entrancy problems. It can be done if sufficient care is taken: the target operation can be implemented using mutual exclusion guards and both sides must agree on the appropriate behavior if access cannot be immediately granted. Should the caller be blocked? Should the caller be returned to immediately with an indication of failure? Should the caller

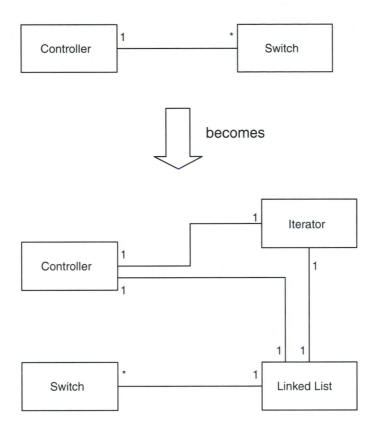

Figure 7-2: *Detailed Design of Multivalued Roles*

be blocked, but only for a maximum specified period of time? All of these kinds of rendezvous are possible and appropriate in different circumstances.

Although directly calling an operation across a thread boundary is light-weight, it is not always the best way. If the underlying operating system or hardware enforces segmented address spaces for threads, it may not even be possible. Operating systems provide additional means for intertask communication, such as OS message queues and OS pipes.

An OS message queue is the most dominant approach for requesting services across a thread boundary. The receiver thread's active object reads the message queue and dispatches the message to the appropriate component object. This approach has a fairly heavy run-time cost, but maintains the inherent asychronicity of the threads.

OS pipes are an alternative to message queues. They are opened by both client and server objects and are a slightly more direct approach for the client to invoke the services of the server.

When the service request must cross processor boundaries, the objects must be more decoupled. Common operating services to meet intra-processor communications include sockets and remote procedure calls (RPCs). Sockets usually implement a specified TCP/IP protocol across a network. The common protocols are the Transmission Control Protocol (TCP) and User Datagram Protocol (UDP). The TCP/IP protocol suite does not make any guarantees about timing, but it can be placed on top of a data link layer that does. TCP supports reliable transmission using acknowledged transmission, and also what is called stream sockets. UDP is simpler and makes no guarantees about reliable transmission.

Lastly, some systems use RPCs. Normally, RPCs are implemented using a blocking protocol so that the client is blocked until the remote procedure completes. This maintains the function call-like semantics of the RPC, but may be inappropriate in some cases.

Using any of these approaches that cross the thread boundary (with the exception of the direct guarded call) requires a different implementation in the client class. The client must now know the thread ID and a logical object ID to invoke the services. So rather than a C++ pointer or reference, *ad hoc* operating system-dependent means must be used.

These methods can be implemented using the Broker Pattern from Chapter 5 or the Observer Pattern in Chapter 6. The Observer Pattern allows the server to be remote from the client, but requires that the client know the location of the server. The Broker Pattern adds one more level of indirection, requiring only that the client know a logical name for the target object, which allows the Broker to identify and locate the server.

Note that this discussion has been independent of the underlying physical medium of interprocessor communication. It can be implemented using shared memory, Ethernet networks, or various kinds of buses, as appropriate. Reusable protocols are built using the Layered Architecture Pattern, so that the data link layer can be replaced with one suitable for the physical medium with a minimum of fuss.

7.4 Operations

The operations defined by a class specify how the data may be manipulated. Generally speaking, a complete set of primitive operations
maximizes reusability. A *set* class template typically provides operators
such as add item or set, remove item or subset, and test for item or subset membership. Even if the current application doesn't use all these
operations, adding the complete list of primitive makes it more likely
to meet the needs of the next system.

Analysis models abstract class operations into object messages
(class, object, sequence, and collaboration diagrams), state event accep-
tors (statecharts), and state actions (statecharts). The great majority of
the time, these messages will be implemented directly as operations in
the server class using the implementation strategy for the association
supporting the message passing (see the previous section).

Analysis and early design models only specify the public operations. Detailed design often adds operations that are only used internally. These operations are due to the functional decomposition of the
public operations. For example, a queue might provide the following
set of public operations:

```
template <class T, int size>
class queue {
protected:
    T q[size];
    int head, tail;
public:
    queue(void): head(0), tail(0);
    virtual void put(T myT);
    virtual T get(void);
};
```

A cached queue caches data locally but stores most of it on a more
remote, but larger data store, such as a hard disk. Operations can be
added to implement the caching so that it is invisible to the client,
maintaining LSP:

```
template <class T, int size>
class cachedQueue : public queue<T, size> {
protected:
```

```
        void writeToDisk(void);
        void readFromDisk(void);
    public:
        cachedQueue(void) : head(0), tail(0);
        virtual void put(T myT);   // new version uses
                                   // writeToDisk
                                   // when cache fills
        virtual T get(void);       // new version uses
                                   // readFromDisk
                                   // when data is not cached

    };
```

These operations are added to support the additional functionality of the cachedQueue subclass.

Functional decomposition of operations is shown in structured methods using structure charts. Since the UML does not provide any means of showing structural functional decomposition within classes, I recommend using structure charts when this view is necessary.

7.5 Visibility

Visibility in the UML refers to *accessibility* of internal object elements by other objects. Visibility is always a design concern. The general guidelines of visibility are as follows.

If clients need it, make it visible, otherwise make it inaccessible.
This first guideline is pretty obvious. Once you are down in the depths of detailed design, you should have a pretty good idea which messages are being sent to an object. If other clients are depending on the service, then they must be able to call it. This is none other than the old "data-hiding" principle in the vogue since the 1970s.

Make only semantically appropriate operations visible.
This guideline seeks to avoid pathological coupling among classes. For example, suppose a class is using a container class. Should the operations be GetLeft() and GetRight() or Prev() and Next()? The first pair makes the implementation visible (binary tree) and the latter pair captures the essential semantics (ordered list).

Attributes should never be directly visible to clients.

This guideline is similar to the previous one in that it wants to avoid tight coupling whenever possible. If clients have direct access to attributes, they fundamentally depend on the structure of that attribute. Should the structure change, the clients all become instantly broken and must be modified as well. Additionally, accessor and mutator operations applied to that attribute can ensure that preconditions are met, such as valid ranges or consistency with other class attributes. Direct access to the attribute circumvents these safeguards.

When different levels of visibility are required to support various levels of coupling, use the Interface Pattern to provide the different sets of interfaces.

Sometimes a class must present different levels of access to different clients. When this is true, the Interface Pattern described in the previous chapter is an obvious solution. A class can have many different interfaces, each providing the semantically appropriate interface to its clients.

The UML provides a simple, if peculiar, syntax for specifying visibility on the class diagram: A visibility attribute is prepended to the class member. The UML defines the following visibility attributes:

Private—accessible only within the class itself

–   Protected—accessible only by the class and its subclasses

+   Public—generally accessible by other classes

Some theorists are adamant that attributes should be private (as opposed to protected) and even subclasses should go through accessor methods to manipulate them. Personally, I find that view somewhat draconian because subclasses are already tightly coupled with their superclasses, but each to his own.

Another approach to providing different levels of access is through the use of friend classes. (Resulting in a kind of "clothing-optional" design, which, although it can be fun, may make some designers nervous). Friends are often used as iterators in the Container Pattern discussed in Chapter 6. Another use is the facilitation of unit testing by making unit testing objects friends of the class under test.

7.6 Algorithms

An algorithm is a step-by-step procedure for computing a desired result. The complexity of algorithms may be defined in many ways, but the most common is *time complexity*, the amount of execution time required to compute the desired result. Algorithm complexity is expressed using the "order of" notation. Common algorithm complexities are:

- $O(c)$
- $O(\log_2 n)$
- $O(n)$
- $O(\log_2 n)$
- $O(n^2)$
- $O(n^3)$

where c is a constant and n is the number of elements participating in the algorithmic computation.

All algorithms with the same complexity differ from each other only by a multiplicative and additive constant. Thus, it is possible for one $O(n)$ algorithm to perform 100 times faster than another $O(n)$ algorithm and still be considered equal time complexity. It is even possible for an $O(n^2)$ algorithm to out perform an $O(c)$ algorithm for sufficiently small n. The algorithmic complexity is most useful when the number of entities being manipulated is large (as in "asymptotically approaching infinity") because then these constants become insignificant and the complexity order dictates performance. For small n, they can only be given as rules of thumb.

Execution time is not the only optimization criteria applied to systems. Objects may be designed to optimize:

- Run-time performance
  - ▼ Average performance
  - ▼ Worst-case performance
  - ▼ Deterministic performance
- Run-time memory requirements
- Simplicity and correctness
- Development time and effort

- Reusability
- Extensibility
- Reliability
- Safety

Of course, to some degree these are conflicting goals, which is why they are called *trade-offs*. For example, some objects must maintain their elements in sorted order. A Bubble sort is very simple, so it requires a minimum of development time. Although it has a worst case run-time performance of $O(n^2)$, it can actually have better performance than more efficient algorithms if n is small. Quicksort is generally much faster ($O(\log_2 n)$), but is more complicated to implement. It is not always best to use a Quicksort and it is not always worst to use a Bubble sort even if the Quicksort is demonstrably faster for the data set. Most systems spend most of their time executing a small portion of the code. If the sorting effort is tiny compared to other system functions, the additional time necessary to correctly implement the Quicksort might be more profitably spent elsewhere (like trying to find some other use for that JATO pack in the garage).

Some algorithms have good average performance but their worst case performance may be unacceptable. In real-time systems, raw performance is usually not an appropriate criterion—deterministic performance is more crucial. Often, embedded systems must run on a minimum of memory, so that efficient use of existing resources may be very important. The job of the designer is to make the set of design choices that results in the best overall system, and this includes its overall characteristics.

Classes with rich behavior must not only perform correctly, they must also be optimal in some sense. Most often, average execution speed is the criterion used for algorithm selection, but as we saw in Section 7.1, many other criteria may be used. Once the appropriate algorithm is selected, the operations and attributes of the class must be designed to implement the algorithm. This will often result in new attributes and operations that assist in the execution of the algorithm.

For example, suppose you are using the Container pattern, and decide that a balanced AVL tree container is best.[7] An AVL tree is named

---

[7] An AVL tree is not a specifically real-time example, but the algorithm is well-known and straightforward and so we will use it here for discussion.

after its inventors—Adelson, Velskii, and Landis. It takes advantage of the fact that the search performance of a balanced tree is $O(\log_2 n)$. A balanced binary tree is one in which all subtrees are the same height ± 1 node. Each node in an AVL tree has a balance attribute,[8] which must be in the range [-1, 0, +1] for the tree to be balanced. The problem with simple trees is that their balance depends on the order in which elements are added. In fact, adding items in a sorted order to an ordinary binary tree results in a linked list, with search properties of $O(n)$. By balancing the tree during the addition and removal of items, we can improve its balance and optimize its search performance.

Let's assume that we want an inorder tree—that is, a tree in which a node is always greater than its left child and less than its right child, such as the one shown in Figure 7-3. Note that node 10 is greater than its left child (6) and less than its right child (12). If we now add a 9 to the tree, we could make it the left child of node 10 and the parent of node 6, but this would unbalance the tree, as shown in Figure 7-4. If we then balance the tree we might end up with a tree such as that shown in Figure 7-5.

AVL trees remain balanced because whenever a node is inserted or removed that unbalances the tree, nodes are moved around using techniques called *tree rotations* to regain balance. The algorithm for adding a node to an AVL tree looks like this:

1. Create the new node with NULL child pointers, set the attribute Balance to 0.

2. If the tree is empty, set the root to point to this new node and return.

3. Locate the proper place for the node insertion and insert.

4. Recompute the balance attribute for each node from the root to the newly inserted node.

5. Locate an unbalanced node (balance factor is ± 2). This is called the pivot node. If there is no unbalanced node, then return.

6. Rebalance the tree so that it is now balanced. There are several different situations:

---

[8] This is a derived attribute. It can be explicitly stored and maintained during addition and deletion, or it can be recomputed as necessary.

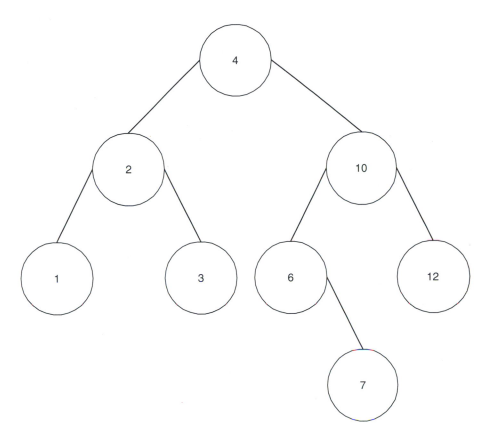

Figure 7-3: *Balanced Inorder Tree*

    a.   Pivot has a balance of +2. Rotate the subtree based at the Pivot left.

    b.   Pivot has a balance of -2. Rotate the subtree based at the Pivot right.

7.   Continue balancing subtrees on the search path until they are all in the set [-1, 0, +1].

    Rotating left means to replace the right child of the pivot as the root of the subtree as shown in Figure 7-6. Right rotations work similarly, and are applied when the balance of the pivot is -2. Many times, dou-

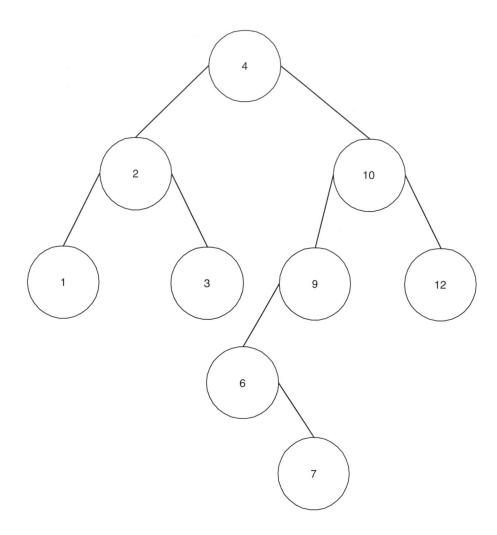

Figure 7-4: *Unbalanced Tree after Adding Node 9*

ble rotations are required to achieve a balanced tree, such as a left-right or a right-left rotation set.

The set of operations necessary to meet this algorithm are:

```
typedef class node {
public:
    data d; // whatever data is held in the tree nodes
    int balance; // valid values are -1, 0, 1
```

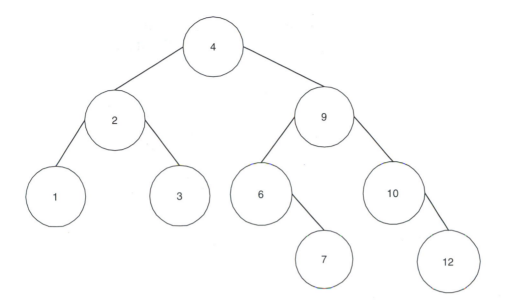

Figure 7-5: *Rebalanced Tree*

```
    node* leftPtr;
    node* rightPtr;
}* nodePtr;

class avlTree {
    nodePtr root;
    void rotateLeft(nodePtr n);
    void rotateRight(nodePtr n);
public
    void add(data a);
    void delete(data a);
    nodePtr find(data a);
};
```

Structured English and pseudocode, as just shown, work perfectly well in most circumstances to capture the essential semantics of algorithms. The UML does define a special kind of state diagram, called an *Activity Diagram*, which may be helpful in some cases.

Activity diagrams depict systems that may be decomposed into activities—roughly corresponding to states that mostly terminate upon

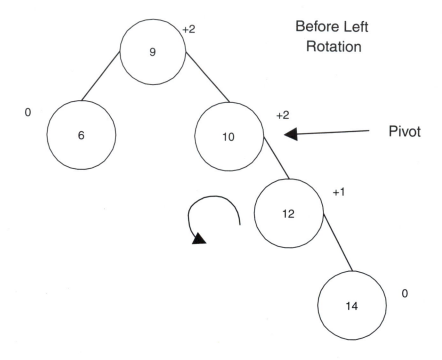

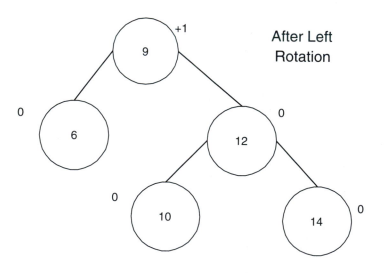

Figure 7-6: *Left Rotation*

completion of the activity rather than as a result of an externally generated event. Activity diagrams may be thought of as a kind of flowchart where diagrammatic elements are member function calls. Figure 7-7 shows the activity diagram for the *add* operation of our AVL tree class.

The full syntax of Activity Diagrams is shown in Figure 7-8

Activity diagrams have several elements in common with statecharts, including starting and ending activities, forks, joins, guards, and states (called *action states*). What is different is the decision points, the use of the states, and swim lanes. Decision points show branch points, based on guards, of program flow. The states mostly represent function invocations that have a single exit transition taken when the function completes. Unlike statecharts, there is no requirement that the action states are all within the same object. Swim lanes visually group the action states. They have no semantics, but are often used to show concurrent threads of execution. Two stereotyped action states can be shown on the activity diagram, one for explicitly sending an event, and one for explicitly receiving an event. These are indicated in Figure 7-8.

Sequence diagrams, shown in detail elsewhere in this book, can also be used to show algorithms within individual objects. Sequence diagrams normally show multiple objects collaborating together by sending messages. These messages can be explicit function calls to show detailed algorithms. Sequence diagrams are weaker than activity diagrams in the sense that they don't show concurrency well.

Action states can themselves be decomposed into more detailed activity diagrams or can use a different notation entirely. Again, pseudocode, text, or a mathematical formulation can be used as alternative representations.

Algorithms prescribe the activities that constitute a desired process [3]. That is, algorithms are, in their very essence, the decomposition of a function into smaller functions. This does not obviate the power of the object-oriented approach, but enhances it.

7.7 Exceptions

In reactive class, exception handling is straightforward—exceptions are events specified in the class state model that result in transitions being taken and actions being executed. In nonreactive classes, the

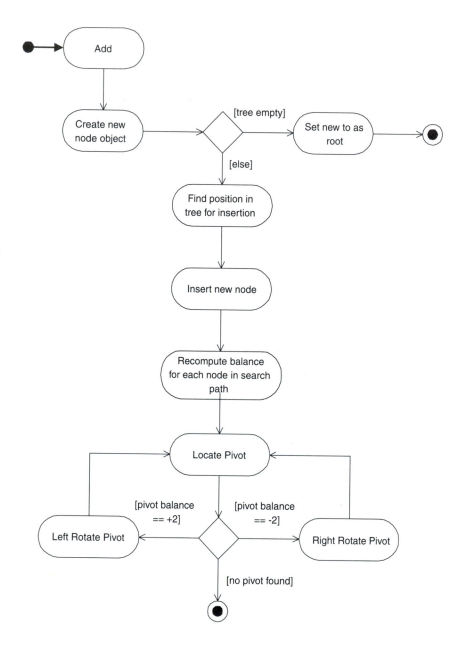

Figure 7-7: *Activity Diagram for Add Node Operation*

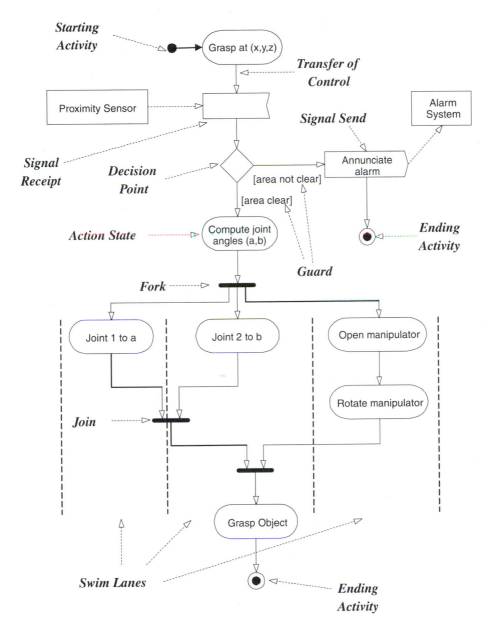

Figure 7-8: *Activity Diagram Notation*

specification means is less clear. The minimum requirements are to identify the exceptions raised by the class and the exceptions handled by the class.

Exception handling is a powerful addition to programming languages. Language-based exception handling provides two primary benefits. The first is that exceptions cannot be ignored. The C idiom for exception handling is to pass back a return value from a function, but this is generally ignored by the clients of the service. When was the last time you saw the return value for printf checked?

The correct usage for the C fopen function is something like this:

```
FILE * fp;
if ( (fp = fopen("filename", "w")) == NULL) {
    /* do some corrective action */
    exit(1); /* pass error indicator up a level */
    };
```

Many programmers, to their credit, always do just that. However, there is no enforcement that the errors be identified or handled. It is up to the good graces of the programmer and the code peer review process to ensure this is done. With exceptions, the error condition cannot be ignored. Unhandled exceptions are passed to each preceding caller until they are handled—a process called "unwinding the stack." The terminate-on-exception approach has been successfully applied to programs in Ada and C++ for many years.

The other benefit of exception handling is that it separates the exception handling itself from the normal execution path. This simplifies both the normal processing code and the exception handling code. For example, consider the following standard C code segment:

```
if ( (fp = ftest1(x,y,z))) == NULL) {
    /* do some corrective action */
    printf("Failure on ftest1");
    exit(1); /* pass error indicator up a level */
    };

if (!ftest2()) {
    /* do some corrective action */
    printf("failure on ftest2");
    exit (1);
    };
```

```
if (ftest3() == 0) {
   /* do some corrective action */
   printf("failure on ftest3");
   exit(1);
   };
```

This is arguably more difficult to understand than the following code:

```
//main code is simplified
try {
   ftest1(x,y,z);
   ftest2();
   ftest3();
}

// exception handling code is simplified
catch (test1Failure& t1) {
   cout << "Failure on test1";
   throw; // rethrow same exception as in code above
}
catch (test2Failure& t2) {
   cout << "Failure on test2";
   throw;
}
catch (test 3Failure& t3) {
   cout << Failure on test3";
   throw;
};
```

The second code segment separates the normal code processing from the exception processing, making both clearer.

Each operation should define the exceptions that it throws as well as the exceptions that it handles. There are reasons to avoid using formal C++ exceptions specifications [2] but the information should be captured nonetheless. Exceptions should never be used as an alternative way to terminate a function in much the same way that a crowbar should not be used as an alternative key for your front door. Exceptions indicate that a serious fault requiring explicit handling has occurred.

Throwing exceptions is computationally expensive because the stack must be unwound and objects destroyed. The presence of exception handling in your code adds a small overhead to your executing code (usually around 3%) even when exceptions are not thrown. Most compiler vendors offer nonstandard library versions that don't throw exceptions, so this overhead can be avoided if exceptions are not used. Destructors should *never* throw exceptions or call operations that can throw exceptions nor should the constructors of exception classes throw exceptions.[9]

Exception handling applies to operations (i.e., functions) and is a complicating factor in the design of algorithms. In my experience, writing *correct* programs (i.e., those that include complete and proper exception handling) is two to three times more difficult than writing code that merely "is supposed to work."[10]

Capturing the exception handling is fundamentally a part of the algorithm design and so can be represented along with the normal aspects of the algorithms. Exceptions can be explicitly shown as events on either statecharts or activity diagrams.

That still leaves two unanswered questions:

- What exceptions should I catch?
- What exceptions should I throw?

The general answer to the first question is that an operation should catch all exceptions that it has enough context to handle, or that will make no sense to the current operation's caller.

The answer to the second is "all others." If an object does not have enough context to decide how to handle an exception, then its caller might. Perhaps the caller can retry a set of operations or execute an alternative algorithm.

At some point exception handling will run out of stack to unwind, so at some global level, an exception policy must be implemented. The action at this level will depend on the severity of the exception, its impact on system safety, and the context of the system. In some cases, a se-

---

[9] In C++, if an exception is thrown while an unhandled exception is active, the program calls the internal function terminate() to exit the program. As the stack is unwound during exception handling, local objects are destroyed by calling their destructors. Thus destructors are called as part of the exception handling process. If a destructor is called because its object is being destroyed due to an exception, any exception it throws will terminate the program immediately.

[10] In contrast to prevailing opinion, I don't *think* this is solely due to my recently hitting 40 and the associated loss of neural cells.

vere error with safety ramifications should result in a system shut-down, because the system has a fail-safe state. Drill presses or robotic assembly systems normally deenergize in the presence of faults be-cause that is their fail-safe state. Other systems, such as medical moni-toring systems, may continue by providing diminished functionality or reset and retry, because that is their safest course of action. Of course, some systems have no fail-safe state. For such systems, architectural means must be provided as an alternative to in-line fault correction.

7.8 Summary

One definition of an object is "a set of tightly coupled attributes and the operations that act on them." Detailed design takes this microscopic view to fully specify the characteristics of objects that have been hith-erto abstracted away and ignored. These characteristics include the structuring of the attributes and identification of their representational invariants, resolution of abstract message passing into object opera-tions, selection and definition of algorithms, including the handling of exceptional conditions.

Attributes are the data values subsumed within the objects. They must be represented in some fashion supported by the implementation language, but that is not enough. Most often, the underlying represen-tation is larger than the valid ranges of the attribute, so the valid set of values of the attributes must be defined. Operations can then include checking of the representational invariants to ensure that the object re-mains in a valid state.

Analysis models use the concept of message passing to represent the myriad ways that objects can communicate. Detailed design must decide upon the exact implementation of each message. Most often, messages are isomorphic with operations, but that is true only when the message source is always in the same thread of execution. When this is not true, other means, such as OS message queues, must be em-ployed to provide interobject communication.

Many objects are themselves algorithmically trivial and do not re-quire a detailed specification of the interaction of the operations and at-tributes. However, in every system, a significant proportion of objects have rich behavior. Although this requires additional work, it also provides the designer with an opportunity to optimize the system performance along some set of criteria. Algorithms include the handling of exceptions and this is usually at least as complex as the primary algorithm itself. Algorithms can be expressed using state charts or activity diagrams. Other representations, such as mathematical equations, pseudocode, or text can be used as well.

7.9 References

[1] Douglass, Bruce Powel, *Numerical Basic.* Indianapolis: Howard Sams Press, 1983.

[2] Meyers, Scott, *More Effective C++: 35 New Ways to Improve Your Programs and Designs.* Reading, MA: Addison Wesley Longman, 1996.

[3] Harel, David, *Algorithmics.* Reading, MA: Addison Wesley Longman, 1993.

[4] Barry, Dave, *Dave Barry's Complete Guide to Guys.* New York: Fawcett Columbine Books, 1995.

[5] Neumann, Peter G., *Computer Related Risks.* Reading, MA: Addison Wesley Longman, 1995.

Appendix

Notational Summary

This appendix provides a summary of the UML notation discussed in this book. It is organized by diagram type to facilitate its use as a reference during development.

Class Diagram

Shows the existence of classes and
relationships in a logical view of a system.

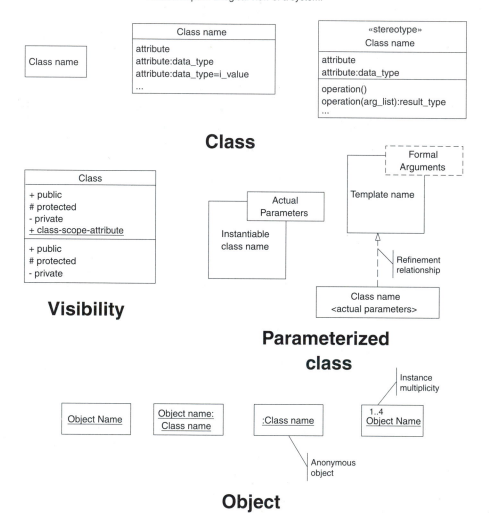

Class

Visibility

**Parameterized
class**

Object

Class Diagram

Shows the existence of classes and
relationships in a logical view of a system.

Indicates speaking
perspective of
association name

Class1 — Association Name — Class2

Class1 — Role Name / Role Name — Class2

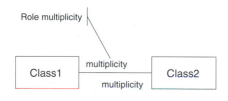

Role multiplicity

Class1 — multiplicity / multiplicity — Class2

**Associations may be labelled using any
combination of names, role names, and
multiplicity**

Multiplicity Symbol	Meaning
1	Exactly 1
0,1	Optionally 1
x..y	From x to y inclusive
a,b,c	Only specific values of a, b, and c
1..n	One or greater
*	0 or more

Bidirectional
navigatable
association

Class1 — Class2

Unidirectional
navigatable
association

Class1 —→ Class2

Association

Class Diagram

Shows the existence of classes and
relationships in a logical view of a system.

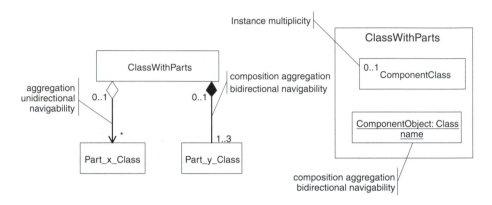

Aggregation and Composition

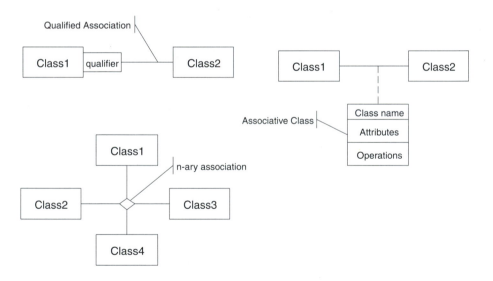

Advanced Associations

Class Diagram

Shows the existence of classes and
relationships in a logical view of a system.

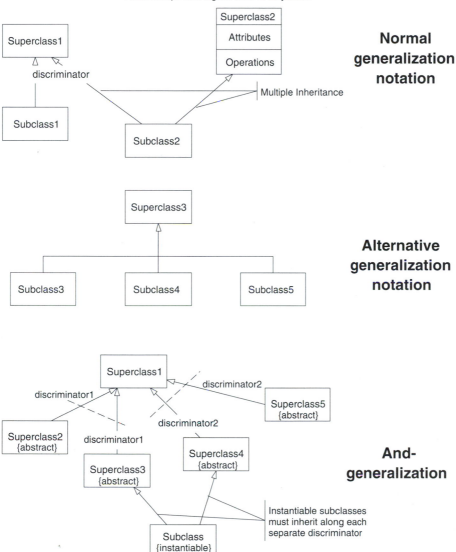

**Normal
generalization
notation**

**Alternative
generalization
notation**

**And-
generalization**

Generalization and Specialization

Class Diagram

Shows the existence of classes and
relationships in a logical view of a system.

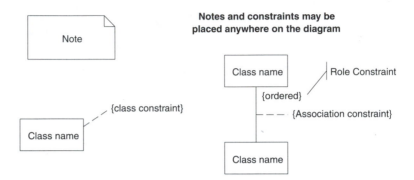

**Notes and constraints may be
placed anywhere on the diagram**

Notes and Constraints

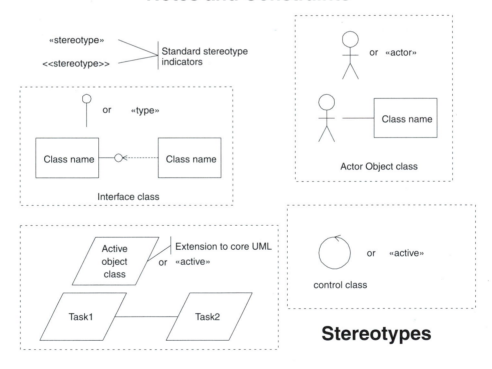

Stereotypes

Collaboration Diagram

Shows a sequenced set of messages illustrating a specific example of object interaction.

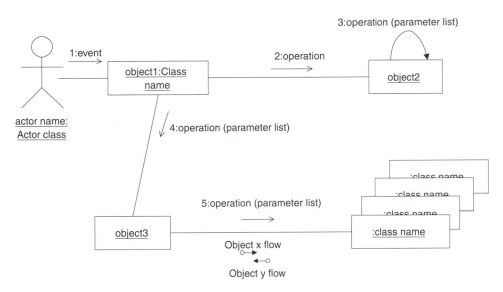

Object Collaboration

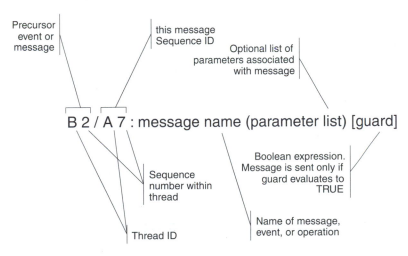

Message Syntax

Sequence Diagram

Shows a sequenced set of messages illustrating a specific
example of object interaction.

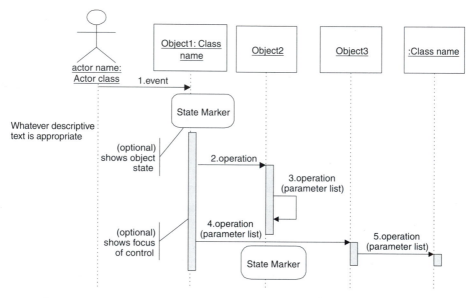

Sequence diagrams have two dimensions. The vertical dimension usually represents
time, the horizontal represents different objects (these may be reversed).

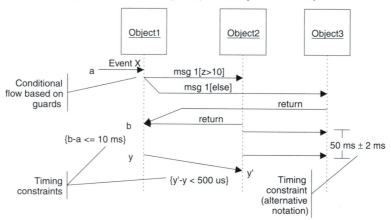

Advanced Sequence Diagrams

Use Cases

Use cases show primary areas of collaboration between the system and actors in its environment. Use cases are isomorphic with function points.

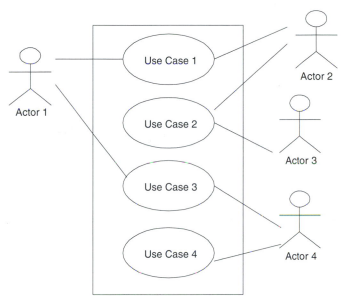

Use Case Diagram

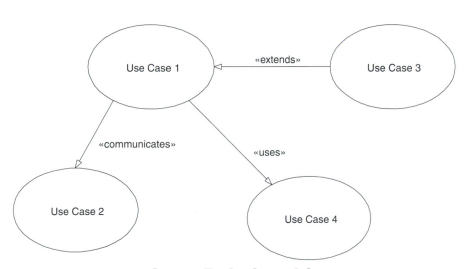

Use Case Relationships

Implementation Diagrams

Implementation diagrams show the run-time dependencies and packaging
structure of the deployed system.

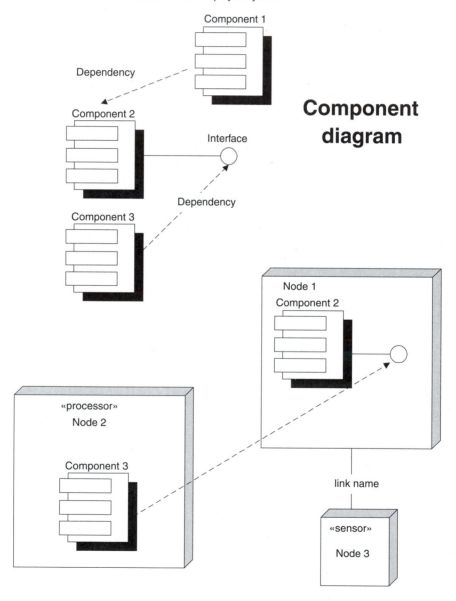

Component diagram

Deployment Diagram

Package Diagram

Shows a grouping of model elements. Packages may also appear within class
and object diagrams.

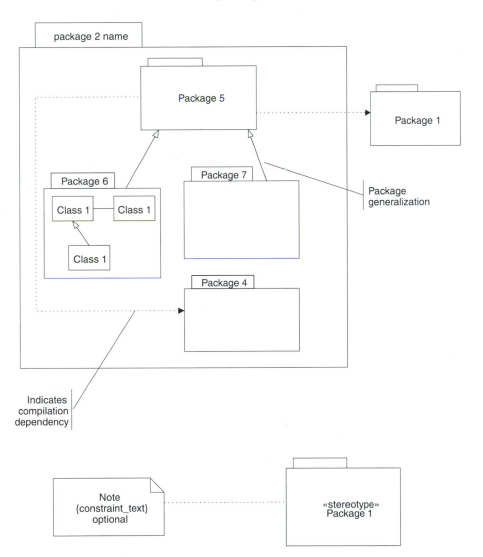

Statechart

Shows the sequences of states for a reactive class or interaction during its life in response to stimuli, together with its responses and actions.

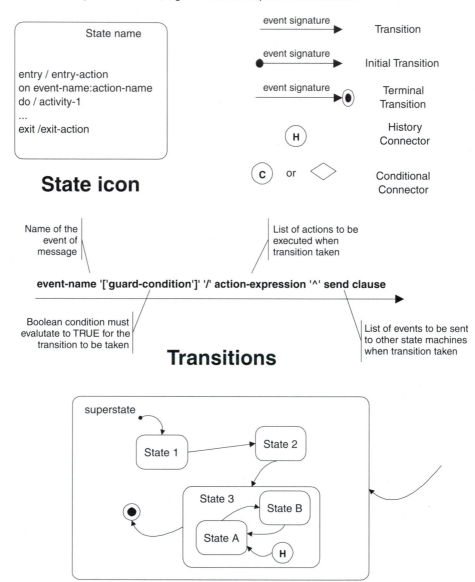

State name

entry / entry-action
on event-name:action-name
do / activity-1
...
exit /exit-action

State icon

event signature → Transition

● event signature → Initial Transition

event signature → ◉ Terminal Transition

Ⓗ History Connector

Ⓒ or ◇ Conditional Connector

Name of the event of message

List of actions to be executed when transition taken

event-name '['guard-condition']' '/' action-expression '^' send clause

Boolean condition must evaluate to TRUE for the transition to be taken

List of events to be sent to other state machines when transition taken

Transitions

superstate

State 1 → State 2

State 3

State B

State A Ⓗ

Nested States

Statechart

Shows the sequences of states for a reactive class or interaction during its life in response to stimuli, together with its responses and actions.

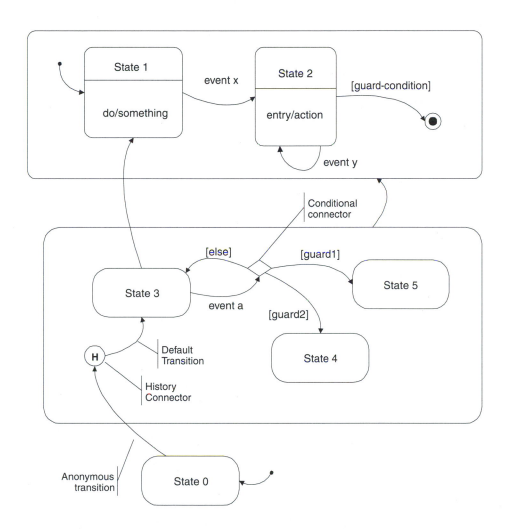

Sequential substates

Statechart

Shows the sequences of states for a reactive class or interaction during its life in response to stimuli, together with its responses and actions.

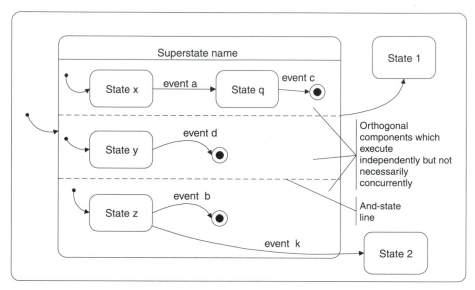

Orthogonal substates (and-states)

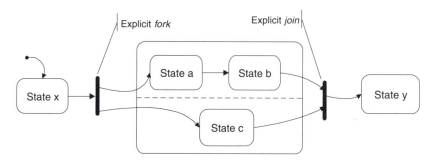

Complex state transitions

Activity Diagrams

Activity Diagrams are a specialized form of state diagrams in which most or all transitions are taken when the state activity is completed.

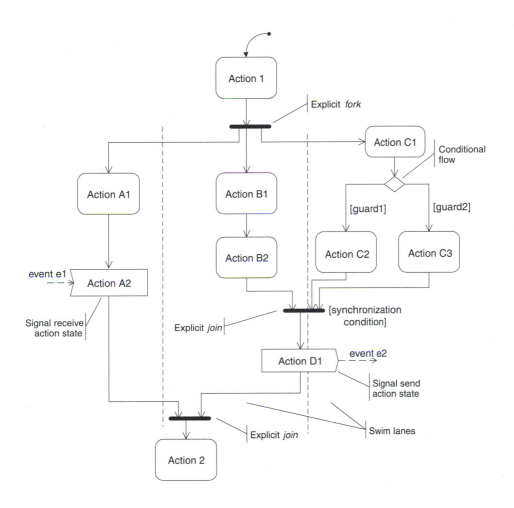

Index

A